In Geronimo's Footsteps

In Geronimo's Footsteps

A Journey Beyond Legend

Corine Sombrun
and
Harlyn Geronimo

Translated from the French
by E. C. Belli

Afterword by Ramsey Clark

Arcade Publishing • New York

First English-language Edition

The authors of this book do not dispense medical advice or prescribe the use of any technique or substance as a form of treatment for physical or medical problems, either directly or indirectly. The intent of the authors is only to offer information of a general nature, based on their experience about traditional Native American and traditional Mongolian healing. In the event you use any of the information in this book for yourself, the authors and the publisher assume no responsibility for your actions.

Arcade Publishing books may be purchased in bulk at special discounts for sales promotion, corporate gifts, fund-raising, or educational purposes. Special editions can also be created to specifications. For details, contact the Special Sales Department, Arcade Publishing, 307 West 36th Street, 11th Floor, New York, NY 10018 or arcade@skyhorsepublishing.com.

Arcade Publishing® is a registered trademark of Skyhorse Publishing, Inc.®, a Delaware corporation.

Visit our website at www.arcadepub.com.

10 9 8 7 6 5 4 3 2 1

Library of Congress Cataloging-in-Publication Data is available on file.

Cover design by Rain Saukas
Cover photo: Library of Congress

ISBN: 978-1-61145-896-1
Ebook ISBN: 978-1-62872-468-4

Printed in the United States of America

To Brigitte. To my Yurt.

To Guu ji ya, the clever one, and to his descendants.

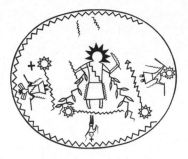

"I know that if my people were placed in that mountainous region lying around the headwaters of the Gila River they would live in peace and act according to the will of the President. They would be prosperous and happy in tilling the soil and learning the civilization of the white men, whom they now respect. Could I but see this accomplished, I think I could forget all the wrongs that I have ever received, and die a contented and happy old man."

GERONIMO

Contents

Introduction

I met Harlyn Geronimo, a medicine man and the great-grandson of the famous Apache chief, Geronimo, in July 2005 in New Mexico, where he lives today. Together, we went on a pilgrimage to the headwaters of the Gila River, Geronimo's birthplace, and were companions of a few months, during which we shared and compared our respective passions for Apache and Mongol traditions, which, according to an Apache legend, have common roots.

Harlyn Geronimo initiated me to the virtues of medicinal plants, to survival in the New Mexican deserts, to the guiding rituals of Apache medicine. And I revealed the mysteries of Mongol shamanic traditions to Harlyn Geronimo.

I was able to write this book thanks to our utterly fascinating partnership, his willingness to share it, and, above all, Harlyn Geronimo's exceptional account, which he granted me permission to record and translate, and for which I again thank him.

My interest in drawing a parallel between the past and present led me to construct this book as a narrative in two voices. Every other chapter is dedicated to Geronimo's life, told for the first time, and as it has never been told before, from his great-grandson's perspective. Together with this, I have interwoven my own account of meeting Harlyn Geronimo and of our trip to the headwaters of the Gila River. In the present-day narrative, I develop three main themes. First, Harlyn Geronimo's take on the social and political conditions of the Apaches in this twenty-first century. Then an unprecedented look at the traditions of the Apaches as compared to those of the Mongols, to explore the hypothesis of a common root. And finally, Harlyn Geronimo's life, his time in Vietnam, his fight as a medicine man to protect the environment and preserve the traditions of his community and his political, cultural, and spiritual choices. This third theme culminates in his participation in the Skull and Bones investigation, which revealed the involvement of George W. Bush's grandfather, Prescott Bush, in the alleged desecration of Geronimo's tomb in order to steal Geronimo's skull and femur bones.

For the details of Geronimo's life, this book doesn't claim to offer any significant new historical information or to amend any part of his known life story. Nor, as his direct descendent, is Harlyn Geronimo exempt from a certain degree of subjectivity in his account, and his memories certainly aren't accurate enough to reconstitute every detail of Geronimo's life in the nineteenth century today. So to re-create this story, I also drew on, among many other sources, scientific theses put forth in Oklahoma by Anthropology Professor Emeritus and expert Morris Edward Opler in his book *An Apache Life-Way: The Economic, Social, and Religious Institutions of the Chiricahua Indians.*

I based myself as well on the account of Karen Geronimo, a medicine woman in her own right and Harlyn Geronimo's wife, who took part in our journey to the source of the Gila River but preferred not to be mentioned in this tale. "I would like the contributions to remain exclusively Harlyn's," she said. I still wish to honor her. Her engagement in preserving her people's traditions and her knowledge of Apache culture (Karen Geronimo is Apache Kid's* great-granddaughter) allowed me to round out the details of Harlyn's account.

---

* Raised on the San Carlos Reservation in New Mexico, Apache Kid was the first scout promoted to the rank of sergeant. After being wrongly convicted of attempted murder, he escaped and, like Geronimo, became an outlaw. The state of Arizona offered a $5,000 reward for his capture, dead or alive, but he was never caught.

By putting these Apache memories into print for the first time, Harlyn Geronimo, Karen, and I hope simply to invite readers to share in this extraordinary journey to the roots of Chiricahua traditions and, by taking these symbolic steps with his great-grandson, fulfill one of Geronimo's final wishes for himself and his people.

C. S.

In Geronimo's Footsteps

The Quarrel between the Wind and the Thunder

An Apache Tale

K'adi díídíí łigo 'ánángóót'į́į́ 'iłk'idą ndii 'ágojiládą.

Ńłch'i'í 'lihndiideíbił dáłe'naa'jiziiná'a.'Áí dáhágoohndii 'iłch'įįgołgóót ǫǫ ná'a.'Ákoo 'iłk'ájałghoná'a. Íquot;Iyáabąą 'iłk'ájałghóó'í 'iłch'įįgołgóót ǫǫ í 'lihndiideí Ńłch'i'í 'áyiiłndí: Íquot;Shíná sheegózhǫ́ ndí doojoń ndeedeeda. Íquot;Ńłch'i'í biłjindíná'a. Íquot;Iyáabąą 'iłk'ájałghóó'í 'iłch'įįgołgóót ǫǫ í 'lihndiideí Ńłch'i'í 'áyiiłndí: Íquot;Shíná sheegózhǫ́ ndí doojoń ndeedeeda.Íquot;Ńłch'i'í biłjindíná'a. 'Ákoo Ńłchi'í 'ágoołndíná'a:Íquot;nDíná neegózhǫ́ ń ndí hį́į́yąąda, ńza'yá nch'ą́nádéshdzá.Íquot;Ńłch'i'í 'lihndiideí yiiłndíná'a. 'Ákoo Ńch'i'í ńza'yá nii'gáshbąąyá goch'ą́'inóódzáná'a. Nágo doońłch'i'daná'a.Dágoosdo náánóółt'eená'a. 'Ákoo 'lihndiideń, Íquot;Shíná sheegózhǫ́,Íquot;ndíń, łą́go naagołtįgo 'ágósį ndah dágoosdo náánóółt'eená'a. Doo'nt'ą́daná'a Doogózhǫ́daná'a. Ńłch'i'ń doohaaeeda Nágo 'lihndiideń doobiłgózhǫ́dána'a. Nágo 'its'os 'ináitsiná'a. 'Its'osí bikázhį Ńłch'i'í ch'édaháshdees'į́ná'a. Nágo doogołgózhǫ́daná'a. Ńłch'i'í bichįį'i'jóół'a'ná'a.'Áałjindíná'a: Íquot;Shik'isę, ndí-doohaaeeda nágo doogózhǫ́da. Doo'nt''ą́da. Dágoosdo'égoosdo. Hį́į́yąąda, nooshką́ą shanáńndá. 'Įshį́ndáse, dánahiłk'eh ndiibikáee naheegózhǫ́daał. Dáłe'naa'iidziidaał. Dáłe'hoot'ashdaał. Nahk'ehgo, ná'nt'įdaał.Íquot;'iihndiideí goołndígo, gooską́ąná'a. 'Ákoo Ńłch'i'í kaanájáná'a. Gojoonáánásndeená'a.

'Áíbee, naagołtįgo, daa'dihndígo ńłch'i'bił. Dáłe'ja'ash náánóółt'ee.

1

Now, here is a story that took place a long time ago, when the Earth was created.

Back then, the Wind and the Thunder worked hand in hand. But they suddenly grew angry at each other. And so they separated. The reason they separated is that the Thunder told the Wind: "I can do it alone even without your help." So the Wind spoke these words to him: "Because you said that, I have to leave you. . . . And so the Wind left to live far away from the Thunder, at the very end of the Earth. There was no more wind. It got very, very hot. So the Thunder, who had told the Wind, "I can do it alone," made more rain, but it was still hot. There were no more crops. This wasn't good. The Wind was nowhere to be found, and the Thunder didn't like it, so he used feathers. But with the feathers he waited in vain for the Wind to come. And because of this, he was unhappy. He finally resolved to bring back the Wind. He spoke these words to him: "My brother, now you are nowhere, and it's not good. There are no more crops, and it's very hot. I beg you to come back and live with me. From now on, we will both do good on the face of the Earth. We'll work together. Thanks to us, there will be good harvests." And so the Thunder begged the Wind. And the Wind returned to live with the Thunder. And became his friend once again.

That's why, when it rains, there is always thunder when there is wind. They are forever together.

Prologue

Paris, February 2005

Dear Madam, following your request, I have contacted Harlyn Geronimo, one of Geronimo's great-grandsons and, without a doubt, the one most invested in keeping his memory alive. I spoke with him about your book project, and I am pleased to inform you that he has allowed me to provide you with his contact information. I am including it here for your perusal. You can tell him I told you to contact him.

I wish you much success in the realization of your project.

Warmly,
René R.

I stand up. I walk in a small circle. It's become a habit whenever I'm overcome with joy. I repeat out loud the words of the Albuquerque journalist: "*You can tell him I told you to contact him! You can tell him I told you to contact him!*" I sit back down. What will Harlyn Geronimo's voice sound like? Will it sound like his great-grandfather's? I reread the email a dozen times, enough to convince myself that it's real. And then I thank the sender for his support and trust, assuring him that I will keep him abreast of developments in the process. I click Send.

And suddenly fear rises in my stomach.

During my childhood, I devoured all of those Indian movies: *Bronco Apache, Broken Arrow, Day of the Evil Gun,* and, of course,

Geronimo! As time went on, Geronimo became, like Superman, Peter Pan, or Mickey Mouse, a citizen of my imagination, a hero of that inner continent. But a fleshless, bodiless companion—a symbol, constructed by my mind, of the fight against injustice. So, you understand, making a phone call to one of his descendants is suddenly as extraordinary for me as having Peter Pan's grandson himself on the line. Inhale. Exhale. I grab the phone, stare at the keypad, my index finger. I smile. So it's not so hard after all to turn dreams into reality. I dial the first three numbers. I stop. What time is it? 4:00 P.M. There's an eight-hour difference between France and New Mexico, I checked. Are they eight hours ahead or behind? Damn, I never remember. No way I'm waking up Harlyn Geronimo in the middle of the night. OK. The United States is west of France. So the sun rises later over there. That means they are eight hours behind. That's right, I can call him! I'm calling Geronimo's descendent! Having a hard time getting used to the idea. OK. I feel inspired. I dial the number. Beep-beep-beep-beep-beep. The tone, like the wick of an old memory, has lit up to cross time. It throws its inexorable sparks at me, tracing a path of light into the present moment, here in my ear. One ring. Maybe he isn't home? Two rings. "Hello?" The voice of a man, a deep voice, has just answered. Is that him? My stomach rumbles. I blank. Surely because of all the emotion. I don't know what to say. The voice grows impatient. "Hello? Who is this?" Come on, courage! Harlyn is a human just like you.

"Um . . . Hello, my name is Corine Sombrun, I would like to speak with Harlyn Geronimo."

"Yes, it's me! Glad to hear from you, Corine, I was expecting your call. . . ."

That simple greeting feels good. Harlyn sounds friendly. And the journalist had informed him that I'd be in touch. So I go for it. I explain to him my desire to write a book on his great-grandfather. And to discuss it with him in an attempt to clear up certain points developed in *Geronimo: His Own Story*, the only existing account of Geronimo's life, told by Geronimo himself, and commissioned by S. M. Barrett.

Harlyn immediately agrees. He says I was right to contact him. He is a medicine man too, just like his illustrious ancestor. So he'll be able to discuss that aspect of Geronimo's life better than anyone. I raise my eyebrows.

"Really? A medicine man?"

Harlyn confirms it. I lower my eyebrows. And I was initiated to shamanism in Mongolia. Isn't that a pretty strange coincidence? One more coincidence on the path that has brought me to this moment. Already some eight years ago, the person I was sharing my life with died. From cancer. I left everything to take refuge in England and then Peru, with a shaman. Surely out of some need or hope to find answers to the question of death. For a few months in the Amazon jungle, this shaman taught me magical chants called *icaros*, which allow human beings to connect with certain plants that can supposedly transmit to humans an understanding of dreams, sounds, and anything else we might need to access the spirit world. At first, I found those prayers ridiculous, and the fact that I was singing them even more so. But it was actually after singing the icaro that corresponds to the ajo sacha, a plant that teaches us to understand dreams, and after drinking a decoction following a very precise ritual that I had this dream about a path to follow—to Mongolia. The dream was so incongruous, there in the middle of the Amazon, that I decided to go. I had nothing left to lose anyway, no ties, no responsibilities. So in 2001, the BBC World Service, the radio news organization for which I had already done a story in the Amazon, allowed me to go and do another on the shamans of Mongolia.* I didn't know at the time that this trip would upend my life.

The shamans there told me that I had been chosen by the spirits. That I too was a shaman. Should I tell Harlyn about it?

* My book, *Mon initiation chez les chamanes* (Paris: Albin Michel, 2004; Pocket, 2006), recounts this episode in my life.

No way! But why not? Harlyn doesn't let me think about it more before asking if I know what a medicine man is.

"Mmm . . . Yes."

And suddenly, I'm not sure why, all of my fears dissipate. I can't help but tell him everything. The Amazon. Mongolia. How there, Naraa, a friend, had agreed to be my guide so I could make contact with some shamans. Thanks to her, I was able to attend a ritual. In Mongolia, shamans go into a trance when they play the drums. One small catch was: the sound of that drum had a very unexpected effect on me, as a Westerner. A deep tremor propagated throughout my entire body. My heart rate rose, my eyes rolled back, my arms began to flail, my legs jumped, my body leaped, images of wolves took over my brain, my nose began to sniff. I really felt like I had become a wolf. I felt myself slip toward this door created by the drum's sound. A strange thing for sure, but the most extraordinary part of it was that I was conscious of what I was experiencing. I just couldn't control it. I kept on slipping toward that door. And then the beating of the drum stopped. In the nick of time, right as I was about to enter. Someone was shaking me. I eventually opened my eyes. The shaman was standing in front of me. Looking worried, he asked, "Why didn't you tell me you were a shaman?!" My eyes finally opened with that remark. As far as I was concerned, he was wrong. I was not, nor had any desire to be, a shaman. But he wouldn't accept my answer. "If the drum causes this reaction in you, then you're a shaman. The spirits have chosen you. You'll have to follow the secret teachings reserved to them." This meant spending three years in the deepest recesses of Mongolia with a master shaman. And if I refused? His response was clear. The spirits would cause me serious grief. According to him, my dream in the Amazon was not a coincidence but a message from the spirits informing me where my "destiny" as a shaman was to be fulfilled. Since then (this was in 2001), I have spent a few months every year on the border between Mongolia and Siberia following the teachings of a woman shaman: Enkhtuya. She's had a costume and drum made for me, she has taught me, thanks to my drum, how to navigate the world of trances, how to interpret its sensations, its messages, its visions.

My story told, I wait for Harlyn's reaction. But he remains silent. The jitters return to my stomach. I feel regret. I never should have told him all of that. Thankfully, I didn't confess the strangest part. It was during one of those trances that Geronimo's name came to me.* It came back incessantly. So real I told myself that this "message," as powerful as the dream I'd had in the Amazon, must have a meaning. But what was it? So I sought to find out by sending an email to the journalist who was an expert in the Apaches' saga. I told him, at the time, about my desire to write a book on Geronimo. My desire to meet one of his descendants. Without revealing the source of my interest—he would have taken me for a madwoman, and he would have been right. Your standard Westerner does not pursue callings revealed in trances. Harlyn's voice finally emerges, revealing what I never could have guessed. . . .

"Your story doesn't really surprise me."

He stops speaking. I wait, having trouble understanding this lack of surprise.

"According to one of our legends," he finally continues, "the Apaches are descendants of the Mongols. And actually our children, like the young Mongols, have a 'blue' birthmark at the bottom of their backs. Sadly, we've lost touch with those roots and traditions. But I knew that one day someone would come and reconnect us with them. And today, you called. So for me, it's anything but a coincidence."

It's my turn to remain speechless. All the pieces of this puzzle start twirling in my brain. Start assembling. Was I this link Harlyn had awaited to reconnect current Apache culture to the ancient Mongol one? Was this the reason for my vision of Geronimo during the trance? But why me? Perhaps Harlyn knows the answer.

---

* *Les Tribulations d'une chamane à Paris* (Paris: Albin Michel, 2007).

No. I mustn't ask him. Not over the phone. And I need to think about it anyway. To give my mind time to accept what I've just heard. It's so beyond any logic or reason.

"Corine? Are you still there?"

"Mmm, yes, sorry, I . . . I was thinking about what you just told me. It's strange, isn't it?!"

I hear a little burst of laughter. Then his voice again. Harlyn suggests that we meet in New Mexico, to see, very simply, where this "strange" story will take us and where it might have begun.

'Íłtséshį́ Bik'ehgo'iindáń gól̜íná'a.
Dájík'eh bédaagojísį.
'Ákoo Isdzánádleeshé 'iłdǫ́ gól̜íná'a.

Bik'éshį́go Tóbájiishchinéń goosl̜íná'a.
Naaghéé'neesgháné 'iłdǫ́ goosl̜íná'a.

'Ákoo dį́į́' jiłt'égo gojíl̜íná'a, dá'íłtségodeeyáshį́.

'Ákoo 'Isdzáńaádleeshéń Tóbájiishchinéń bizhaaná'a.
'Ákoo Naaghéé'neesghánéń ndé doonzhǫ́dashégo ndé 'át'į́ná'a.

Ghéé'ye hooghéń 'iłdǫ́ gól̜íná'a.
nDéí doobáńgólaadaná'a.
Isdzánádleeshéń bizhaa goyaleełná'a.
Isdzánádleeshéń bizhaań 'it'a bizą́áyégo, Ghéé'ye hooghéń kaayinłndéná'a.

In the beginning there lived the Creator.
Everyone knows this.
Then there lived White-Painted Woman.

Later, Child of the Water was born.
And Killer of Enemies too.
And so there were four, in the very beginning.

9

And Child of the Water was the son of White-Painted Woman.
And Killer of Enemies was also the son of
White-Painted Woman.

The one called Giant existed too.
He wouldn't allow humans to live.
When the children of White-Painted Woman were born,
The one called Giant wanted to eat them.

In the Beginning

IN THE BEGINNING, everything was darkness. There was no sun, no stars, no moon. But then the sun, stars, and moon were born, and began their watch. . . .

So begins our legend, Grandfather. The legend of the Apaches. The legend of our family, told to me by your wife, Kate. About you, Geronimo, many things have been said. Good things and the worst, but none of them *your* truth. The truth you told Kate and that she passed on to me throughout my childhood. And today, Grandfather, as if for the first time, I have finally been given the opportunity—yes, me, Harlyn Geronimo, your great-grandson— to retell the story of our heritage so dear to my heart and in doing so, to reveal the fate allotted our people.

Long ago, the Wind, the Thunder, the Lightning, and other forces came into being. Thirty-two powerful elements in all. They created Earth. At first, she was tiny, but then she grew and grew, in a spiral. Ribbons of iron plunged deep in her center, to keep her in place. Then everything blended together, and that is why iron can be found everywhere on earth.

In those days, two tribes ruled the world. The feathered creatures, the birds, and the furred ones, the beasts. The chief of the bird tribe was the eagle. The world was in perpetual darkness, and the birds wanted to invite the light in. But the beasts refused. And so they made war. The eagle alone knew how to use a bow and arrows. He taught other tribe members, and they won the war against the beasts.

And so light was allowed on Earth. The sun brought heat, which made the waves that shuddered in the air. And thanks to this, the Apaches were created and humanity could develop. In honor of the eagle, who was responsible for this victory, men would wear feathers as an emblem of justice, power, and wisdom.

Millions of years ago, the one we call Yusn created a girl named, by my people, White-Painted Woman. She was submerged in the ocean and, according to legend, this took place off the coast where San Diego is in California. A few moments later, Yusn caught her by her feathers and laid her on the beach. There, he told her: "White-Painted Woman, you are the precursor to the Apache nation. You shall bear two boys. Killer of Enemies and Child of the Water. The latter shall be the son of Rain of the Storm. He must walk to where the sun rises, then marry, and multiply to give rise to the Apache nation."

But after Yusn left the girl on the beach, the one we call Giant, who at that time lived under a giant seashell, came to see her and told her: "White-Painted Woman, you may stay here a while, but no one other than you may live here. If I see a single human being around, I will have to kill and eat him."

Yet a few months later, the two boys were born. Remembering Giant's threat, White-Painted Woman dug a tunnel to hide her sons, and several years passed like this. Yusn had given the boys bows and arrows. He also taught them how to use them to hunt, and they were very skilled.

But by accident one day, Giant discovered the truth. He told their mother: "I had forbidden you to have any children. Now I'm going to have to kill them and eat them." But before he could do anything, Killer of Enemies shot an arrow straight into Giant's heart. The arrow didn't kill him right away. So Child of the Water shot another one into his heart, then another, and another. The fourth arrow killed him.

Child of the Water began his journey to find a place to settle. Yusn taught him how to prepare herbs for cures and how to fight his enemies. He was the first Indian chief and wore eagle feathers in honor of the one who had helped the birds bring light to the Earth.

1

The car's in drive. Accelerate and brake is all you have to do in these automatic-shift cars, unlike in France. I yawn. Not, as we say in French, *aux corneilles*—"at the crows."* There are none here, only eagles scratching the sky with their beaks. One etches a furrow around the sun. I wish he'd take me in his claws so I could explore the sky with him. The landscape is far too dull in this place. Outside of El Paso, I passed through fields of houses that stretched for miles, planted in the middle of the desert and lining the roads in a perfect grid pattern. I felt like I was moving through an electronic circuit. Like I was nowhere. *Nowhere.* And the worst came right after that: the gray cube. First it was small, far off under the deep blue sky, lost between the rocks, the cacti with their long white feather dusters, and the ochre land, but then the cube slowly grew on the horizon, nestled comfortably in the loneliest place you could imagine. It turned into a huge building surrounded by multiple layers of barbed wire.

When I realized it was a high-security prison, I looked away and muttered a quick *Shit* as you would if your eye involuntarily caught sight of something shocking. I counted the cacti, the rocks, the shrubs, the busted tires scattered like black carcasses along the road that was utterly straight and monotonous, without a turn or curve, without anything soft about it. But I couldn't stop thinking

---

* *Bailler aux corneilles* is a French idiom that literally translates as "to yawn at the crows" and is said of someone who is yawning excessively or deeply.

about those hallways of death. The electric chair. The terror just before it. Humans are more barbaric than this so-called inhuman desert. I turn the AC to max. The freezing air strokes my face. I think about Harlyn, about the Apaches. They too had to suffer under the law of the strongest. I wonder, does the reservation where they were stuck look like this desert?

I didn't dare ask Harlyn what type of dwelling he lives in. Certainly not a tipi. I reached a home phone—perhaps a trailer? I saw a whole bunch of them outside El Paso. More boxes, but this time made out of cardboard and with wheels. Unsightly, and I bet without AC. Summer is probably scorching hot. And to think I brought sweaters and my down sleeping bag. Between minus forty Celsius in Mongolia and this BBQ pit here, I seem to have a knack for turning up shamans in the most extreme places. Anyway, you're a lot better off than the residents of the gray cube over there behind the barbed wire, just a few miles away. A road sign blinks to my right: SPEED LIMIT 70 MPH. What's the equivalent in kilometers per hour? No idea, and no intention of doing the conversion. A glance at the speedometer: *80 mph.* You end up speeding without out even realizing it on these infinitely straight roads. Instantly, I lift my right foot. I really have no desire for a run-in with the police in this country. The sun beats down on the red hood of the car. Not a cloud in the sky. And the water on the asphalt in the distance playfully disappears when I draw closer. A mirage. The only possible game in this enormous valley of quivering heat.

I turn my head to check that my blue water bottle is still next to me. It is. Without letting go of the steering wheel, I grab it and place it between my thighs to unscrew the lid. One gulp. This, water, is the only way to catch you here. I'm suddenly jolted by a honk. Quick glance at the rearview mirror. A huge truck is behind me. A red cabin with silver exhaust pipes, and my car is reflected in it because it's so polished. Why is he honking? I check my speedometer. *70 mph*, exactly. Well, you can just pass me if you want to go faster! No way I'm accelerating. I move over a bit to the right and let him pass.

He draws closer. His great shadow swallows a little bit of my car. The cabin is now at my level. I keep my eyes on the road ahead of me. I don't feel like staring into the driver's angry face. There. The monster has pulled past me. I get to stare at its rear end now. With a great big sticker in the shape of a ribbon with the colors of the American flag. I squint to read the words: SUPPORT OUR TROOPS. I remember this country is at war. You wouldn't know it, sitting here. No gunshots, no fighting. I was reminded of it briefly at the Atlanta airport when I heard some applause in a hall. Some people were holding up banners: WELCOME TO OUR HEROES. The heroes were coming off the plane in their camouflage uniforms and matching backpacks, with combat boots on their feet and big smiles. Two of them walked past me. I was able to notice that the patterns on their uniforms were pixilated. Thousands of little green and beige squares coming together to create that look. Probably to enhance its effect from a distance? I put my bottle of water back on the seat.

All good in the rearview mirror now? No. Maybe? A gray cylinder seems to have dropped from the sky back there, on the horizon. I turn my head to see. It looks like a dusty tornado. I slow down, pull onto the shoulder, and open the window. The heat tumbles in. Yep, it's a big dust devil. I see it move forward, turn, twist. Is it as far away as it looks? Hard to say in this great expanse. It looks small from here. I hope it doesn't land near me. What do you do in that case? First things first, avoid being in one.

I start the car again. Maybe that's why the truck was in a hurry? He was probably honking to warn me to get out of there. I accelerate. Surely you can break the speed limit in case of a dust storm. *80 mph, 85, 90.* That's what I'll tell the cop who pulls me over. Is it coming this way or not? Quick glance in the rearview. Still just as small. Okay. I lift my foot off the gas pedal. *85, 80, 70 mph.* The landscape slows down with me. Cacti, stones, brush, stones, ochre earth . . .

The clock in the display shows 2:30 P.M. If the dust devil stays where it is and my best guess is correct, the Mescalero Apache Indian Reservation shouldn't be more than two hours away.

Harlyn told me the Apaches are spread out across different reservations throughout the Southwest. Two here in New Mexico, two in Arizona, and one in Oklahoma. There are apparently approximately fifty thousand Apaches. I don't know if I'll be staying with him, but he told me to call when I get there. Anyway, I have my camping gear with me. Tent, headlamp, electric flashlight, Swiss Army knife (the big multi-tool model), two survival blankets, dried apricots, vitamins. In Mongolia, at Enkhtuya's, there was only dried meat and flour to live on, so now I come prepared.

I also brought a bottle of wine for Harlyn from the Graves region of Bordeaux. He's probably never tasted wine before. Enkhtuya made a face the first time she tried it. The second and third times too. She prefers vodka. I hope I didn't forget my two plastic jerry cans. No, I remember putting them in. They're convenient, since they're collapsible. They can be completely flattened to fit into your suitcase and then unfold in the form of a water bag when you fill them. I use them a lot in Mongolia, since there's no water except for the river or lake where we make camp for the reindeer and yaks to graze nearby. They're sure to be useful on the reservation. I hope at least there's a watering place not too far from Harlyn's. It probably only rains once every three years in that desert, and you can bet I've picked a drought year. Enkhtuya taught me a ritual to find water underground but none to make it fall from the sky. That, she simply can't do. And she doesn't need to anyway, since it rains where she lives. I've noticed, after spending so many years in the company of shamans, that each people tends to develop the rituals most useful to them.

And, to a certain extent, that's what shamanism is. A collection of recipes for surviving in a hostile environment. A trick to reassure humans by giving them the illusion they control whatever might fall into their hands and on their heads. Psychologists call it the illusion of control mechanism. I'm guessing that the Apaches must have come up with a ritual that makes the rain come, since there is none. I mustn't forget to ask Harlyn about it.

A first house, then a second. Ah! A lot filled with school buses to my left. There must be at least a hundred of them, all yellow and black, parked next to each other. Maybe a school bus cemetery. And here's a gas station. Quick look at the gas gauge. Half full. All good. Ah! An intersection. The first in three hours. I hope I don't have to go straight. Turning the steering wheel might finally wake up my arms. I look at the signs. Albuquerque, Alamogordo . . . Tularosa, to the left! I make the turn. And see another endless straight line. Oh well. At least the landscape has changed. Gas stations alternate with lots of car carcasses, wooden houses without fences, and now a large sign advertising pistachios for sale. Another similar sign on my right. This time around I put on my blinker and give a quick glance in the rearview. Only out of instinct, since the only car I've encountered since the red truck was a pick-up with a guy sleeping in the back under his sombrero, arms crossed.

I pull onto a road leading to a parking lot with a building in the middle. The store, apparently. I park the car, open my door. The heat is oppressive. Breathing the scalding air, I feel like I'm some sort of frozen good being shoved into an oven. It's uncomfortable. I shake my numb legs, stretch my back. There are fields of trees behind the building. They look like fruit trees, of average height, with pretty green leaves. I'll take a look. The sun is beating down on my skull. I create some shade by holding a hand just above my head. The hand heats up immediately. I come to a white wooden fence. Here are the trees. Clusters seem to be hanging from the large oval leaves. I climb over the fence and go closer. These are indeed pistachios in their green velvet shells. I touch them. They're soft. But it's no time to linger; the sun is beating down too hard. Immediate return to my icebox. And to think I brought sweaters with me but not a single hat. I considered it, but they make me look like a turtle. Ludicrous. If I can find a store in this hole, I'll buy a cowboy hat.

The road has been climbing for about a half hour. Now it's winding through big hills covered in pine trees. I haven't found a single place to buy a hat, only some antique stores. I wonder what they could possibly sell in there, but the heat prevailed over my curiosity and I didn't stop. There's a bit more traffic here. I passed a few pick-ups and a white truck that said WAL-MART. And look, among the pines I see some firs! Or larches, I can never tell. If only Harlyn lived nearby. My gaze lingers on some paint along the road. Graffiti? I crack the window and stick my nose out. It's much cooler here. Yep, it's graffiti on a wall. I slow down when I come to it. There's a big Indian figure painted in black on a white background. Three feathers extend from his headdress. There's also a moon painted in a black sky and tipis, conifers. It looks like my wish is coming true. I'm entering Indian territory.

I turn off the AC and keep the window down. The smell of pines fills my nostrils. Deep breath in. Eyes closed. Eyes open again. Just in time to see the sign: WELCOME TO MESCALERO.

A tingling feeling of joy fills me. I'm here! Harlyn told me to keep going until the RUIDOSO sign and then stop to call him. Where is my phone? Do I have his number? Yes. Okay. In my contacts. I was right about the sweaters, it turns out. A tipi! There, to the right, in a clearing in the middle of the forest. And horses grazing next to houses made of wood and painted almond green. So pretty. Maybe Harlyn doesn't live in a trailer after all? The four-lane road crosses a field of mauve thistles. Still no sign of Ruidoso. Maybe I missed an intersection? Some big 4 x 4s are passing me. I notice another sign, APACHE FRY BREAD, in front of a wooden cabin. Fried bread? I switch on my blinker and pull into the parking lot. Maybe someone will be able to give me directions. I enter the sky-blue building, a kind of grocery store with dream catchers and photos of Indians on the walls. An obese lady with long brown hair, wearing jeans and a pink T-shirt, appears behind the counter. She asks me with a smile if she can help me. I look at her, moved.

"Are you Apache?"

She laughs.

"Of course! You know, you're going to see a lot of us around here."

I apologize and explain that I live in France. She doesn't really seem to know where that country is but welcomes me anyway.

"Why have you come here?"

"I'm here to see Harlyn Geronimo. Do you know him?"

She thinks.

"No."

Her answer is a little disappointing. I'd imagined him to be some sort of celebrity here. Apparently not.

"Are you going to be staying with us for long?"

"A month."

She raises her eyebrows.

"A month? In Mescalero?"

She seems quite surprised. But I refrain from asking why. I don't really want to know. Anyway, she continues:

"Do you want to taste our specialty?"

She shows me a large platter filled with a kind of donut.

"Is that fry bread?"

"Yes. We fry the bread in a big pan. How many would you like?"

A quick glance to estimate. Each piece is the size of a plate.

"Um . . . one will be fine, thanks."

She gives me the once-over from head to toe, kind of like, *One of these donuts is not going to fill out those curves, Missy.* But she doesn't put any words to her thoughts. She simply points at the walls of the store.

"I also sell dream catchers. The net in the center of the circle catches the bad dreams and lets only the good ones through. Do you have those in your country?"

"No, we have sleeping pills."

Shrug.

"We do too, but I prefer dream catchers. Do you want one?"

"I don't have nightmares."

"It's a nightmare here, you'll see."

How should I interpret that statement? As a threat? A warning? Or simply a gloomy statement of fact? Again, I'm not going to dwell on it.

"Okay! I'll take one."

She asks me to take it down, since moving around is hard for her. I choose a purple one, about four inches in diameter and with three leather strips decorated with feathers and beads, and lay it out on the counter. A smile finally returns to her tanned face, and she points to a glass case on her right.

"I also sell Apache crafts. Necklaces, bracelets, and belts decorated with beads."

I go over to it, hoping she won't make me buy her entire stock before letting me leave, but what I see is very beautiful. I even spot a large belt with red and blue geometric motifs and two leather straps instead of a buckle. I love it. I ask the price. She takes the belt out of the glass case, turns over the price tag.

"Sixty-six dollars."

I grimace and apologize. A bit too expensive for me. She seems a little sad but doesn't insist. I take a last look at the belt, uncertain for a moment. Should I get it? No! my reason replies. Okay. I pay sixteen dollars for the rest.

"Am I on the road to Ruidoso?"

"Yes, straight ahead."

She wishes me good luck and a nice stay among the Apaches. I thank her and leave, holding my fry bread with my fingertips.

About a quarter of the fry bread later, I feel like I've swallowed a stone. How could you possibly eat more than one of these? I gently lay the bread back down on its wrapper and attempt to wipe off my greasy fingers. It was a good idea to bring the dried apricots. Still no Ruidoso. But more and more fir trees along the road. The air is actually cool now. It feels like the Vosges region in France with these pines among the fir trees. I've really been unfair to the Americans. This reservation seems pleasant, and my stay might even end up feeling like a fitness vacation. Ah! There's an enormous billboard in the shape of a lollipop up ahead. It's blinking. An ad? I get closer. My eyes widen as I come to a digital screen that's at least twenty feet high and reads: AT CASINO APACHE . . . CASH BACK FOR SLOTS . . . TABLE GAMES . . . PLAY . . ." I close my eyes and open them again. BIG JACKPOT TODAY! No, I'm not dreaming. All of the day's games and possible winnings are even listed.

Behind the lollipop there's a huge parking lot with not too many cars and a large, rectangular two-tone building, green and beige, on which an enormous sign-board that says CASINO APACHE is completely lit up with neon lights. I smile. And I was expecting three trailers, two tipis, and horses with their manes floating in the wind! I have to admit that my French middle-class imagination is somewhat shaken. The Apaches certainly don't seem to have followed the example of their Asian ancestors, who still live in tipis and survive on flour and water.

And the surprises aren't over. A half mile later, the road is all decked out with fast food restaurants, motels, hotels, banks, cell-phone stores. I suddenly feel as if I'm in the urban development zone of a small French city. Except there are Dollar Stores and Wal-Marts instead of the local Leclerc or Carrefour supermarkets, there are Motels 6s instead of our Formula 1s, and certain distinctive signs mark this town as belonging to Indians. For example, Lincoln Rent A Car has a tipi on their sign, the store at the gas station is called Big Chief Store, and I passed a motel with the evocative name of Arrow Head.

Don't I look like a fool now with my tent, my survival gear, and my vitamins? When I think that all I had to do was Google "Mescalero Reservation" to get the right info. But there you have it: Madame doesn't ever care to know in advance. She'd rather be surprised. She'd rather experience culture shock in her innards, her nostrils, her eyeballs. Well, this time, it's a bust. The only shock I'm experiencing is at my own stupidity, which encounters with other people's cultures tend to bring out. Ah, the Ruidoso sign at last. And a traffic light, the first since Tularosa, a few hundred yards ahead. Red. I stop next to a black 4 x 4. That's all you see around here. Each one bigger than the last. I peer at the driver's face. He certainly looks Indian. But his face is swathed in a layer of fat. The light turns green. I follow the arrow telling me to turn left for downtown. First City Bank, Wells Fargo, Best Western, ah! Lincoln Hospital, that's handy, and a vet, maybe. Another McDonald's and an . . . Apache Motel! The perfect name for my first stop. I can use the parking lot to call Harlyn. Blinker on. The car in the next lane over stops to let me through. People around here are chill. In Paris, someone would already have rammed my door in. After thanking the driver with a hand signal, I drive onto the parking lot.

The motel is a one-story building in a U configuration. The door of each room looks out onto its own parking space. I park in front of reception to turn on my cell. PIN code. The little bars in the upper left-hand corner seem to move. I wonder what name the network will be here. Apachetelecom? Nope. Nothing shows. No reception? That's the last thing I need. Come on, phone, connect! Still no bars. It worked in El Paso, though. In Atlanta too. New search. Sometimes, it takes a while. Nope. Still nothing. Sigh. Sigh again. Even deep inside Mongolia there's a network! I'm in the United States—it should work, shouldn't it? I get out of the car to see if I can get some information at the registration desk.

Behind a wooden counter, a skinny young Indian man with a black ponytail greets me. "May I help you?" Oh yes! I explain my problem. "That's normal," he says with a big smile that reveals a green line over his teeth, "we have a special network on the reservation. But you can buy another phone in one of the shops in town." He smiles again. I stare at his mouth, intrigued. He's wearing braces, and the green line over his teeth is the elastic connecting them. I wore them too. But all metal ones, not as fun. Apparently ignoring my stare, he continues his explanation.

"There's an Alltel store two minutes from here, but they'll be closed."

"Closed?"

I glance at my watch. It's not quite five!

The young man confirms that's closing time in the States. OK. No need to panic. I'll go tomorrow morning. I ask him at what time the store opens tomorrow morning. A slightly embarrassed look.

"Tomorrow's the Fourth of July, our national holiday. But it'll be open two days from now."

Seeing my irritation, he says, "Sorry," and shrugs his shoulders. I thank him for the information anyway. The smile returns to his face. He asks me where I'm from.

"France."

"France? Cool, my grandfather was French! He married an Apache . . ."

While I'm getting over my surprise, I answer that I actually came here to meet an Apache man. But without the intention of marrying him.

He bursts out laughing.

"And are you planning on staying long?"

"A month."

He opens his eyes wide. A month? In Ruidoso?

I look at him. A slight concern registers in my tired brain, which is feeling the jetlag.

"Why is everyone asking me that? It's not normal to stay for a month?"

"It's just that there's not much to do here in summer. . . . Except for the casinos."

I furrow my brows. The casinos, plural? I've only seen one. So there are more?

"Two to be precise. One on the main road, which you drove past, and the other half a mile from here. It's bigger and has a golf course. Do you play golf?"

I'm speechless. Two casinos? A golf course? To put an end to the surprises, I ask him to tell me what other things I might enjoy this vacation.

"In the winter, people ski here. That's the region's main attraction. There's a resort about twenty miles away. Haven't you seen lots of rental cabins all over town?"

"Cabins?"

"Yes. Little wooden chalets. One room with a fireplace in the middle of the forest. They're very nice. But in July, with no snow, no skiing, the resort's closed. You can go hiking there if you like. It's a nice walk. By the way, though, who is your Apache friend?"

"My friend? Oh, right. Harlyn. Harlyn Geronimo. Maybe you know him?"

A doubtful look. Clearly, no one has heard of him around here.

"I'm supposed to call him. Do you have a phone?"

"Is it a local call?"

"Yes, well, I hope it is."

I show him the number. He confirms it is. Phew. I'm starting to doubt Harlyn's presence in the area. The young man points to phone behind the counter. I pick up the handset. One ring, two, three, four, five. I look at my watch. 5:15 P.M. Maybe he isn't home yet? Finally, a voice. "You have reached Harlyn Geronimo . . ." Damn, the answering machine. "I'm away from the phone. Please leave me a message. *Beeeeeep.*" My turn to speak. "Um, hello Harlyn, this is Corine. I am in Ruidoso but my cell phone doesn't work. I'll call you later or you can leave a message at the reception desk of the Apache Motel. Their number is . . ." I look over at the receptionist, who hands me a card with seven digits. I read them out loud and hang up. Harlyn didn't give me an alternate number in case I couldn't reach him. But considering the quality of life on this reservation, I don't doubt he has a cell phone.

I ask the receptionist if he has any rooms available for tonight, glad I don't need to use my tent. No worries, he says with a laugh, there aren't any tourists in the summer. OK, OK, I get it! He offers to show me a room. I follow him to a wooden door. He opens it and invites me into the bedroom. It's hot, but it's roomy and has a big bed, a white wooden table, a chair, and a kitchenette equipped with a microwave, an electric coffee maker, and a stainless steel sink on top of a small cabinet, and a fridge. The carpeting is brownish and a little worn, but that matches the terry cloth bedspread. The young man shows me a bathroom behind the door. Sink, shower, and toilet. And to think I brought my collapsible jerry cans thinking I'd have to fetch water. I thank him. "You're welcome!" he answers, handing me a gold metal tipi to which the key is attached. Number nine. He heads for the door, pointing out the AC. The AC? "Of course," he replies, surprised at my bewilderment. With this heat, it's everywhere. He goes over to the machine. The heels of his suede cowboy boots make the carpet hiss. "You want me to turn it on for you?" Please do. He presses a large gray button. The motor starts up. Not very quiet, but quite the luxury compared to what I was expecting.

Before leaving, he says to feel free to come by reception to phone my friend. I thank him again. The door is barely closed before I hop onto the bed. A pleasure I can never indulge in in Mongolia, since I have to sleep on the frozen ground in the tipi. Two *boing boings* later, I get up with a smile on my face to do a brief inspection of the room. I open the fridge, which feels cool. I open the freezer. No ice tray. I'll have to ask for one. I open the cabinet door under the sink. Two mugs, two glasses, two plates, four pieces of tableware. I fill my water bottle at the sink. I'm going to assume the water's fine here. In Mongolia, I have to boil it first, since we take it from the lake or the rivers. I have a little metal pot just for that, and I always leave it on the wood stove. The Mongols drink it as is. Which is a good thing, since my boiled water alone consumes more wood than a whole family uses for heat. Around the lake, you can actually see the effects of nomadic families beginning to settle there. Little by little, the forests are giving way to large clearings dotted with tree stumps.

I still have to go fetch my luggage from the trunk of the car. Only two large bags with wheels. Yes, I've always been inclined to comfort. Even in the steppe, I roll them into the tipi, which makes Enkhtuya's husband, Doudgi, laugh. He prefers to carry them for me. He's no weakling. One, two, and they're out of the trunk. I roll them over to my room. One of them will be useless, since all it contains is my camping gear. I fetch my shaman's drum too. It's a monster, about three feet in diameter with eight-inch sides. No wheels. I've never been able to find a case the right size for it. So, whenever I travel, it doesn't leave my shoulder.

I probably won't need it much here, but I thought Harlyn would enjoy learning about the shamanic traditions of his "cousins." I also brought my costume, including the hat with feathers from the *soïr*, the sacred Mongolian bird. I lay the drum on the table. Enkhtuya has always told me to keep it elevated. I don't know why, but I follow her instructions. Spirits anger easily, it seems. . . .

Now all I need is to shower and take a nap. I'm exhausted. It's eight hours ahead in France, so about two in the morning. I set the alarm clock on my cell phone to 8:00 P.M. Harlyn should be home by then, so I'll call him from the front desk. What if I can't reach him? Well, I'll put my dream catcher on the nightstand for starters. Maybe it will spare me that nightmare.

’Iłk’idą, inndaaí ’it’ago hąhé łą daolaahát’édadą,
nDéí ’ił’ango ’ádaahooghéí díík’eh joogobago daahindáná’a.

’Íyąąda k’adi, Chidikáágo hooghéí ’ásht’į.
Shinndéí, biłnndénshłįí, dásídá’át’égo ’iłk’idą daahindáná’aí
baanałdaagoshndi.

Daanahitsóyéí dáłeezhíighe’yá daahindáná’a.
Dátł’ohná beekooghąshį dá’ádaa’ílaa.
Tł’oh bégoos’eelyá naasjé.

Ch’ide yá’édį.
Beekooghaní yá’édį.
Dooha’shį ła’jóláhát’éda.
’Iban ’ádaat’éí gotł’aazhį k’édaadeesdizná’a.

Naagołtįgo, tóí gok’izhį nkeedanłį.
Zas naałtįgo, zasí gokázhį naadaałtį.
Hago, dák ǫǫ ná daagoch’ide.

Góghégo nDé góĮíná’a.
Díík’ehí yá’édįná’a.
Béésh yá’édįná’a.
Bee’itseełntsaaí yá’édįná’a.
Bee’itseełbizą́ąyéí yá’édįná’a.
Dátsédeendíná gobeedaa’itseełná’a.

A long time ago, long before white men existed,
All of the people called Indians lived poorly, so they say.

I am one of those called Chiricahuas.
About my people, the people among whom I live, I will tell you

What was said of their customs in the past.

Our ancestors lived in the dirt, so they say.
Their houses were made only of grass, so they say.
They lay in the grass.

There were no blankets.
There were no tents.
No one was safe anywhere.
The people were wrapped in buckskins, so they say.

When it rained, water fell on them.
When it snowed, snow fell on them.
In the winter, fire was their only blanket.

The Indians had a hard life, so they say.
They went in need, so they say.
There was no metal, so they say.
There were no axes, so they say.
There were no hatchets, so they say.
Their only axes were chipped stones, so they say.

The Day You Were Born

THE GILA, OUR RIVER, forks at the spot where you were born, Grandfather. You couldn't know then that this split would be the symbol of your life—always between two attitudes, love and hate. The river's clear, elusive water flows through six beautiful red boulders, spaced like the web of a dream catcher. Watching that water gush in joyful gurgles was always your favorite thing to do. Many times you came here to quench your desires. And even more often to drown your nightmares.

From the Mogollon Rim on the Arizona border, the Gila took millennia to dig its way to this land of our people, the Chiricahua Apaches. The hills that surround it are covered in a tangle of shrubs. They make walking arduous and slow, but you loved dragging your legs through them. Your father, *Taa di tlish hn*, would always say to you, "Facing the enemy, your legs are your only friends." He was right. They often saved you and each time you thought of him. Your father was a righteous man. His Apache name in fact was that of a being from our mythology who is often invoked to make children behave. "If you aren't good, we'll call *Taa di tlish hn*!" That was enough to quiet even the most unruly among them.

Your birth name, dear Grandfather, was *Guu yuu le n*, referring to the stag's back tendon, which we used to make our bowstrings, but a few months after your birth your father also called you *Guu ji ya*, the clever one. A Chiricahua Apache could have many names, depending on his personality or the events that marked his life.

The name Geronimo was never yours. That was given to you later by your worst enemies, the Mexicans. But I will speak of this at the proper time. Not in the chronological way that white men value, but in the Indian way, by what seems important.

And so I'll begin by telling of the time when this territory still belonged to the Biidaa-hikahnde our "band," which came from one of the three main bands of Chiricahuan Apaches. There were six in all, and they were defined by the territory they occupied, from the far southeastern corner of Arizona to the Rio Grande in New Mexico and into the northern parts of Sonora and Chihuahua states in Mexico.

Back in those days, these borders didn't exist for the Apaches. It is the whites who determined them later, without consulting the Apaches. Your territory, Grandfather, the Biidaa-hikahnde territory, lay in western New Mexico, extending around what is known today as the Gila National Forest.

Your mother, *Gha den dini*, often told you that on the day of your birth the light and the air were mercilessly bright, the shadows deep and sharp as razor blades. It was the season we call Little Eagles. The Chiricahuan year is divided into six periods, from nature's regrowth to its period of rest. Little Eagles corresponds to the start of summer and is followed by Many Leaves, Large Leaves, Large Fruit, Earth Is Reddish Brown, and Ghost Face, the coldest time of winter. The whites said you were born in June of the year called 1823. Or perhaps 1829. Your mother never remembered exactly. But of this she is certain: the berries were beginning to ripen on the sumac bush in whose branches the midwife, a woman from your tribe, placed your umbilical cord wrapped in the buckskin on which you were born. Each newborn had his or her own tree. The trees returned to life each year, and, through this act, the Chiricahuas gave prayer that the child's life would be renewed as well. The cord was never buried, for wild animals might have dug it up and eaten it, bringing the child bad luck.

After placing it on a branch, the midwife blessed your cord with pollen, the yellow powder collected from cattails, and said to the tree: "May this child grow and live long enough to see you bear fruit many times. . . ." On that day, this place became sacred for you. You would have to return without fail to die here for the great cycle of your life to be complete.

When she found she was pregnant, your mother, like all Chiricahua women, had to respect the restrictions imposed on her condition: cease having sexual intercourse, cease riding horseback, and avoid sitting for too long. Especially after the fifth month, since it might have prevented you from descending into the right position. She also eliminated from her diet any foods made with animal entrails, so you wouldn't be strangled by your umbilical cord, and avoided eating meat fat, so you wouldn't be too big and the delivery would be easier.

Some say shamans are able to determine the unborn's gender. Your mother never believed that. To her, only Yusn, the creator, had this power. But she knew you were a boy, Grandfather. You moved in her womb more than a girl would have! She had eight children altogether, four boys and four girls. And you were the fourth.

Just before labor began, your mother swallowed four yucca leaves from the tender part at the center of the cactus, with some salt, to speed your passage and shorten the amount of time she would suffer. When it came time, your father and the men of the tribe went away. The midwife accompanied your mother to an oak pole that she would be able to hold onto. She knelt on a buckskin, with her thighs spread wide over a receptacle filled with a decoction made from the mashed roots of a small plant with white flowers from the Xanthum family, and into this your mother dipped her genitals. (You yourself later learned to collect this plant.) Then the midwife massaged her belly, from top to bottom, until you came out.

She said you'd grow to be robust since you didn't scream very loudly. She couldn't have imagined just how robust, Grandfather!

She cut your umbilical cord with a long black flint blade and wrapped the filament from a yucca leaf around your navel. After checking that your mother's uterus was returning to its normal place, she cleaned you with warm water and lay you on a buckskin. Then she coated your body with animal fat and red ochre, a sort of clay, to prevent blemishes or sores. While praying, she threw pollen to the four directions, starting with the east, then lifted you high and presented your body to the four directions.

To help your mother recover, she had her drink a decoction of roots and tied a rope around her belly, so her stomach wouldn't hang. The following day, your mother lay down for several hours. The day after that, she rested a little less. One week later, she resumed all the activities of an Apache woman. But, to ensure that her milk would be rich and abundant, she boiled deer bones to make soups. She offered you her breast the moment you cried. And, since you already had the appetite of an ogre, you cried a lot.

The construction of your cradle was done by a shaman. Your parents had given her a horse and a buckskin decorated with a turquoise. She used pieces of ash for the frame and wove together yucca stalks for the back of the cradle. Above the head, to protect your eyes from the sun, she affixed a sort of canopy made from the stems of Apache plume, a small plant with white flowers, whose seeds develop into bundles that are very soft to the touch. She then dressed the inside of the cradle with wild mustard leaves and crushed bark to absorb your excretions, and garnished the upper part with leaves of nightshade, a plant in the potato family, to make a pillow.

Finally, she placed the amulets. A bag of pollen, beads of turquoise, and a turkey's beard to ward off fears, which in the Chiricahua tradition are the cause of many diseases. To protect you from evil spells, she also hung a young shoot from the creosote bush, a small resinous plant with yellow flowers that grows in desert areas. Then she chanted prayers for your cradle, that it might bring you luck and a long life.

The fourth day after your birth, the shaman held a ceremony for your entry into the cradle. In the early morning, she threw pollen to the four directions, dabbed your face with four dots of pollen, then raised your cradle from east to south, to west, to north. She set it down facing east, placed you inside, and, last, tied the straps tight to prevent you from falling out. Your mother would never remove you from it except to change the crushed bark and wash you. Not even to breastfeed.

Your ears were pierced when you were two months old, a tradition meant to allow you to grow faster but also to improve your hearing and make you more obedient. Yet you never obeyed anyone, Grandfather. And you weren't very tall either. But these traditions remain sacred. So your mother applied something hot to each of your earlobes and pierced them in one go with the sharpened tip of a bone. You screamed, of course. But your mother blew onto your ears to soothe your pain. The Apaches are very gentle with their children. She then whispered into your ears the first rule that little boys learn: "A future Apache warrior must dominate his pain." I don't know how you were able to understand her words so young, Grandfather, but you apparently stopped screaming immediately.

When you began to sleep less, turquoise beads were hung above your head to stimulate your attention. Your mother would also sing you a lullaby. A short little song you'd always remember, for your first wife sang it to your children too. Long afterward, even during your captivity, you still used to sing it. It ran along three simple notes and was whispered with a smile. "Little baby, go back to sleep, you're my little baby, you're my little baby. . . ."

At seven months, you were taken out of your cradle. You were already very curious, constantly exploring, visiting every last corner of your wickiup. You would crawl on all fours over to the buckskin that served as the door and poke your head out, playing hide and seek with the sun. You climbed into your bed of branches and watched the smoke rising from the fire, as if by some magic, through the open hole in the top of the wickiup. You also loved to poke your nose into the big stalks of bear grass that covered your bed. The scent of those bundles remained in your memory always. You could still imagine their smell even when the walls of your prison cell sent you their own dull scent, a sickening odor. It kept you from beating your fists against those walls.

It was your mother who always replaced the grasses when they dried out. She tied the stalks with yucca threads. It was the women's job to build the wickiup, and it took about three days. The men sometimes helped carry the willow saplings that the framing was made of, but that wasn't their role. They hunted, made war with rival tribes, or went on raids in Mexico to steal livestock.

The wickiup was your most comfortable home. The tipi, used when you didn't have time to stay long, was made of three oak poles, tied together at the tip with yucca string. You then covered it with brush like the wickiup, the layers of branches more or less thick, depending on the season. And sometimes buckskin was the cover too. That way, your homes remained cool in the summer and warm in the winter. It was very pleasant, but that didn't entice you to stay put, Grandfather.

Even when you were crawling, you never stopped exploring the camp. You were already very fast, said your mother, who had to watch you constantly. She made especially sure that no dogs went near you. They might have bitten you, of course, because you liked to pull their fur, but for the Chiricahuas that wasn't the most serious danger. According to our beliefs, if one of them had frightened you, that fear might have penetrated you and weakened your heart. This is the main reason the Chiricahuas avoided dogs.

Weaning began when your first tooth came in. But, since you continued to ask for the breast, your mother dabbed chili where you would ordinarily place your lips. You never asked for it again! She was smart, your mother. In fact, her name, Gha den dini, meant The One Traversed by Light. She certainly passed that trait on to you.

Between the pregnancy and the weaning lasted about three years. During this time, couples were expected to practice abstinence. As an adult, you understood how strict that rule was, and you never broke it. As a true Apache warrior, your mind knew how to control your body. Certain men—though not most—would secretly visit women who were easy. Those men had no will power. They were the first to go over to the whites. They were the men who, according to you, Grandfather, caused your downfall by enlisting as scouts with the United States Army. Those men would suffer your wrath. Knowing how unyielding you were, they would come to fear you more than anything.

2

I wasn't able to call Harlyn last night. Once I lay my head on the pillow, I slept straight through to the morning. The problem is that around eight thirty, when I went to reception, there was still no message for me. I tried calling Harlyn, but the voice of a man, not his, answered: "He's out for the day." I explained that we were supposed to meet. He didn't seem to know anything about it and just recommended I attend the "ceremonies." Harlyn would be there. When I asked where they would be taking place, he mustn't have heard because he hung up. I started to panic a bit. Had Harlyn changed his mind about us meeting? Or maybe he'd left a message on my cell phone? But I had specifically said that he should reach me at the motel because my cell didn't work. Maybe he hadn't listened to his messages?

So I decided to follow the man's advice and attend the "ceremonies." Alfred, the receptionist, explained that this was some big four-day Apache festival, celebrated each year in honor of Independence Day. It would be taking place a half mile from here. He showed me how to get there. He also told me I'd be able to fill my fridge if I stopped at Wal-Mart, which he said was open every day except Christmas.

At nine, I was pushing a gigantic cart through dozens of aisles overflowing with consumer goods ranging from aspirin to electric drills, not to mention underwear, firearms, televisions, stationery, sports gear, camping equipment, cosmetics, and wines from California, Chile, and, of course, France. And I thought I'd surprise

Harlyn by bringing him a bottle of wine. He almost certainly has already tasted the mysteries of the Bordeaux vineyards and may even be better versed on the subject than me.

I bought everything I needed, and, after depositing the provisions in my room, making myself a cup of coffee, and eating two banana muffins, I'm back in my car and on Harlyn's trail. Alfred's map has led me to an enormous talus slope dominating the road I arrived on yesterday. A young Indian woman is directing the cars into the parking lot. She's wearing jeans, a white v-neck T-shirt, and an orange safety vest with a reflective neon-yellow strap around the waist. When I get to her, I roll down my window and ask if this is where the "ceremonies" are taking place. Without answering, she signals for me to park a little farther down to the right.

After getting out of my car, I follow a flood of Indians making their way to an unpaved path at the head of the parking lot. At the end, on the left, a tipi has been erected that doesn't quite resemble "my tipi" in Mongolia. This one seems to have just come out of the wash. It's perfectly white with, running from the tip to the base, two bands of blue triangles facing each other like sharks' teeth. A canvas door conceals the interior. I feel like going over and raising it to see if there's a stove in the center like in Mongolia, and skins, pots, bottled oil, sacks of flour, noodles, and pieces of dried meat hanging from strings stretched out between the poles of the frame, with buckskin bags filled with clothes and blankets lying all around.

But I don't dare. I don't want to stick out. There is also some sort of dome covered with branches and with an opening instead of a door this time. I take a quick look inside. Just two benches. I continue to follow the flow of people until we reach an area surrounded by fences, with an entrance preceded by what must be some ticket booths. Is it here? It looks like it. A cardboard sign reads ADULTS $5. I walk up, and a rather large lady with one blue eye and one brown eye and short black hair asks me how many tickets I'd like. One. She takes my ten dollar bill, returns some change, and tells me that the ticket is good for the entire day, that the ceremonies end at midnight, and that I get one free meal. She hands me a light-blue program with the name of the event printed in black, *Mescalero Apache Ceremonial*, with a drawing of an Apache in traditional dress. I ask her if by any chance she knows Harlyn Geronimo. Again, the answer is no. There are four thousand Apaches on this reservation! Sigh. I don't stand a chance of running into him. I thank her and walk away to present my ticket at the entrance. A man in an orange safety vest with a reflective neon-yellow strap around the waist checks my ticket. Unsmiling. But he lets me in.

The smell of old frying oil is sharp in my nostrils. My gaze falls upon a fry shack, hot-dog stand, corn-dog stand, and sausage-covered-in-some-fried-dough-topped-with-ketchup stand lined up in front of a crowd of obese young Indians wearing XXL T-shirts and baggy jeans. Stay calm. I walk over to a booth selling belts, sunglasses, and Apache crafts to study my program in what seems like a quieter corner. Four photocopied pages, with the names of the sponsors on the first page. I scour the list, hoping to find Harlyn's name but having no luck. But I do see the name Inez Cochise. Maybe a descendant of the other famous warrior? I gaze up at the sky. As though on a big blue screen, I see images from my favorite childhood movies scrolling by. Geronimo, Cochise. And suddenly I realize how lucky I am to be here, surrounded by their descendants. Close enough to touch them, speak to them. Now all I have to do is find Harlyn.

The other pages in the program are a schedule of events. 10 A.M.: *Mescalero Parade*. 10:30 A.M.: *Navajo Dinah Dancers*. So there aren't just Apaches? 11:30 A.M.: *Buffalo/Eagle Dancer*. 12:30 P.M.: *Apache War Dancers*. 4:00 P.M. *Comanche Youth Group*. 9 P.M.: *Dance of the Mountain Gods*. And starting at midnight, in the big tipi, the *Ceremonial Maiden Dance*. No idea what that's about. I know the word "maiden" is an old-fashioned term used to describe a young girl. Never mind, at least I'll be able to sit in on a ceremony.

Oh, no! There's a notice: "Midnight curfew for all non-Indians." I don't think I'll be allowed in with this face. I'm really not having any luck with the Apaches! I look at my watch. 12:45 P.M. A quick glance around. The crowd is getting denser and denser. I'm not going to ask every last Indian here if he knows Harlyn! I'll call him again tonight. I hope he'll be easier to catch than his great-grandfather. It took the American soldiers more than ten years.

Zigzagging through the stands, I notice an enormous tipi. Probably the "big tipi" mentioned in the program. It's surrounded by a sort of enclosure made of branches. I don't even try to enter. This non-Indian, a little vexed, will proceed to the bleachers. Probably where the dances take place? Correct. Everyone is seated in front of a sort of dance floor covered in sand. It's empty for now. I walk up the bleachers. Huff, puff. Obvious shortness of breath. At last, the top. Maybe Harlyn will spot me up here? I'm the only skinny one in all these rows.

I take a seat next to a little girl of ten or twelve in a turquoise T-shirt. She's holding a huge serving of French fries covered in ketchup that's enough for six people. She scoots over a bit. I settle back, and in one sweeping vista I can take in the whole site occupied by these proceedings. It's like a raft of ochre earth covered with cars, tipis, and the smoke from frying things, floating in the middle of an enormous forest. And here I am, suddenly thrust into this present without really knowing why. How was a vision able to lead me onto this raft? To what movement of the world's energies am I once again going to bear witness? Is my mission really to reconnect Apache tradition with its Asian roots? A kick in my back derails my thoughts, making the record skip. An Indian man, visibly encumbered by his size, looks at me apologetically. In his left hand he's holding a large plastic cup with blue and red shaved ice. Droplets of sweat run down his temples. They're lined up along the angle of his jaw, waiting for the first movement of his head to leap down onto his khaki T-shirt. He's all wet in the area where the droplets are falling, leaving only a damp halo as evidence of their suicide. Maybe he knows Harlyn? A noise in the crowd draws my attention to the dance floor. Some men carrying cylindrical drums with what looks like a clay base form a circle. What if Harlyn is among them? No, they seem too young. He had the voice of an older man. But maybe I'm wrong? A quick calculation; Geronimo died in 1909, around eighty years old. His descendants are Lana Geronimo, his daughter, and Juanito Via, his grandson and Harlyn's father. Count approximately twenty years on average per generation, and he should be in his sixties. So he can't be one of the dancers who are making their way onto the dance floor. Their enormous bellies hang over their belts. It doesn't seem to bother them. In a single file, they begin a round dance, shouting and firing into the air. Little girls clothed in long deerskin dresses with fringes, who up till now have been sitting on the edge of the dance floor, go and join them. The sound of the drums suddenly takes me back to the movies of my childhood. I'm moved, really, to see that world reborn before my eyes. Would Geronimo be proud of his people today?

When the drums stop, the sun is already setting. I make my way down the bleachers amid the crowd, touching the ground again, the present. Maybe Harlyn left me a message at the motel?

Alfred welcomes me with his wide green-wired smile. I like him. He's always in a good mood. Any messages?

"Your friend called. He'll be here in not too long!"

My heart skips a beat. I look at my watch. 7:40 P.M. I look at Alfred.

"What do you mean by not too long?"

With his mouth drawn downward toward the tip of his chin, he shrugs.

"What do I know? He just said, 'in not too long. . . .'"

In Mongolia that expression can mean in three days, in an hour, or twelve moons from now. OK, don't panic. I simply ask Alfred to be kind enough to give Harlyn my room number. I'll wait for him there. He answers with a "Yes, cousin!" that makes me chuckle. He then takes two plastic cups from behind the counter and goes over to a machine to the left of the entrance. The heels of his ostrich-skin cowboy boots scrape the gray floorboards. *Boom, boom, boom*. He always drags his feet. As though he had to push them ahead in order to move forward. It makes his body seem like a flag floating limply in the wind.

"If you need ice, it's in this machine. You can come get some whenever you want."

Now I understand why there was no ice tray in the fridge in my room. He fills both plastic cups to about three-quarters full.

"Do you want a Coke?"

"I'd rather have some water."

He goes back behind the counter. His ponytail follows the movement of his heels. I smile. Alfred's energy is like a duster. Hard in the center and very diffuse on the outside. He must have a difficult time centering himself. There we go, it's starting again. I didn't use to feel these sorts of things. It's been happening ever since I started playing the drum. The shaman told me it would develop "powers" in me. When I asked her to reveal them to me, hoping, I have to admit, that they would be something along the lines of Samantha's in *Bewitched*, she simply answered: "Play your drum, and like watering seeds in the ground, you'll know the names of the powers once they've blossomed. Mind you, it will take years of practice to really develop them!"

For the three years of my apprenticeship, nothing blossomed. But one day, I did begin to sense strange things in people. Like a kind of music, at higher or lower pitches, deep, soft, or round, quite unique to each person. Like a kind of vibratory ID card. The problem is that I don't know at all how to interpret this information, even though it is becoming more and more defined. Today, for instance, I feel a sort of blockage at the level of Alfred's stomach, in addition to his feather duster energy. Like some sort of barrier. Perhaps due to an old trauma? Or something else, I can't be sure. But there is something, I'm certain of it.

According to the scientists I work with in France and Canada, for whom I have agreed to be a research subject, the practice of trances or meditation plunges our brain into "a state of modified consciousness," which supposedly "awakens" certain of its abilities that are usually more or less dormant when we're in our normal state. Physiologically speaking, this heightened state is caused by the overexcitement of the vestibular system, a part of the inner ear responsible for balance. The hyperventilation you experience as a result of practices that can bring on altered states of consciousness—like playing the drums in my case—apparently leads to a decrease in CO_2 and an increase in oxygen in the brain. All of this, along with cerebral vasoconstriction, results in a decrease in oxygen in the tissue. And, apparently this decrease in oxygen is better handled by the older parts of the brain, the regions that have to do with emotions and instincts. The regions that are "less" deprived of oxygen than others now become more active. And that is how abilities that we don't have access to, or have very little access to, in a normal state, become active and stand out. The phenomenon of "superhuman" strength, for instance, has been studied and catalogued as one potential feature of these modified states of consciousness. It has even been proven that the strength exhibited in these states is not commensurate with muscle mass. I've experienced this personally with my shaman's drum.

It weighs an average of eighteen pounds, and I normally can't use it for more than ten minutes without my arms aching quite intensely. Yet, during a trance, I can hold the drum for hours without ever feeling its weight. Apparently, it has also been proven that in this state an individual's resistance to pain is heightened. It's happened before that I've banged myself, fallen, or been hit in the nose by the drum without or almost without feeling any pain. As though the pain didn't hurt as much.

These phenomena seem to stem from the fact that your conscious mind is less "present" in such states because of the reduced oxygen and cannot amplify pain or even send messages along the lines of "I am incapable of . . ." or "I don't have the strength to. . . ." So this state would allow our true physical abilities to come to the fore.

In December, I'll be heading to Edmonton, Canada, where Professor Pierre Flor-Henry, a neuropsychiatrist at Alberta Hospital and the director of the Center for Diagnostics and Research, will be performing multiple electroencephalograms of my brain while I am in a trance state. I may finally get to know whether it's physiologically normal or there is a "bug" that might explain my transformation into a "wolf" every time I play the drums. This state is of all the more interest to scientists because, if, for example, they can succeed in understanding its mechanisms, they may be able to use it as a means of managing pain. Alfred hands me a plastic cup full of ice.

"You really don't want a Coke?"

I decline. He fills mine with mineral water and his with Coke. We drink in silence. I'm wondering how to broach the subject of his stomach. I ask him his age. Nineteen. If he's always lived in Ruidoso . . .

"Yes, my parents . . . Well . . . My father has a house here."

"Your father? Do you live with him?"

"Yes."

His right hand twirls the Coke that remains in his plastic cup. The ice cubes make a dull sound.

"And does your mother also live in Ruidoso?"

He tosses his head back to drink the last drops of the Coke. Ice cubes touch his nose. He tilts the plastic cup upright again. Wipes off his nose and mouth with the back of his hand. And stares me straight in the eyes, as if to bar my access to his inner thoughts.

"My mother is no longer with us."

I don't dare push it, but maybe that's the reason for what I felt? In a single motion I finish my water. The moment I put the cup down on the counter, a man enters the room. Harlyn?

No, he asks for a room. I decide to make my way back to mine. Small wave good-bye to Alfred. I need to shower before

Harlyn arrives. My navy blue tunic is white from the dust, and the smell of grease is stuck in my nostrils.

10:30 P.M. My ears, eager for any sign of Harlyn, grab on to all the traffic sounds around the motel. Four cars have parked, three have started, one has started up again, and if I knew the names of the different engines, I could probably describe them to you in perfect order. This is getting annoying. But as much as I tell myself to stop waiting, I can't manage to do anything else. This trip will end up being called *Waiting for Harlyn*. All right. Maybe I should leave my door open? At least then my pulse wouldn't race every time someone passes on the walkway. I suppose I could take Alfred up on his offer of a Coke. He must be so bored. Harlyn won't show anyway, it's way too late now. *Knock knock*. Did someone just knock? I get up and go to the door. It must be him. There are butterflies in my stomach. I'm moved to recognize a little of Geronimo's eyes in his great-grandson's. Our eyes, our actions, our voices bear the mark of our ancestors. We are the true time machines. I open the door. A thin man in his fifties with a direct gaze, about my size, wearing jeans, a turquoise shirt, and a white Stetson on his head appears in the doorway. A cowboy? I almost tell him he's come to the wrong room when I suddenly notice, beneath his hat, an angular face and a broad, strong nose, features we've come to expect in Native Americans. "Are you Harlyn?" He smiles and nods. His ponytail swings, seeming to acquiesce, and little crows' feet form around his black eyes. "Hi Corine," he says, moving his right hand forward. I would like to leap into his arms, but I just shake his hand. The tips of his fingers are a little rough in my palm. Geronimo's were probably even more so—but the shape of the hand, wide and firm, must have looked just like this. I feel a swell of tears rising in my eyes.

Harlyn asks if he can come in. I'm such a fool. I apologize, inviting him to sit in the only chair in the room. He walks past me. A circle of turquoise hanging from his right ear oscillates, because

of his slightly stiff gait. As though the air around him were squeez-
ing in on his body. The heels of his black cowboy boots don't even
hiss on the carpet. Nothing like Alfred's, which make the air pop
around him, giving his gait the semblance of not being quite stable.
Before sitting down, Harlyn looks his chair over, lifts it. Is there a
problem? No. He sets it back down softly and seats himself in it
with a smile. You can never be too careful with chairs, can you?
I nod. This man definitely seems very cautious. Would you like a
Coke? No. He'd prefer some tea. Phew, I have some. He drinks a
lot of tea, he explains. With honey. It's good for your throat, and it
helps with allergies. I take the two mugs from the little cupboard
under the sink, fill them with water, and put them in the microwave. Press Start. One minute. The sound of the machine fills the
silence of the room. Makes it more obvious. I'm not sure what
to say anymore. Yet so many questions are jostling in my mind.
Aphonia. Harlyn clears his throat. Crosses his legs. Uncrosses them.
His jeans are deep blue, not faded like mine. The microwave dings.
I open the door, put a bag of tea in each cup. It's ready. I bring his
over to him. His stocky shape conveys a certain strength. Calmness
too. He thanks me for the tea. His voice becomes slightly husky
when he speaks softly. This gives it warmth. "It's Mongolian tea,"
I tell him. "Green tea. I always have some in my suitcase." I sit on
the bed. He uncrosses his legs, places the mug on his right thigh.
He looks at me with a smile. I like his eyes. They glimmer with
mischief. They're direct, but also in their expression there is a tinge
of softness and languor maybe, characteristic of people whom life
hasn't spared. I wonder what kind of hardships he's had to overcome. But I simply ask him the stupidest question in the world.
"Did Geronimo drink tea too?" He looks at me, amused.

"Do you mean tea, like this, in a little bag?"

He bursts out laughing. A funny laugh, a little like a duck call
with the cadence of an automatic weapon. I ask him if Geronimo
had a similar sense of humor. He lets his laughter end before beginning to speak again, appearing serious once more.

"My great-grandmother, Kate, Geronimo's wife, told me that he often played tricks. For example, he liked to hide in order to scare his mother. Unfortunately, one day he fell asleep in his hiding place, and since he was too young to find his way back in the dark, he had to spend the night outdoors. He never did it again!"

We both laugh. Then he takes a sip of tea. I noticed a necklace around his neck. A piece of turquoise, a small red bead, turquoise, red bead. Something appears to be hanging from the bottom of it, but the end is hidden inside his blue shirt. He places the cup carefully back on his thigh. His movements are meticulous. Precious almost. As though he's applied himself to perform them well.

"It's good. We Apaches also have a kind of tea that's made from a small desert plant. I'll show it to you if you're interested."

That offer sounds like the most beautiful gift. I accept it with joy. And suddenly remember the bottle of wine. I get up to fetch it from under the window next to the AC unit. Harlyn opens his eyes wide with pleasure when the bottle lands in his hands.

"It's one of my favorite drinks! I haven't told you about it yet, but my father, Juanito, was there on D-Day, in Normandy. He lived in France for a while, and he always appreciated the red wine in Bordeaux. When I drink it, I'm always reminded of the way he used to talk about different varieties of grapes, Cabernet, Pinot. . . ."

His voice stops, suspended. He looks at the bottle, turning it to read the label. He seems moved. I remain silent, unable to accompany him in his memories. His eyes finally come back to me, in a very gentle movement.

"He landed at Omaha Beach. Have you heard of it?"

"Of course."

"His unit climbed the cliffs, reached Saint-Lô, and then crossed your country to Germany, where he remained for several months. Do you know what the war cry of the American paratroopers was at the time?"

"No."

His eyes suddenly sparkle with joy.

"They'd jump out of the plane screaming 'Geronimo!'"

My eyes widen.

"Really?"

"He wasn't treated as a celebrity, though. He was a simple American soldier, and the fighting was so violent, he said he often felt like he was watching fireworks on Independence Day."

His voice drops.

"His best friend actually died right beside him during a bombing."

"Was your father injured?"

Before answering, Harlyn places the wine bottle gently on the floor. His tea is still balanced on his right thigh.

"He wasn't injured a single time, no, despite remaining there till the German surrender in 1945. It seems unbelievable, doesn't it?

I nod, raising my eyebrows.

"But he had a secret. Do you know what I mean?"

"Mmm . . . No."

"The *medicine*, the strength of his Apache 'power' protected him!"

"He was a medicine man, like you?"

"No, but his grandmother Kate was. She performed some magic rituals for him. Apache *medicine* is strong enough to protect at a distance! He was even decorated as a hero. My wife's father too, it turns out. He was in Africa, going after Rommel. Have you heard of him?"

I nod, my mouth agape in astonishment.

"It was Kate, my great-grandmother, who gave me this gift, the gift of Apache *medicine*, by blessing me with pollen when I was only five years old. So you work with a shaman in Mongolia, if I understood correctly?"

"Yes, it's been seven years now. But before we talk about that, I'm curious to know if for you there's any difference between a shaman and a *medicine* man?"

"Not really, no. Both terms mean the same thing for us. Although I don't really know the origin of the word 'shaman.'"

"All I know is that it comes from the word 'saman,' a word used by the Tongouse people of Siberia to describe a kind of sorcerer. Originally, it only applied to Siberian and Central Asian shamanism."

His head nods slowly, and he utters an "uh, huh" as though to confirm his interest.

"And where exactly does your shaman live?"

"In the north of Mongolia, right on the border with Siberia. Her name is Enkhtuya. The funniest part is that she doesn't even live in a yurt, which is the traditional Mongolian dwelling with a circular wooden frame covered in white felt, but in a tipi."

He raises his eyebrows.

"A tipi like the ones the Indians live in?"

"Yes, the same."

"You see, they really are our ancestors! According to oral Apache tradition, a branch of one of the nomadic tribes that used to occupy the territory where your shaman lives migrated to Alaska through the Bering land bridge. At the time, the sea level was much lower than today, the strait didn't exist, and populations could migrate from Asia to America over the frozen land without even getting their feet wet!"

"When was this exactly?"

"About ten thousand years ago. Apparently, they went to Canada where they founded the Athabaskan tribe, whose dialect is the root of our Apache language. Then in the middle of the fourteenth century, an offshoot of the Athabaskans migrated here, to the Southwestern United States. The Navajos and the seven Apache tribes—the Mescaleros, the Lipans, the Jicarillas, the White Mountain, the San Carlos, the Chiricahuas, and the Fort Sill—are descended from that second migration.

I drink a sip of tea, enough time to process all of this information and appreciate the confidence he seems to have placed in me, pulling me into his world already.

"You told me on the phone that Apache babies are born with a blue mark on their backside, which is a feature Mongolian babies have too. Do the Navajos and Athabaskans have it as well?"

"They do. As do all the tribes that descend from the branch that went to Alaska from the land of Genghis Khan.

"And no other Indian tribe has this birthmark?"

"Nope."

It's his turn now to swallow a sip of tea, then place the mug delicately back onto his thigh.

"Does your shaman know that certain North American Indians live like she does, in a tipi?"

I remain silent for a bit, assembling the elements of my response. When I met Enkhtuya, she lived in her tipi without electricity or running water, and her knowledge of the world was bound by the horizon within her gaze and the legends her parents had told her. For her, her world was simply that of her ancestors, a very small population of reindeer breeders called Tsaatans, who were originally from Siberia. She'd never heard of Indians. But for two years now, thanks to the tourism boom in Mongolia, she's been able to sell her crafts, little sculpted objects made from reindeer antlers, and buy herself a television, a solar-powered charger, and a satellite antenna.

"When I arrived last April, right away she told me: 'I saw the Indians in America and the tipis you were telling me about!'"

Harlyn starts laughing. Praising the benefits of television.

"So, do you also live in her tipi when you visit her?"

I nod, adding that on my first visit, I hadn't been able to suppress a little shriek of joy when I saw it. As a child, I had transformed my room into a tipi. It was my domain, where I used to re-create the life of the Apaches I'd discovered in the movies, in which Geronimo was already my favorite character. So when I found myself on all fours in front of Enkhtuya's tipi and pushed open the canvas door, and then, inside, discovered the wood stove in the center, the smoke hole at the top, the skins on the ground, I really had a strong impression—the feeling—of entering my child-hood imagination again.

"Reality caught up with me fast, though. Living in a tipi at minus fifteen Fahrenheit, with no water, no electricity, and no insulation on the ground other than yak skins, which also served as our mattresses, turned out to be a lot less fun than I might have supposed. But by then I had no choice!"

He flashes a broad smile, revealing his straight white teeth. He seems really amused by my Tintin adventures in Mongolia.

"You're more Apache than me, it turns out! We only use the tipi for certain ceremonies. And I wouldn't swap my house for it for anything in the world!"

He finishes his tea with a laugh. I tell him about my day at the Mescalero Ceremonial and ask him what those round houses covered in brush are called. Wickiups, he answers, but they're also called wigwams. I tell him I asked other Apaches about him, to try and find him, but that no one seemed to know him. He smiles. That's normal, he ends up admitting. It's like a code among the Apaches. If a stranger comes asking questions, don't say anything, don't know anything. He narrows his eyes slightly, as if to fixate his gaze in mine.

"It's a relic of the times of persecution, you know what I mean?"

I can only confirm that I do, under the power of Harlyn's gaze in which he has poured all of his determination to have the suffering inflicted on his people recognized. If Geronimo served up some of the same to his enemies, I can understand why they wanted to flee. OK. Well, what if I asked a different question? The meaning of the maiden ceremony, for instance? A smile returns to Harlyn's face. Phew.

"Yes, it's very simple. When a young girl has her first period, we organize a ceremony to prepare her for her future life as a woman. Following a specific ritual, she's informed and prepared for four days, shamans chant prayers, and she has to dance, but unfortunately it's the last ceremony from our traditions that's still actively performed. And only Indians are allowed to witness it."

That I know. I offer him another tea. He appears to think about it, looks at his watch, and looks at me. The little wrinkles begin to show around his eyes, and I wonder what thought is causing a smile to form, but I don't dare ask. He finally opens his mouth to speak.

"No, thank you. I'm going home. And tomorrow you have to get up early, since we're going on a trip."

"A trip? For how long? Should I bring my sleeping bag and my tent?"

He smiles.

"Don't panic! You're not in Mongolia. There are motels everywhere here! Just bring the clothes you need."

"But where are we going? Very far?"

His head bobbles.

"Yes and no."

My eyebrows assume a perplexed position, slightly furrowed. He remains silent for a moment and, as if he'd sensed the tempest brewing inside my skull, finally agrees to give me a few additional clues.

"You're here to write a book, aren't you?"

"Mmm . . . Yes, of course."

His eyes scrutinize me all of sudden. I feel like he's guessed there's something else I need to tell him. The book, yes. But the vision I had of Geronimo. Should I tell him about that? The little turquoise circle at his ear starts to oscillate again, and he continues:

"So you can write this book, I have to take you on the path of my people and . . ."

He pauses, seeming to search for the right words.

"To a place where, let's say, the past can meet the present."

His gaze is full of mischief.

"Be ready tomorrow by six, and trust me, that's all you need to know."

My eyes continue to question him, but he concludes with a non-negotiable "Uh huh," then gets up, places the cup softly on the table, and thanks me for the tea. He really seems to like Mongolian tea. He then turns, walks to the door briskly, opens it, and closes it softly. It doesn't even make a click.

I remain speechless, my head full of questions. And moved too by the trust he's shown me. We hardly know each other, and, from the outset, he's making the way of his traditions available to me. Of course, there's a book to write. Or did the medicine man in him actually "see" that I had come because of my vision of Geronimo? No. You're crazy, poor girl. Still, he didn't have to take me on this trip to retrace his people's footsteps. OK. Well, it will all come clear with this journey. Harlyn is right. I just need to trust him.

'Ádą 'iłk'idą, joogobago daajindáná'a.

Ndah nDéí 'isdzą́ą́yóí biche'shkéne gózhǫ́go yaahihndíná'a.

Biche'shkénei ndédaahaleeł ndah,

keekę́yóí 'isdzáńdaahaleeł ndah,

díík'eh bik'ehnaakaná'a.

Íquot;Shishke'é, doo'jódzįda.

Doháń k'eshíndiida.

Doháń bich'įįlójigoda.

Doháń baajadloda.

Dohyáabaajó'įįlee'át'édań goshinsį́.

Yóósń Tóbájiishchinéń bichįį'itédahdlii.

'Áń dá'gobiłk'eh gok'ehgodaanndá.

Niigosją́ń́ yáí 'ágoił'į́.Íquot;

daayiiłndíná'a.Íquot;

'Indaanałį́í, dákogo,

díídíí 'iłk'idą ndé doo'ikóńzįdaí gólį́ ndah,

dá'át'égo kooghą gótǫ́ǫ́yéí goos'ą́í bighe'yá

dá'át'égo gózhǫ́go biche'shkéne yaahihndíí,

nahí doobégonasįda.

Yóósń Tóbájiishchinéń goche'shkénei beebich'įįyájiłti.

53

Bikooghạí baajoogobááyéégo naagoos'ạ́ ndah,
bighe'shị saanzhóní híndínzhóní yeeyádaałti.

In those days, a very long time ago, the Indians lived in poverty.
But Apache women tended their children well, so they say.

Even when their children became men,
Even when their little girls became women,
They all remained obedient, so they say.

"My child, we do not curse.
We do not hate anyone.

We do not act intemperately with anyone.
We do not laugh at anyone.
We treat with respect those for whom we can do nothing.
Pray to our God and to Child of the Water.
We are alive today thanks to them both.
They created the Earth and the Sky,"
The women taught this to their children, so they say.

You, the whites,
Don't realize that,
Even if our ancestors knew nothing,
They taught their children to be righteous
Within their pitiful camps.

They spoke of our God and of Child of the Water to their
children.

Even if their camps were pitiable everywhere,
Out of the depths of their souls they spoke with kind words
and kind thoughts.

The Good Days

At sunset, Grandfather, the land of the Gila turns in places the color of an old bloodstain. Even as a child, you would come sit in those reddish puddles. The earth smelled of heat, dry grass, and rabbit droppings, with a bit of the taste of the poplar buds you used to chew for hours. In those endless sensations, stretched out on your back, gaze perched in the sky, you sometimes felt like you were in the exact moment when the past and present could meet, suddenly freed from the constraints of time.

But unfortunately, on this day you were squatting low with your loins twisted by your first diarrhea. It was picking season, the one you called Big Fruits, and the day before you had over-indulged in the yucca fruits that your mother, Gha den dini, had gathered from around the camp. The problem, though, was not your diarrhea but that the red earth on which you'd released the product of your sickened loins was in the path you took to fetch water. When your mother discovered your foul-smelling offense she hadn't been able to suppress her anger. It was the very first time she'd scolded you. The Chiricahuas weren't accustomed to remonstrating with their children. When you screamed or cried, she simply placed a blanket over your head. Your cries stopped instantly. When you happened to pee on the blanket you slept in, she likewise resolved the problem without loud words. The following night, she'd place a bird's nest under your bottom. The following day, your bed was dry. She'd throw the nest to the east, and for several moons you wouldn't pee in bed.

But, on that morning, her cries made the stags of the Gila flee as far as the Mogollon Rim. Hands pressed to your ears, you had to wait for her to calm down to grasp the seriousness of your offense. "Do you realize that if a sorcerer takes this path and slips on your excrement, he'll cast a spell on you!" And she made you erase even the smallest trace of your passage.

You must have been just seven, Grandfather, but this anecdote remained engraved in your mind. It helped you realize that the world could be dangerous for those who didn't know, or didn't respect, the invisible forces. It was on this day that your mother chose to teach you the first rituals that would allow you to move along the path of life without falling into its "traps," where, as surely as a panic-stricken rabbit, you could easily let yourself be caught at any moment.

She began by preparing medicine from the flowers of a plant in the gnaphalium family with fuzzy gray-green leaves. This decoction was to stop the diarrhea. Then she tied a small, fringed buckskin bag around your neck containing the shoot of a creosote bush. This would protect you from illnesses. She also advised you to avoid all contact with what the Chiricahuas considered the source of illnesses: snakes, owls, bears, coyotes, and ghosts. As for sorcerers, she added, with the firmness of a mother fearing her child's recklessness, if you happened to meet one, you had to avert your head so there was no chance of your gaze engaging theirs.

You followed her advice for at least five moons, Grandfather. But the season of Little Eagles had hardly begun, and the buds on the trees had barely pointed their noses out, when you couldn't resist the urge to test the validity of her rules. You went in secret to visit the sorcerer who lived in the canyon after the third meander of the Gila. Those people usually lived in remote places. They were feared because they were suspected of using their powers for dark magic. In fact, those who were caught in the act were burned alive. But you didn't care, you simply wanted to know what was so terrible about this sorcerer that you weren't even allowed to meet his gaze.

Since the sun was already very hot, you placed a crown of willow leaves on your head as your mother had taught you, then you made your way south toward the canyon. A long distance, but you were toughened. Apache warriors could walk up to fifty miles in a single day. And along the way, hummingbirds accompanied you. There were many in that region. You sometimes gave them honey, which you found hidden in stems of the mescal plant, a kind of agave, or in the stems of the yucca. In a pouch of animal skin, you had placed a few strips of dried elk meat. Your mother had told you that if a sorcerer ate this meat, it would make him vomit. So you decided to offer him some to see his reaction. A good way, you thought, of proving or disproving whether he was a sorcerer.

Having finally arrived near his house, you slowed your pace. The bigger his wickiup became in your field of view, the louder your heart beat. What terrible thing would happen to you if you met his gaze?

You were bold for your age, Grandfather, but you still jumped when he suddenly emerged from his house. When he saw you, he frowned. That's when you met his gaze, which was as hard as the heartwood of an oak. You immediately lowered your head and waited. But nothing happened. So, slowly you raised it again. Seeing his smile, you found your courage and felt you'd been a fool to fear him. From that day forward, you refused to respect any prohibition without first confirming its accuracy.

With your little head held high as a pheasant's during mating season, you went toward him. His face had the shape of a horned owl's, and a big wrinkle across his forehead formed a cross with another between his eyes. He invited you into his house. But you began to feel a pain in your head and you wondered whether your mother might not be right after all. This man was dangerous, and you had better break your own speed record and get out of here. The man again invited you into his home. Smiling. So you followed him. Convinced, now, that never again should anyone ever dictate your actions.

The interior of the wickiup was just like yours. With a hole in the center, where a fire burned. Duck eggs waited in a receptacle of carved wood. Your mother cooked them under hot ash, but she wouldn't eat them if she feared becoming pregnant. A large woven basket contained hazelnuts, and two deeper ones were full of mescal stems. The women picked them right before the flowers bloomed and roasted them over the fire.

The sorcerer offered you water, indicating a jar. But you refused his offer. This jar was different than yours, which were made of woven baskets that your mother had coated with pitch, which she collected by slashing the knots on the trunks of pine trees. He smiled, as if he had recognized your distrust. He told you the water would ease your headache a bit. You wondered how he knew. His "power," surely. He didn't insist on the water, but he walked toward a buckskin bag, opened it, and let some powder spill out that he poured into a small bowl carved out of wood. "It's osha root powder, don't worry." You knew what it was, for your mother often gathered the dark brown roots of this plant. Shamans mixed it with wild tobacco leaves and had you chew the mixture to cure a cough or sneezing whenever a chill penetrated your body. If the chill had already entered your lungs, they boiled the osha root powder in water and made you drink it. You, Grandfather, hated this remedy, so bitter it made you vomit. Yet it was extremely effective!

In the sorcerer's house, you recognized the smells of wild celery and osha root, and were reassured by it. He wasn't trying to trick you. He mixed his powder with water, not too much so the mixture wouldn't be too liquid, and approached you with the bowl. "I'm going to spread this paste on your forehead. The pain will dissipate." You didn't know whether it was because of his owl head or everything your mother had told you, but you felt the fear rising in your belly, and suddenly you remembered the elk meat. If you offered him some and he drew back, you'd refuse his remedy. He'd be a sorcerer for sure and would clearly want to hurt you.

So, brusquely, you took a piece of meat from your little bag and handed it to him, right under his nose. His reaction was immediate. When he saw it, he pulled back sharply. You had your answer. Without another thought, you jumped up and ran.

To avoid angering him, you shouted back at him from a distance, "Goodbye, the sun's low, I have to go home. Thank you for the remedy, but the pain's gone!"

On the path home, you began to eat the meat that had made the sorcerer back away. But you'd hardly tapped your supply when a flash of lightning tore the sky above the canyon. Yet not a single drop of water fell. You couldn't help but think that the sorcerer had cast this lightning against you. Your mother had told you that certain people had this power. This time, preferring to follow her advice, you immediately stopped eating. You weren't supposed to swallow food during a storm, for it was said to increase the number of lightning strikes and could make your teeth fall out. You also made sure you weren't wearing anything red, since that color drew the lightning, and you then spat noisily, as your mother had taught you, to ward it off, while saying in a loud voice: "Do it, Brother Lightning, split the sky with all your might!"

Nothing could happen to you now.

3

Lightning just split the sky. A gust of wind makes my hair fly up. According to these signs, Harlyn should appear shortly, riding the thunder. I place the loose hairs back behind my ears. Sigh. It's almost eight o'clock. Harlyn is two hours late. Luckily, Alfred felt sorry for me. A while ago, he invited me for a drink of coffee. He's really nice, and I think a bond is starting to form between us. He spoke again about his French grandfather. He dreams of discovering Paris. I offered to host him. He was very happy, but he doesn't have enough money yet, so he's going to save up. He also wanted to tell me about his mother. She was killed a year ago by a reckless driver. He was never able to find him, and so his anger remains, lingering in his stomach. A large, cherry red Dodge Mega Cab 4 x 4 with tinted windows appears in the parking lot. Harlyn? There's a white hat behind the windshield. It's him!

I grab my backpack, in which I've tossed a pair of jeans, two shirts, two pairs of underwear, a toothbrush, toothpaste, a towel, three notebooks to write everything he's about to tell me, two apples, three apricots, and my sleeping bag in case the place "where the past and present meet" doesn't have bedsheets. In any case, Harlyn has succeeded in his little plan. I wondered all night where such a place could be. I also brought a mini yurt made of felt to show him what Mongolian dwellings look like, as well as my shaman's mouth harp and my drum with its cover.

Not getting out of the vehicle, Harlyn rolls down his tinted window. He's wearing Oakley-style anodized sunglasses that follow the curve of his eyes perfectly. Ideal for sports, motorcycling, skiing . . .

"Nice glasses!"

He thanks me, smiling. "They're very light, too!" and then invites me to put my stuff in the back. Two minutes later, the back loaded and shut, I climb into the cab next to him. Two little girls with their black hair done up in ponytails are in the back. Harlyn introduces me to Harlie Bear, his daughter Kate's daughter, and Shania, his son Rocky's daughter. A great big smile splits their round faces. I greet them. Harlyn tells me he has another son, Lyle.

"Does he have children?"

"No," Harlie Bear answers in a soft and polite voice. "He has no children."

I ask her how old she is. Ten.

"I'm seven," Shania chimes in with a very deep voice for her age. "And you?"

"Me? I just turned five!"

They burst out laughing. Their two little ponytails make the same bouncing motion. They're funny. Harlyn buckles his seatbelt. He's wearing a T-shirt with a white Nike logo on it. After checking that the girls have buckled theirs, he motions to me to buckle mine. Done. The car starts. Harlyn asks me questions like, have I had time to visit Ruidoso yet? Only the Wal-Mart. With a precise movement, no more than necessary, he activates the blinker and makes a right onto the street. Words start to jostle around in my mind. I'd like to tell him already how moved I am that he's taking me with him on this journey. And I'd like to know too why I'm worthy of such trust. I look at him. Always quiet, he seems focused on the road. Should I ask him anyway? I look again in his direction. He really does have a nice profile. OK. I'm going for it.

"I'd like to thank you for taking me on this trip in your ancestors' footsteps. I'm really touched and moved by the trust you've placed in me."

He shoots me a quick glance, as if to thank me in return, but seems a little discomfited by my confession. Without responding, he focuses on the road again. I stop talking, when suddenly his voice emerges. It's a little hoarse, like mine when I'm moved.

"You know, here, white people aren't too interested in us or our history. Never, not once, for instance, has anyone come to find me to hear what I have to say about Geronimo's life. Even though he's my great-grandfather and my account could be worth something, don't you agree?"

I acquiesce silently. He continues.

"So I'm very happy, and very moved too, that you, a French woman, came all this way simply to write a book on us, the Apaches. That's why it seems perfectly natural to me to open the door to our traditions to you and take you on this journey. You're going to learn many surprising things, believe me, and it's the least I can do for you."

I thank him with a nod, too moved to utter a word. We remain silent for a while. I observe the landscape. Lots of larches, or maybe pine trees, among which have sprouted fast food places and banks. More questions assail my mind. Now that I know why we're all here together in this car, I'm burning to find out our destination. Do I dare ask? No. Harlyn would have told me if he wanted me to know. Maybe he could at least tell me if we're going to be gone for very long? I finally make up my mind to ask him, but he simply smiles, seeming to understand what I'm trying to get at. So I let it go, realizing with glee that a French woman doesn't stand a chance at outwitting an Apache. We pass by a small agglomeration of perfectly aligned chalets.

"The *cabins!*" says Harlyn. "You can rent them in winter."

"They told me over at the motel that there's a ski resort here?"

"Yes. Many Apaches work there during the ski season. The reservation is about eight hundred square miles in size, and the rest of the year they're busy taking care of the forests, raising cattle—there's lots of cattle—and producing lumber. We even have a brand-new sawmill."

"What about the casinos?"

"My daughter, Kate, manages one of them. But only about forty percent of the Apaches on the reservation work there. The others don't have enough schooling."

"Who comes to gamble in the casinos?"

"Many of us, unfortunately, but also some people from around the area."

"Do you gamble?"

"Occasionally, but only when the signs are favorable."

"Meaning?"

Harlyn pushes a button. His window rolls down. The smell of pine enters the car. He seems to be peering at a sort of cabin perched at the top of a hill. The girls look out in the same direction. They're both wearing hot pink T-shirts but not the same jeans. Shania's are embroidered with yellow flowers. Harlyn rolls up the window. It's a fire tower, he explains. With all these trees, fires are a real scourge at the moment and all Apaches are doing like he is, keeping a close watch on their forest. He adds that his son Rocky is a smoke jumper. He jumps from an airplane into areas close to the fire that can't be accessed by other vehicles. And this with a hundred pounds of equipment on his back so he can carve out firebreaks and prevent the fire from spreading.

"It's a very dangerous job," Harlie Bear interjects, her voice full of pride for her uncle.

"So what are the signs that it's good to go to the casino?" Shania asks, her hands posed neatly on the flowers on her jeans.

Harlyn smiles. For the Apaches, he explains, muscle spasms are considered to be a warning sent by the spirits. If, for instance, your left eyelid starts quivering, it's a bad sign. A problem might occur. To avoid it, you must recite some prayers while smoking a sage cigarette and then bless the eyelid with some pollen, or apply some ash to it. On the other hand, a quivering of the right eyelid presages some good news. But these muscle spasms can have different meanings and each person has to judge by his own experience. Once, he said, his great-grandmother told him that some soldiers were about to catch Geronimo, but just in time he felt his eyelid quiver. So he jumped on his horse and eluded them. His men asked him later how he'd done it, how he'd known. He said he didn't know, but that, by quivering, his eyelid had told him to leave. Harlyn glances at me full of mischief.

"I'm going to tell you a little secret. . . ."

The girls and I prick up our ears.

"One day when my right eyelid was quivering, I went to the casino to see if it meant I'd have some good luck."

"And did you win?"

"Yes, a lot of money! But it was just a test, I'm not really much of a gambler."

I tell him that in our culture, usually, a muscle spasm is a sign of a magnesium deficiency, and we run to the closest pharmacy. Laughing, he suggests I try a casino next time. I promise, also laughing, that I'll put his winning formula to the test. He's serious again.

"Are there casinos in Paris?"

"No."

"No? But there are some in France, aren't there?"

I nod.

"Are there a lot of you on this reservation?"

"About four thousand."

It was created in 1872, he continues. Each member of the tribe received a plot of about five acres where they were allowed to build a home and that they could pass down from generation to generation. They could also buy more land, and today only tribal members have that right. His land is about twenty-five acres. He raises cattle and horses.

"I've been riding since I was five!" Shania proudly shouts from the back.

I tell her that Mongolian children begin before they can even walk. She frowns, with a look full of doubt. I'm about to answer her when Harlyn resumes. The reservation also has its own constitution, which was created in 1936 and revised in 1968. The government is divided into three branches: the executive, legislative, and judiciary. The executive branch is comprised of a president, a vice president, a secretary, and a treasurer. It conducts the daily activities of the tribe, manages the operations of the different departments, such as the one for businesses like the casinos and the ski resort. The judiciary branch is run by a head judge and two associate judges. The legislative branch is composed of ten members elected by the tribe. He shoots me a glance.

"Five years ago I myself was elected to sit among the members of that council. Its role is to manage the affairs of the reservation and its natural resources, to set the annual budget, sign contracts for the tribe, loan money, and grant tribal membership."

Harlyn interrupts his explanation to show me the road we've come to. I'm speechless. It's bordered with stores that are built like chalets and painted in colors of bright yellow, sky blue, or pink. Like our Megève ski resort in France but multicolored, with flowers, pretty storefronts, and café terraces! Harlyn and the girls laugh at my response. Pretty, isn't it? He parks the car in front of a violet storefront where in black letters are the words SKI AND SNOWBOARD RENTALS. Time for me to replace my old board. We get out of the car. Harlyn locks the doors. I go over to the window. I imagine how proud I'd be snowboarding in the Alps on an Apache board. Harlyn seems just as intrigued as I am by the gear on display. I ask him if he skis.

"Like a champ!" he answers, laughing.

I give him a doubtful look, but the girls reply in unison, "It's true! He's really good!"

"So if I come back this winter with my board, you'll take me up on the slopes?"

He accepts the challenge. I immediately start dreaming of the moment when our tracks will lie side by side in the powder on the Mescalero peaks.

"I'm hungry," announces Shania, brushing back behind her ear a strand of hair apparently too short for the ponytail.

Good timing. I am too. At five thirty this morning, I couldn't swallow a thing, and then I was waiting for Harlyn. So, I happily get in line with my glossy black clogs when he suggests that we have breakfast at his favorite spot. In single file, we pass by Indian artisan stores with lots of turquoise jewelry, memorabilia, sports gear, hats, and cowboy boots. I even spot a snow globe with an Apache instead of the traditional fir trees. There are also life-size sculptures of bears carved out of wood. It's a tradition in this area, Harlyn tells me. It goes back about fifty years, to the day when a bear was saved from a blaze by some firefighters. Nicknamed Smokey Bear, he became their mascot and a symbol for the campaign to prevent forest fires. On the radio you could hear him say, "Don't forget: Only You Can Prevent Forest Fires!" He died in 1976 in the Washington Zoo at the age of twenty-six.

"The sculptures depict him," Harlyn continues, "and people buy the Smokey Bears to put in their yards."

I ask him if he has one. Silence. Shania raises her deep voice. Her brow furrowed and with a serious air, she tells me that Apaches don't buy bears. I ask her why, but Harlie Bear answers instead.

"The bear's spirit is very strong, and the Apaches respect it. You can't buy one just to make your yard look nice."

I look over at Harlyn, hoping for more details, but he simply concurs and starts walking. OK. We continue like this, in silence, until we reach a Harley Davidson store in front of which Harlyn find his voice again.

"I have one."

"One what?"

"A Harley!"

Well, well, I think.

"He took me on it!" says Shania, the tips of her white Nikes and her little nose pointed at me.

She's a hoot. Harlyn eyes a black leather belt with an enormous silver buckle. Not for long, though. Harlie Bear's getting restless; she's really hungry. We pass the Café Rio.

"They make my favorite pizzas here," Harlyn tells me. "Are there pizzerias in Paris?"

I say yes.

"And stores too?"

My eyes widen. Yes, of course. Appearing satisfied, he goes over to a chalet painted hot pink from top to bottom, with a fenced-in patio with a sculpted wooden balustrade where some white cast-iron tables are set up. This is the Gourmet Bar. The girls run to pick a table. We follow them. Before sitting down, Harlyn asks Shania to lift up her shirt a bit and show me her blue "mark." She complains, but Harlyn insists. So, with a great big sigh, she turns around, bends forward a bit, and lifts up the bottom of her T-shirt. And there it is, a mark of about three-quarters of an inch square, a very pale purple in hue, just over her right kidney.

"Is it the same for young Mongols?" Harlyn asks.

I nod. It's really amazing. Shania pulls her T-shirt back down, then walks over to the chair next to the balustrade. She pulls it toward her, making a face. The cast iron is heavy. Harlie Bear reaches to help her, but Shania vehemently shakes her head no. She can do it on her own! Harlie Bear, obviously used to this, doesn't insist, and settles on the chair next to her. I sit between her and Harlyn. A waitress arrives. Brown, short hair, hot pink apron to match the Gourmet Bar's hue. The girls order a Fanta, a Coke, Harlyn a hot chocolate, and a coffee for me, all this is accompanied by some croissants and *pains au chocolat.* The specialty here, Harlyn explains, putting his sunglasses on top of his hat.

"My dad loves croissants!" says Shania, raising her chin. "My dad's very strong!"

Harlyn explains that Rocky is also part of a helicopter emergency response team. Fires, tornadoes, natural disasters. It's dangerous, but he's really glad to have a job.

"Only sixty percent of the members of the tribe have one!" he points out. "The other forty are seasonal workers, or retired, or students."

"What's the average yearly salary here?"

He thinks for a minute and gives me a number of around $20,000, to which is added, three times a year, in June, August, and December respectively, a portion of the profits from the casinos and the ski resort. On average $1,800 per person per year.

"The American government doesn't provide anything?"

"They signed treaties to subsidize the schools and hospitals and improve roads and infrastructure. But that's it."

Our drinks arrive. Shania licks her lips when she sees the four enormous croissants and as many *pains au chocolat* arrive. I'm shocked by their size. At least twice the size of our Parisian *viennoiseries*. She grabs a *pain au chocolat*. Harlie Bear, who definitely takes very seriously her role of older cousin, picks up the bottle of Coke to pour some into Shania's glass. But once again Shania refuses her help. Harlyn looks at me, smiling. Their quiet circus amuses him; he doesn't intervene. I take a sip of coffee. Far from a decent espresso but considerably better than what you normally get around here.

"Do you have a hat?" Harlyn asks.

"No, why?"

"The sun is very strong where we're going."

"Oh really? Where are we going?"

He grabs a croissant and smiles. I won't get my answer.

"Your shoes are weird!" Harlie Bear tosses at me after putting down her glass of Fanta.

I bend over to peer at my shiny clogs.

"You don't like them?"

She twists her mouth downward. This makes Shania, who seems to approve of her cousin's judgment, chortle, but Harlie

Bear simply bites into a huge mouthful of *pain au chocolat*. Three people arrive onto the terrace. Two adults and a child. All of them obese. Harlyn has followed my gaze. For him, obesity has become a real problem. In earlier times, young Apaches underwent rigorous physical training, and they hunted too. Nowadays, they'd rather watch TV and pig out on junk food.

"You have to remember that shows are interrupted every five minutes by advertisements for hamburgers, cheese fries, chicken nuggets. Food that's way too fatty! And that's not counting the ads for beer. Which is also a scourge. Thirty-five percent of young people between twenty and twenty-six are alcoholics. But you realize those ads are promoting a lifestyle that young people unfortunately want to identify with. . . ."

I ask him if he has any ideas for solutions. He swallows some hot chocolate.

"We must never stop being what we are: Apaches. The only solution would be to interest young people in the traditions of our ancestors again—like bow hunting, tracking, desert survival, long-distance running—but the more obese they are, the less exercise they can do because of heart problems. It's a vicious cycle."

"You know, in Europe too, obesity has started to become a problem. Statistics predict that by the end of the decade fifteen million people will be obese."

Harlie Bear adds that Cody and Mario, her brothers, spend all their time playing video games when they get home from school.

"You know," says Harlyn, "I'd rather play football."

"His favorite team is the Dallas Cowboys!" says Shania, who has dropped her *pain au chocolat* to mimic the gestures of a cheerleader.

Harlie Bear bursts out laughing. But Harlyn, obviously used to being made fun of by his grandchildren, continues with dignity.

"I also like playing baseball, like Geronimo, actually."

Point for Harlyn. The girls look at him, suddenly very intrigued. Yes, Harlyn says, delighted with his comeback. The Chiricahuas of the time used to play a game that was very similar. They placed four stones in a square, each spaced five yards apart. A player in the center tried to reach each stone without being struck by a leather ball, thrown by an opponent. The first player who managed to reach all four stones without being hit won the game.

"And what game did you use to play?" Shania asks me, swinging her legs under the table.

"Cowboys and Indians!"

She raises her eyebrows. To prove it to her, I tell her about the Indian costume my mother bought me for Christmas when I was seven. A red skirt, a bolero with fringes, and a headband ringed with black and white feathers. I hadn't wanted to take it off for a family visit. My mother warned me that everyone would make fun of me in the street, but my pride in wearing that costume beat out all her warnings.

"And did they make fun of you?" Shania asks, truly worried.

"Not at all!"

A smile returns to her face. Harlyn offers me a pastry before the girls wolf down every last one. I grab a croissant. He continues to sip his hot chocolate, looking preoccupied all of a sudden. My croissant tastes like flour, but I don't dare tell him or ask him the reason for his silence. He ends by tilting his head up.

"I was thinking about the drug problem in the schools on the reservation. Cocaine and marijuana, mostly. It comes in from Mexico."

He looks at the girls. He warns them never to agree to take any in school. And to tell him about it immediately if they're offered any. They swear. The young victims of it can't work anymore, he continues. To prevent the problem from spreading, certain adults still connected to the old traditions, like he himself, have begun to develop a program for teaching the values of the past. His wife, Karen, for instance, gives some classes in the Apache language, which most members don't speak anymore.

"You know, if we lose our language, we lose everything."

"Karen teaches at the Mescalero Apache School," says Harlie Bear. "And I've started learning it. The word 'Apache' is pronounced 'uh–PAH–chee' and means 'enemy.'"

"In the Zuni language," Harlyn clarifies. "That's a tribe from northeastern New Mexico. But Apaches are traditionally called 'Nde,' which means 'the people' in our language."

I ask Harlyn if many Apaches still speak their language today. He thinks for a while. The girls trade a croissant for a *pain au chocolat*.

"Around fifteen thousand out of a population of fifty thousand."

"Are they all Chiricahuas, like you?"

"No, there are about six distinct Apache tribes. Chiricahuas, but also San Carlos, Jicarilla, Lipan, White Mountain, and Mescalero."

"Where do they all live exactly?"

"On five different reservations in the Southwestern United States. The White Mountain and San Carlos live in Arizona. The Fort Sill ones, in Oklahoma, and the Jicarilla and Mescalero tribes live here in New Mexico. But we don't all speak the same Apache. There are two dialects, actually. The Apache spoken in the west and the Apache spoken in the east. The Mescaleros and us, the Chiricahuas, speak the Apache spoken in the east."

Harlie Bear asks Harlyn if she can eat the remaining *pain au chocolat*. Yes, he answers, before going on. His wife Karen also teaches the Apache language to young adults. Many more than they knew, it turned out, were interested, and so they decided to add some nutritional counseling to enhance the program. Harlyn himself teaches traditional combat and desert survival classes. He finishes his hot chocolate.

"But I teach those techniques outside of regular school hours, since we don't want any non-Apaches to discover them. They're our patrimony, our treasure. White people mustn't take that from us too. Only Apaches will have the benefit."

Harlyn looks at his watch. It's time to go. I finish my coffee. Everyone gets up. Harlyn takes a look at my shiny clogs.

"Let's buy you a hat and some real shoes!"

I protest. But I like my shoes! Harlyn smiles. Harlie Bear chimes in, "But your heels stick out."

"So what? Isn't it nice? I won't be as hot!"

"As you wish," says Harlyn, "but I'm warning you, we'll be walking in rattlesnake, coral snake, scorpion, tarantula, and black widow country. So one last time, do you really want to keep your shoes?"

Harlyn and the girls burst out laughing, and the shopping queen suddenly feels an intense desire to go on a spree. . . .

"Are there really a lot of snakes where we're going?"

"There are snakes everywhere outside the cities."

I obviously won't get to know what our destination is. But I'm really curious.

"How did the Apaches protect themselves from snakes if they only wore moccasins?"

Harlyn doesn't answer. He suddenly starts looking for his sunglasses, takes three steps back to check that he hasn't forgotten them on the table, but the girls make fun of him.

"They're on your hat!" they shout in unison.

Nágo Tóbájiishchinéń Ghéé'yeńbił 'iłaanaagot'aashná'a.
Naaghéé'neesghánéń 'iłk'idą́ ndé silį́ ndah, biłgóghégo hichago,
goch'į̨sidáná'a.

'Áko, k'adi, Ghéé'yeń Tóbájiishchinéń 'áyiindíná'a:
Íquot;'Áhąh, k'adi, 'iłnnłt'ó. T'éhéńdiidaí bégoozį̨.Íquot; Tóbájiishchinéń
yiiłndíná'a.

Íquot;'Áhąh.Íquot; Tóbájiishchinéń goołndíná'a.

Nágo Ghéé'yeń Tóbájiishchinéń 'áyiiłndíná'a:
Íquot;nDí 'iłtsé ǫǫ shánanńndá. Shí 'iłtsé ninsht'ó.Íquot; goołndíná'a.

'Ákoo Tóbájiishchinéń: Íquot;'ÁhąhÍquot; goołndíná'a.
'Ákoo 'áńdeeda kánanńyáná'a. Nágo Ghéé'yeń dį́ín góńłt'oná'a. Díík'een
gosiiná'a.

'Ákoo Tóbájiishchinéń Ghéé'yeń 'áyiiłndíná'a:
Íquot;K'adi ndíída ǫǫ shánanńndá.Íquot; yiiłndíná'a.

Ghéé'yeń kánanńyáná'a.Ghéé'yeń béshgai'é dį́í'go 'Iłkáá'sijaago bi'édená'a.
Dooka'ólídaná'a.

Tóbájiishchinéń góńłt'oná'a. 'Ikáshį́go béshgai'é go'édení
goghahnaadzóółteelná'a.Náábik'eshį́go, náágóńłt'onágo, 'áíłi'í
goghahnaanáádzóółteelná'a. Táán hilaaee náágóńłt'oná'a.Táánee go'édení

73

goghahnaanáádzóółteelná'a. Nágo dágon'oshį gojéí naahihndáná'a.Dįįnee
náágóńłt'oná'a. Gojéíí dásí'iłndíyá 'ijóósiná'a.

Then Child of the Water and Giant quarreled.
Killer of Enemies was already a man, but, afraid and in tears,
he just sat down.

Finally, Giant spoke these words to Child of the Water:
"So let's aim our bows at each other and see who is bravest."

"All right," answered Child of the Water.

Then Giant spoke these words to Child of the Water:
"You stand before me. I'll shoot first."

Then Child of the Water spoke these words to Giant:
"All right," he said.
And then he stood in front of him. And Giant shot at
him four times.
He missed every time.

So Child of the Water spoke these words to Giant:
"Now, you, stand before me," he said.

Giant stood facing him. His coat was made of four layers of flint.
He wasn't afraid of Child of the Water.

Child of the Water shot his first arrow. The first layer of flint fell.
The next arrow took off the second layer. He shot a third time.
The third time, Giant's coat fell off. And then Giant's beating
heart appeared.
Child of the Water shot a fourth time.
The arrow impaled itself into the very center of Giant's heart.

Apprentice Warrior

LARGE LEAVES, THE SEASON when the sun was warmest, had just begun, Grandfather. To protect you from snakes, whose season this also was, your mother made you a little buckskin braid decorated with two pieces of turquoise that you tied above one of your ankles. She also made you chew some osha leaves and then had you spit the saliva onto your feet and legs. That plant's spirit was said to repel snakes. Finally, you placed a pinch of pollen inside your moccasins—buckskin moccasins that came up to your knees with the top turned down, into which men sometimes placed a knife.

Thus protected, you could finally begin your training as an apprentice warrior. You'd just turned eleven and the men in the tribe considered you strong enough to start. A second level in a way, because from the age of seven you had been trained to hunt squirrels and birds, first with a slingshot and then with a small bow specifically adapted to your size. You were also taught to ride a horse without a saddle, controlling him with just a rope around his nostrils and prompting him into a fast gallop, then stopping him instantly before an obstacle or making him jump over it. While riding, you learned to lean down on either side to catch some target, often a wild turkey. They didn't run that fast, so they were easy to hunt this way. With your friends, you brought them back to the camp for your mothers to cook. Rabbits were a harder game. Dipping down on one side of your horse, you would strike their heads with a wooden club.

You were also trained to jump into ice-covered rivers and emerge from the freezing water without being allowed to warm by the fire; or to stay outside for a day and a night without sleeping, just to guard the camp. Without uttering the slightest cry of pain, you spent hours hardening your hands against the bark of a tree, hours trying to break branches as thick as your thighs with those same bare hands and setting sage alight on your skin until the ash turned cold.

But all of this was nothing compared to what awaited you next.

That morning, for the first time, your father woke you before sunrise. You had barely finished putting on your moccasins and securing your snake-repelling charm when he ordered you to run without stopping to the top of the canyon that towers over the Gila. It was a very steep climb but one your well-trained legs had little trouble making. So doing it at a run didn't seemed impossible. But your father added a formidable condition. . . .

You had to run this distance holding water in your mouth and return before sunset without having swallowed a drop or spat any out.

You didn't let your worry show—the face of a warrior must remain impassive in any circumstance—but you really thought you wouldn't be able to accomplish such a feat. Without a word of encouragement, your father simply said: "Running with water in your mouth will teach you to breathe better. You'll increase your endurance and strengthen your lungs. If you want to stay alive, never forget that no one must be able to run faster than you."

Your mouth full of water, torso naked, with only a loincloth around your waist, you set out, Grandfather. But you'd hardly begun the climb when your feet got tangled up in your moccasins, which had somehow twisted back around the big toe, you never understood why. You tripped, spitting out the precious water like a spurt of vomit onto the nearby shrubs. There was no question of giving up; that would have been the greatest shame for a warrior. So you kept going, running faster, promising yourself that at least you'd complete the test before sunset. To no avail. Halfway down, when some stones dislodged by your running rolled under your feet you pitched forward and fell, coming face to face with a snake whose spot you'd surely disturbed. You needed to come to a stop instantly, for it was standing erect, ready to strike. Looking it straight in the eye, you recited the phrases your mother had taught you: "I want to be your friend. You must not hurt me." The snake finally disappeared into the bushes, but the race was lost. The sun, in a halo of orange light, had just set the horizon ablaze.

When you arrived home, completely out of breath, your father said only: "You will start again every day until you succeed."

You repeated this exercise for three moons until you finally returned before sunset with your mouth still full of water. But after that, Grandfather, you were able to catch rabbits with your bare hands and run beside your trotting horse without lagging behind!

But your warrior's training did not end there. Sometimes you even regretted not being a girl because of how difficult it was. Girls were also trained to run, but only enough to escape as fast as possible and shelter the children in case of an attack. Their main responsibility at the camp was watching over the young ones, fetching wood and water, and picking berries, yucca fruits, and nuts. Then they learned the names of medicinal plants, how to dry them and prepare them, how to sew moccasins and clothes, how to weave baskets, prepare meals, preserve foods, dry them, store them.

But you weren't a girl, and an apprentice warrior isn't allowed to complain. Soon after passing this last test, an even harder one awaited. There were eight of you young boys. You were separated into two groups of four, spread out at half a stone's throw. One of the groups, not yours, was equipped with slingshots and tasked with aiming projectiles about the size of three rabbit droppings at you. Your group had to stand in front of the attackers but was forbidden from running off to avoid the stones. You were allowed to move in only a small perimeter of about an arm's length around you. This exercise was meant to improve your reaction time.

For an hour you served as a target. At first, in a complete panic, you jumped, spun around, or dove to the ground but couldn't avoid the stones. They hurt badly, especially when they hit your face. You kept the scars for a long time. But after much practice, you finally understood something essential. You had to focus on your opponent's movements. His gaze. He'd show you where the stone would go. So you learned to decipher each of your opponent's moves, to discover his thoughts in order to anticipate each movement, to unsettle him because of your self-assurance and to make him lose his. You hardly moved anymore, only an arm, a leg. You would lean your head a bit to the right or left. You felt the slight wind from the stones, but none of them touched you anymore.

Your trainers then replaced the slingshots with bows, not the same ones as those used by warriors but smaller, though still equipped with reed arrows whose bone points were as sharp as a needle. Now, you were truly afraid. You were all afraid. You thought it would be impossible to avoid those arrows, which were much faster than the stones. But to your fears, they answered: "Your mind must dominate your body, make it faster than those arrows, stronger than your doubts. Nothing is impossible for an Apache warrior."

Deeply focused, you faced your opponents again. Standing solidly on your legs, chest straight, eyes locked on their eyes, the hardest thing was to control the terror that rose in your stomach when, suddenly, beside you, one of your companions fell, quickly stifling a cry of pain for an arrow had planted itself in his eye.

If you came out of this test unscathed, a test that was repeated for many moons, you'd have to run at a trot the entire night with an enormous load on your shoulders, just to inure you to exhaustion. This was how they selected the best runners. The time after that, the best runners were armed with long, thin branches to whip the poor runners and force them to go faster. Luckily, you were among the fast ones, Grandfather.

But to improve your speed further, you were put into a sort of wickiup where they threw water on some embers to make you sweat. Once sweating, you had to go out, run over the hills around the Gila, and then come back, sweat, and run again some more.

Finally, you had to ride horseback for two-day journeys during which you were allowed neither to eat nor to sleep. And since you were cunning, an adult would follow to make sure you followed the rules. . . .

That is how, when you were barely fourteen, Grandfather, you became a true Apache warrior, as dangerous and elusive as lightning.

4

Our car has just left the center of town, which is actually the main stretch where the Gourmet Bar and the stores were. I tried on all kinds of cowboy boots until a hot pink model in natural leather finally struck my fancy. It matches our T-shirts! the girls exclaimed. I also bought a super lightweight straw cowboy hat, a square turquoise ring, and, ah yes! . . . a shot glass decorated with a photograph of Geronimo. It's a souvenir, I told Harlyn, who looked at the thing with knit brows like, *You're not going to buy that thing, are you*? But I did. I bought it. And with my cowboy boots on my feet, we're finally all back into the car, where, with the AC blasting, we're on our way to our mysterious destination.

"That's my hospital!" Harlie Bear shouts suddenly, pointing behind her window at a midsize building painted beige and gray. "That's where I go for my asthma."

I just have time to read RUIDOSO PRESBYTERIAN HOSPITAL on the façade before she shows me another unit. The emergency room. Her mother brought her there the first time she had an attack.

"Do you have bad asthma?"

Without answering, she takes a green and red inhaler out of a small denim backpack. Becotide and Ventolin.

"I have to always carry them with me."

The problem with inhalers, Harlyn explains, is that she doesn't really know how to use them properly. Since she isn't able to empty the air from her lungs before she inhales the medicine, it doesn't work very well during an attack and she panics, so we have to take her to the ER. Luckily, she doesn't have too many.

"That's because you give her plants," Shania explains, in a serious voice.

I look at Harlyn. He nods. Medicine men use more than three hundred medicinal plants. Over the years, his great-grandmother Kate showed them to him, one by one. She taught him how to recognize them, how to prepare them. Certain ones must be ground, others cut into pieces, and the cooking time matters too. Everything is very precise in these arts. The same plant may not have the same virtues when mixed with this or that other plant. I ask him which plant he uses for asthma.

"Apache plants, you wouldn't know them."

"Can you tell me their names anyway?"

"They only work on Apaches."

"OK, but it interests me. In Mongolia, for instance, to cure indigestion, shamans use a decoction made from wolf's tongue, a small plant whose leaves have that shape."

Harlyn's only answer is to continue scrutinizing the road. I don't want to insist. But a few moments later, he points with his index finger over the steering wheel.

"See that tree, there . . . ?"

I turn my head to the right. I see a big tree in front of a wooden house. It's too far away now for me to see it well. It was an oak, Harlyn explains, a *Quercus gambelii* to be precise. He smiles. People often have one in their garden and don't even know that it has powers.

"Apaches made coffee with its bark," Harlie Bear says, redoing her ponytail.

Shamans dry the leaves, Harlyn explains, grind them into a powder, and mix them with the leaves from a bush called *Diotis lanata*. You can recognize it by its bunched white flowers. When someone is the victim of some ill fate, the shaman does a ceremony. He asks the individual to bring four relatively inexpensive objects as offerings to get the spirits' cooperation. Generally, a knife with a black handle, a new item of clothing, some tobacco in a small leather pouch, and money, between thirty and fifty dollars. He then puts the powder from his plants in some rolling paper and makes a stick that he gives to the person to smoke. The spirit of those plants has the power to protect the person and drive off the bad spirits, to purify him. He clears his throat.

"To purify himself before the ceremony, the shaman also has to smoke little white sage cigarettes and recite prayers. Do you know about sage?"

"Yes, there's a lot of it in France. My grandmother even used to say that keeping sage in your yard could avoid a visit to the doctor."

"Was your grandmother a shaman?"

"No. Well, not officially, anyway. And what about asthma?"

He smiles, like, *You and your one-track mind* . . .

"We'll get back to that later. First, tell me how you become a shaman in Mongolia."

Before I can answer, Shania's forearm appears to the left of my face.

"Look!"

She proudly displays a five-pointed star, freshly and meticulously tattooed on the inside of her wrist. Now I understand why she has been silent for almost ten minutes. Harlyn bought her the tattoo at the souvenir shop.

"I put it on," Harlie Bear points out softly.

The forearm disappears. Shania examines her star, eyebrows knit, mouth pursed. Harlyn tells me that the Apaches used to tattoo themselves. On the inside of their arms, for the most part. The tattoos represented stars, like the one Shania has, or constellations. Shamans also tattooed themselves with lightning, to show the source of their power.

"And do you know how they did their tattoos?" Harlie Bear asks me.

I shake my head no.

"With cactus spikes dipped in charcoal or cactus juice, I can't remember which."

"Prickly pear or *Opuntia humifusa*," Harlyn specifies.

"The spike must have hurt so bad," Shania adds in her deep voice, lips twisted in disgust. "I prefer to stick them on!"

I feel like laughing but refrain because Shania is staring at the blue drawing as if imagining what she has escaped. Harlyn, who definitely hasn't lost the thread of our conversation, asks the question about Mongolia again.

"So how do you become a shaman?"

After clearing my throat—the AC never does it any good—I answer that most often it's hereditary. But you can also be chosen by the spirits. In that case, the person will suddenly start having a string of problems, like some of their cattle dying, or the deaths of family members. They also may start having little episodes of madness or losing consciousness, or epileptic fits. In Mongolia, all of those events are interpreted as warnings from the spirit world, cautionary signs meant to lead their "victims" to the understanding that they're shaman. I hear a huge yawn from the back. I turn around. Shania's mouth is wide open. Harlyn, one eye in the rearview mirror, tells her to put her hand in front of her mouth. Done. He stares at the road again. I conclude.

"But having those types of problems doesn't necessarily mean you're a shaman."

"Well, then, how do you know?" he asks.

"The individuals who have been 'targeted' visit a shaman, who questions the spirits to find out whether or not they are."

"And you, did the spirits choose you?"

"In a way. In fact, you can't really decide to be a shaman in Mongolia. You are one if the spirits want you to be, if they send you the gift, the 'power.' Otherwise, you're not one."

"For the Apaches it's the same thing!" Harlyn tells me, seeming delighted with this similarity.

He, for instance, inherited his shaman status, he explains. His great-grandmother Kate had chosen to transmit her "power" to him. But this power could have refused the transmission. So, when he was five, Kate held a ceremony to call the power to him. She recited prayers meant to protect him from evil forces. And then, four times, she applied pollen to his mouth. The fourth time, the power was supposed to enter him. But it could have not done so. He shoots me a quick glance.

"Is that how it works in Mongolia?"

I nod yes. He knew for sure that the "power" had chosen him because he'd instantly managed to memorize the prayers. Without it, he would have been unable to. So Kate organized a celebration where all of the food, the meat, the cabbage, the fruit, and the nuts were blessed with pollen. In the years that followed his great-grandmother passed her knowledge on to him. How and with what plants to cure illnesses, care for cancers, soothe headaches. She also taught him how to develop certain extrasensory perceptions, another characteristic of Apache shamanic traditions. He swallows.

"For instance, I know when someone is going to come visit me. Especially people coming about the puberty rite, you know, the sacred ceremony for young girls I told you about?"

He shoots me a glance. I nod. He continues:

"As soon as one of them gets her first period, a member of her family has to visit a medicine man to organize the ceremony. Well, I get a vision of that person at least two weeks before they arrive. In my dreams, they walk toward my house. I know then that they're going to be asking me for a ceremony. And it never fails."

With his index finger, he softly massages his forehead, right above his glasses.

"That's also how I knew in your case."

I look at him, waiting for the explanation. He smiles.

"I told you during our first conversation that I knew someone would show up one day, as you have, to reconnect me with my Mongol roots. . . ."

"Oh, yes! So it was a dream that told you about it?"

He nods with a mischievous look. I smile. I'm glad finally to have an explanation, even if it isn't exactly rational. But I'm in no position to discuss rationality. Am I not here because of a "vision" of Geronimo? I clear my throat to suppress a giggle that really wanted to get out all of a sudden.

"And the anonymous letter?" Harlie Bear asks. "Tell her about it!"

"Oh, right! I once received an anonymous letter that was pretty unpleasant—like all anonymous letters. So I prayed to Yusn, with the letter in front of me, and I asked the spirit to let me know, within the next four days, who the person was. Two days later, I received a message. The person appeared to me in a dream. I recognized him and was able to respond!"

"They were so embarrassed!" says Harlie Bear, laughing.

"These dreams are very powerful," says Harlyn, his hands still firmly on the steering wheel at 10-and-2.

It took him a while to understand it, even though his great-grandmother had told him about those types of powers when he was still small. According to her, all you had to do was pray to Yusn for it to work. He hadn't really taken her seriously. But one day, after he'd become an adult, he wanted to try it. He said a prayer and it worked. Only then did he understand how strong the power was, and he was happy he hadn't realized it sooner, since he might not have used it with all the wisdom it required. Despite having been utilized by the Apaches very effectively for centuries, this power still has to be handled with the utmost caution.

"Anyway, I started having dreams in which 'the power' told me, little by little, what I was capable of, like driving off a tornado or causing it to turn, for instance."

My eyebrows go up. Luckily, Harlyn doesn't notice, since he's still looking at the road.

"It's true," says Harlie Bear.

Harlyn looks at me, as though trying to convince me.

"Do you remember the hurricane that struck New Orleans two years ago?"

"Katrina?"

He nods.

"I had the strong feeling that if I had been within five miles of the storm, I would have been able to make it deviate a bit. I was certain I could do it. It's like when I pray for snow or rain now, it actually comes. But I don't do it for fun. I do it when it's necessary. In the case of severe drought, for example. When that happens, I pray to my medicine. It's incredibly powerful. Even if I don't understand why and how it works."

I stroke my right eyebrow with the tip of my index finger. A way to collect my thoughts.

"Could you explain to me why you speak sometimes of your *medicine* and sometimes of your *power*. Is there a distinction?"

"No. Both terms have the same meaning."

"Yuuuuuck!" cries Shania from the rear.

I turn around. With a disgusted look, she hands me a transparent lollipop I had bought in the Ruidoso store. A large worm, like the one at the bottom of a bottle of mescal, sits at its center. His gaze in the rearview, Harlyn tells Shania to please put the lollipop back where she found it. You don't go through other people's stuff! She looks down, using her fingertip to replace the object of her crime in its paper sack. I tell her that, if she wants it, she's welcome to have it. A new cry of disgust. Harlie Bear bursts out laughing. "That'll teach you!" Shania, apparently offended, settles firmly back in her seat, arms crossed, nose and eyebrows scrunched in a frown, mouth contorted. All her little mannerisms really make me want to laugh. But I'm in complete control—not a hint of glee shows on my face. Nor on Harlyn's, for that matter. He's still concentrating on the road. We're passing fields, meadows with horses, colorful sheds covered with chili peppers drying out. It feels like Mexico isn't far.

"Back to the subject of shamans," Harlyn resumes. "Each receives a 'power' that is unique to him or her."

"Yes, but how do they receive it? Only by inheritance, like in your case?"

"No, not only. If the person doesn't inherit their power, then they might have a vision one day or 'hear' an animal speak. Like Geronimo, but I'll tell you about that later. So each shaman, man or woman, receives a very specific power. Some are able to heal people, others to predict the future. Others know how to lead a hunt."

"So you visit a shaman based on their qualifications?"

"Yes. For example, Geronimo was a war shaman. He said prayers before each battle, and his power would come to tell him where to go, what to do or not to do in order to win. He was rarely wrong, and as a result people would consult with him before each battle. That's why the American soldiers were never able to capture him."

"He surrendered!" Harlie Bear shouts, noticeably very invested in her ancestor's path already.

"Yes," Harlyn confirms, "the soldiers had kidnapped his entire family and were threatening to kill them or never let him see them again if he didn't give himself up. A typical ploy used by the military to destroy tribes and force the warriors to surrender."

A large truck passes us. Indraft. They drive really fast here. Harlyn keeps the car over on the right. We watch the black mass slip in front of us. I'm surprised not to hear any comment from Shania. Is she sulking? I turn around. Yep. Her nose stubbornly turned toward her window, her gaze locked on the trees that go by. She's going to get carsick, if she keeps this up. Harlie Bear shoots me a glance in which I can read, *Don't worry, she'll get over it.*

"And the shamans in Mongolia, what do they do, are they healers?" Harlyn asks.

"We don't call it healing in the context of a shamanic ceremony in Mongolia, we call it mending. According to the Mongols, spirits are sensitive, thin-skinned. If you do something they don't like, they're offended and punish you. So the shaman's role isn't to 'heal' but simply to arrange a ceremony in order to ask the spirits the reason for their anger and then to convey it to the person consulting them, along with instructions for what to do to 'cure' the offense."

"For Apaches too, the origin of a problem is often attributed to an act that might have made our god, Yusn, angry."

"Like what, for instance?"

"Well, whenever there was an epidemic, the shamans would ask all the members of the tribe to try to recall some act that might have provoked Yusn's ire. Such as having profaned our religion, or abandoned parents or relatives in need, or being unfaithful or cowardly or lazy."

"And when the fault was identified?"

"The shaman would hold a ceremony to ask Yusn to please forgive the mistake. But the person who was responsible was still banished from the tribe."

"Banished?"

"The Apaches had no prisons," Harlie Bear interjects.

"That I suspected, but Mongols needed only to present offerings to the spirits in order to appease them. They weren't banished."

"Banishment was the worst punishment too," Harlyn adds. "Because any Indian who no longer belonged to a tribe was not only no longer protected by its laws but was also considered an enemy by all the other tribes. So he could be killed at any moment."

I frown.

"Killing an enemy, or stealing from him, wasn't considered wrong?"

"No. That's a girl's question! Do you think they put soldiers in jail nowadays for having killed an enemy in Iraq? It's like in every war, the more you kill, the greater a hero you are when you come back."

I nod without comment, since, precisely because I'm a "girl," it's hard for me to understand that kind of heroism. Harlyn continues.

"So, in Apache culture, being banished was much worse than prison. It was very simply the equivalent of a death sentence. The person who was banished was forced to live entirely alone in the wild and couldn't count on help from any other Apache. His only chance, really, was to band together with other banished individuals. But this system of punishment worked against us when the whites arrived. The ones who had been banished ended up forming small bands. To survive, they would pillage here and there, which the whites unfortunately pinned on the tribes. And since they weren't subject to our laws anymore, we could do nothing to reason with them. They weren't bound by our peace treaties with the Americans either."

"I feel sick," Shania's deep voice suddenly intones.

Without looking at her, Harlyn tells her to open her window. I turn around. Her face is totally white. Still sullen, she presses the button. Heat rushes into the air-conditioned car. Her little nose perks up.

"But if someone has hurt himself, after a riding accident, for instance, what can the shaman do?" Harlyn continues, obviously used to his granddaughter's capricious moods.

"The same principle applies. If you're the victim of an accident, it's because the spirits are angry and your soul is a mess. So the shaman must first of all hold a ceremony to mend the offense and ask the spirits to let you be."

"And what about the injury? What do they do about it? We Apaches we make poultices with plants like *i-ah-i*. I'll show you some if you like. We apply the boiled leaves to the wound to stop the bleeding. We also make decoctions from it to help bones fuse faster, and they mend in two weeks with that plant. To fight infection, we also give infusions of Mormon tea."

I explain to Harlyn that to purify a wound, the shaman merely applies some juniper ashes to it. Mongols today are more likely go to the hospital to heal a wound and then to the shaman to mend their soul.

Harlyn nods, lost in thought apparently. Shania is still resting her head on the edge of her wide-open window. It's hot. Loose strands of her hair fly in the wind. On the side of the road, I notice a sign for ROSWELL. I ask Harlyn if that's the place where an extraterrestrial was supposed to have been found in the fifties. He shoots me a quick glance before staring at the road again. I wait. His answer will come in a few minutes probably. Just as his movements are studied, he always seems to reflect carefully before answering. We skim the entrance to a ranch. There are fences as far as the eyes can see.

"There have always been lots of aliens around here," he finally says. "But Apaches don't talk about it."

"Oh really? And why is that?"

"We mustn't. That's all."

He looks into his rearview mirror. Asks Shania if she's feeling better. But with the wind in her ears, she doesn't hear. Harlie Bear touches her shoulder and asks her the question again, loud enough this time. Shania turns to face her, a smile finally back on her face.

"I need to pee!"

Harlyn puts his blinker on with a sigh. A hundred yards down the road, he parks the car on the shoulder. Everyone gets out. The heat envelops us. Dry. Harsh. Harlyn hands some Kleenexes to the girls. They disappear. As far as the eye can see, the road extends through enormous spaces of yellowed grass, fenced in by a single line of barbed wire.

"This land all belongs to the same owner?"

"Yes."

"In France, there'd be at least twenty different farms in the same amount of space."

He smiles. Then he asks if I wouldn't like to take advantage of the pee break too. Sure. He immediately hands me a Kleenex. The girls come back skipping, hand in hand. They climb into the car in a good mood. It's our turn now to go relieve ourselves. Harlyn in the little ditch below the fence, me behind the car, since the road is deserted. Two minutes later, our little troop is reunited and once again driving along with the wind in our ears.

"Close your window, Shania, I put on the AC."

Without grumbling for once, she presses the little black button. An electric sound. Clunk. We are now insulated from the heat. Shania settles back in her seat, seatbelt pulled tight. We are still skimming along the same fence. This ranch is really huge.

"So tell me how a ceremony goes in Mongolia," Harlyn asks.

Concentration, deep breath in. Go. Before the ceremony, the shaman speaks with the person who has come to consult him, and she tells him about her life and why she came to see him. It's a bit like what a psychologist does. The shaman then crafts an *ongot*, a construction made of pieces of cloth meant to represent the person seeking advice. Next the shaman places the "problem" on the ceremonial altar. He tells the person that if his problem is there, in front of him, it's because he must have made a mistake in his life and offended a spirit. To be forgiven and to calm the unhappy spirit, he'll have to make him some offerings.

"What kind of offerings?"

"Sweets, cakes, cigarettes, vodka, milk. . ."

"Everything humans like, then?"

I nod. After having made the offerings, the person asks the spirit to please forgive him. The shaman then puts on his ceremonial costume, plays the drums to enter into a trance, and asks the spirits the reason for the problem's existence. That is to say, whatever the person seeking advice or one of his ancestors has done to offend them.

"What offends the spirits?"

"Some of the reasons given to the shaman can be quite surprising. Like, *You walked around your yurt three times*, or *Your ancestor ate the meat of a stolen animal.* . . . But whether or not the reason seems valid doesn't matter, because its restorative function lies solely in the fact that it provides the shaman with an identification of the problem, and through that the diagnosis that's needed for the mending process."

His eyes still on the road, Harlyn nods in silence, as though thoroughly digesting this information. I go on.

"Penultimate step: the shaman purifies the *ongot* that symbolizes the problem. In purifying it, he eliminates its evil power by transforming it into a new ally for that person. Then comes the final step in the ceremony: the shaman gives the person protective amulets for him and his home."

"And the ritual is always the same?"

"With some variations depending on the problem or the goal to be achieved. But no matter what, it's the spirit that instructs the shaman on the procedure to follow. If the spirit doesn't care to speak to the shaman, if he's protesting, the shaman will be unable to give the person a single answer. He's only ever an interpreter."

His mouth slightly open, Harlyn nods and utters his usual "Uh, huh." A kind of linguistic tic. Like a little beat, a little tap on the cymbals to emphasize his words or his interlocutor's.

"It's exactly the same for the Apaches," he says finally. "The shaman is nothing without the intervention of his 'power.' A bit like the way metal conducts electricity. It's the electricity that has the power to light the lamp. Not the shaman."

I smile. I like that image. I add that, during a trance, the spirit usually manifests itself as an animal. And each shaman has his own, which is supposed to give him the information he needs.

"And you? What is your animal? Does it speak to you?"

Breathe in. I always find it hard to "admit" this type of thing.

"It's . . . It's a wolf."

Anxious glance at Harlyn, who doesn't seem in the least surprised. He hasn't even taken his eyes off the road. I continue.

"But I still haven't completely understood the wolf's words yet. During the trance, I see him before me, he howls like a wolf, and I begin to do the same as if all of a sudden I had become a wolf, but I don't know yet how to translate what he's telling me. Though I do start making gestures that my mind doesn't control.

If a person is in front of me, for example, I start to 'see' the parts of his body that are suffering. Without anyone having spoken to me about it beforehand, of course. My hands go to those parts, making very precise, very distinct motions, along a particular geography known only to them. Sounds, breaths, and chants also come out of my mouth. As if my entire body was suddenly guided by, let's say, a kind of perceptual intelligence?"

Again, I glance over at Harlyn. He nods his head and seems to be following. Still not surprised either. I ask him if he "suffers" from those sorts of symptoms. No. He doesn't really practice trances. Not in that form, at least. But he'll talk about it later. First he urges me to continue my explanation about the hand gestures.

"It's really hard to say, but I have the deep conviction that I'm being 'pushed' to make these gestures, as though to restore some kind of energy flow."

Harlyn punctuates with his usual "Uh huh," then remains silent, lost in deep thought, apparently. I remain quiet. Not the moment for comments, since he must already think I'm nuts. The girls are asleep. The effect of the motor's purring, surely. Harlyn finally opens his mouth.

"So your wolf speaks to you."

I look at him, bewildered. This time, I've ended up with a bigger nut than me.

"What do you mean, he speaks to me? I told you, I can't hear any words."

He turns his head toward me with a smile that says, *Okay, girlie, it's time for me to explain . . .*

"So what? Words aren't the only way to transmit knowledge! If you're making hand gestures, sounds, if you're chanting, it's because your wolf has transmitted his message and you've understood it. The gestures are proof of it. So you're playing your role of interpreter the way you should."

I answer with a sober "Mmm." He continues, glasses glued to the road again.

"The spirit of the wolf exists among the Apaches too. My great-grandmother spoke of a white wolf that came to 'see' a woman who had been bitten by a dog. In the dream, the wolf told her to touch its four paws and to pray that her leg be as strong as his paws. She did what the wolf asked and was healed."

"Mmm," once more, then I ask if Geronimo also had a spirit animal.

"Eagle."

Suddenly, I feel like laughing. I want to say, *Welcome to the kingdom of loonies!* but don't. Anyway, Harlyn goes on. The coyote ceremony, he says, is used when someone gets bitten by a dog, a wolf, a fox, or a coyote or catches some disease that was contracted through their intermediary.

"Those four animals are associated in your tradition?"

"Yes, completely. Even if certain shamans draw their power from the wolf, the dog, the fox, or the coyote, they're animals that inspire fear. In our culture, if a man even crosses their tracks or smells them, he risks becoming cross-eyed, having convulsions or tremors, or he might bare his teeth, and, worse, his lips might stay pulled back like that."

I smile.

"That's exactly what happens to me during trances when the wolf is in front of me! I feel like I have chops and paws. I also start trembling. Except I become 'normal' again when it's over."

On the side of the road, three crows in a line watch us go by. I show Harlyn the birds. The crow is Enkhtuya's animal. A coincidence? No, says Harlyn. Just a manifestation of the invisible bonds that make up the world. Knowing how to discover them and recognize them is the very essence of shamanism. Its secret facet. I purse my lips. Secret, maybe, but isn't it time for an explanation now? I turn to face him.

"The information I perceive in my trance state, which prompts me to make gestures and sounds, isn't it—rather than a message from 'spirits'—just information emitted in the form of vibrations or waves by what surrounds us?"

Harlyn turns to face me with a disappointed look, and without another word turns back to his road. I feel like I've just uttered the dumbest sentence in the universe. His earring followed the movement of his head and is still oscillating. Like the air that ripples near the horizon of this plateau we're driving across. The AC had better not break down. Harlyn suddenly finds his voice. Clear, precise. According to him, each element in nature possesses a spirit equivalent. It is these spirits that speak to us to give us information. Not sound waves. I toss a dubitative "Mmm" his way. I won't let it drop, and insist.

"Have you heard of the discoveries made in quantum physics?"

His head says no. A moment to gather my thoughts, then go! It's a branch of physics founded on the study of quantas, particles. As we now know, matter is made of atoms, which themselves are made up of different particles, including protons, neutrons, quarks, and electrons. Advances in the technology for measuring these particles have allowed scientists to go farther in the study of their mechanics and confirm that electrons, for instance, may have the physical properties not only of matter but also of waves. In fact, an electron might not be an unbendable sphere orbiting a nucleus, as was believed for a long time, but a bendable cloud, a blob, that would have the peculiar ability to be both here and there, making its speed and position impossible to establish. The "blob" state would explain why, if we act on one part of the cloud, the rest reacts instantly. Particles capable of interfering with each other in this way exhibit the behavior of waves—whose defining characteristic is precisely the ability to cause interferences. I look at Harlyn. He's staring at the road. Even the piece of turquoise is immobile. "Are you following this?" His head starts bobbing, and he asks me to continue.

"Well, my question is, if electrons indeed behave like waves, why wouldn't those waves carry, just like radio waves, information that our brains would have the ability to perceive and 'translate'?"

Harlyn stares at the road in silence. I wait. The girls are still asleep. We are driving among small hills dotted with low bushes in the shape of balls. It looks like some poorly kept French garden. Harlyn finally opens his mouth.

"So the messages from the spirits that shamans perceive would in fact be 'waves' that carry information?"

"Yes."

"And every brain would have that ability?"

"Sure."

"So everyone would be a shaman?"

"Or would have the potential to be one. But today only individuals who have developed those abilities, for whatever reason, are officially granted the status of shaman."

"So the gestures and sounds that you start to make during a trance would be the brain's response to those waves carrying the information?"

"Just a hypothesis, of course. But during a trance, when my hands start moving about the person in front of me, it's because they're responding to some kind of stimulus. As a rule, they're not mistaken. The body parts they 'work on' are always areas that are suffering. I never know it ahead of time, but, thanks to this state, my hands sure seem to 'know' where to go. So where do they get that information?"

Harlyn glances at me again.

"Are you asking me?"

I nod.

"Um . . . no doubt from that person."

"I wouldn't know from where else. Their body must be sending out emergency signals, or some signal of an energy imbalance or I don't know what, that my brain has the ability to discern and interpret in having me make those gestures and sounds, whose purpose is maybe to restore some kind of balance that existed before the problem."

Lips pursed doubtfully. I go on.

"Anyway, it all remains to be proven. Research in this field is in its infancy, you know."

"And what would be the point in promoting this type of research?"

"Well, to understand the human brain and the invisible mechanisms of the universe!"

"But shamans have already explained them!"

"Yes, but not in a scientific way. Because of that, shamanism continues to be associated with practices that are more or less debatable."

"Yes, but that often work."

"But precisely, that remains to be proven."

"Proven by what means?"

"Well, for instance, by agreeing to work with scientists . . ."

I tell him that on my next trip to Canada I'll be staying in a psychiatric hospital. He bursts out laughing his duck-call laugh and says it's not starting out too well for me. I merely shrug, while his laughter stalls. It doesn't matter, I like very much how interested he is in the path I've chosen. His mere willingness to listen, his questions, his way of bouncing back and even making fun of me a bit show me to what extent, little by little, we're becoming accomplices. I go on with my explanation.

"In that hospital, a neuropsychiatrist is going to run a series of tests, including multiple electroencephalograms of my brain. This is a first step to discover the physiological mechanisms responsible for modified states of consciousness—which areas of the brain are activated, what the consequences are."

"And granted that our brain has this capacity to perceive information present in the environment, which I call messages from the spirits, do you really think there will be a way to develop these abilities?"

"The whole point of the brain recordings would be to try to elucidate the mechanisms in order to learn how to develop these abilities. But first we have to prove that wave-particles do in fact carry information that the brain is capable of perceiving, analyzing, and utilizing to provide the appropriate response. We would also need to know whether these responses, like for instance the gestures and sounds I make during a trance, actually have a restorative function."

He smiles.

"It'll take hundreds of years!"

"Yes, I know, but the study of particles is also moving things forward."

"Meaning?"

"Apparently, there may exist between certain atoms a correlation that causes the atoms to be interdependent. Even at a distance . . ."

Harlyn frowns. I continue.

"Imagine two atoms, A and B. Well, certain studies have shown that if the atoms are correlated, they start to depend closely on each other. Even at a distance."

"Do you mean that if I disturb atom A—"

"And atom A only, B will instantly be disturbed too, no matter the distance between them."

Harlyn graces me with an "Uh, huh" this time, but asks me where I'm going with this.

"I just mean that atoms have a way of communicating with each other at a distance."

A mischievous smile starts to form at the corners of his mouth. Careful now.

"It's because they have a telephone!"

He bursts out in his jerky laugh. I'm not laughing, though. He must have noticed, because his laugh brakes to a stop immediately. He starts talking, serious again.

"I'm joking, of course. But here again, shamans have known for a long time, even if they haven't provided any scientific proof, that there are other ways of communicating besides speech and touch! For instance, I don't use trances to get information, I also don't have a specific animal, like you and Geronimo, but the spirits . . ."

He looks at me.

"Yes, I prefer to continue saying 'spirits,' if that's OK with you."

I nod. Anyway, his look doesn't leave me a choice. He resumes his explanation, staring at the road again.

"Well, these spirits communicate with me through dreams or in a kind of waking vision."

His voice has become hoarse. He clears his throat before continuing. Once, he had a very bad backache. It was in 1997. He had been working in the forest but didn't know if that was the reason for it. One night, the pain became so intense he couldn't do anything anymore. Even the plants had no effect. So he said some prayers. Four "Hail Marys, Full of Grace" and four "Our Fathers" . . .

"But those are Catholic prayers! Are you Catholic?"

"Yes, I belong to the Roman Catholic Church."

"We go every Sunday," suddenly says the deep voice of Shania, who has probably just woken up.

I loosen my seatbelt a bit and turn to face her. Big smile and unkempt hair, her arms already raised to redo her ponytail. Harlie Bear wakes up too, stretches, smiles at her cousin, then me, then looks out the window.

"Where are we?"

"Near Capitan," Harlyn answers. "Smokey Bear country," he adds for my benefit. There are huge forests all around—"

"And a great rodeo in the summer," Shania interjects, arms still around her head.

Harlie Bear leans over to help her, but as usual gets rebuffed. Harlyn continues.

"Geronimo was converted to the Christian faith during his incarceration."

"Which faith?"

"The Reformed Church."

"And he continued to practice Apache rituals?"

"Yes. He couldn't see any disagreement between the two practices. I don't either, by the way. It means I have twice as many chances for my prayers to be answered."

He laughs again. I like his pragmatic way of analyzing life. He asks me about my religion.

"Catholic. But I've never practiced it."

A shrug.

"You do what you want."

Along the road, there is a guy in a neon vest signaling us to slow down. There is some roadwork a little farther on, so they're alternating traffic on a single lane. The girls straighten up to see. We stop in front of a temporary red light. A cluster of cars is coming from the opposite side. The road runs through green hills covered with paths and full of little rivers bordered by tall trees. Harlyn takes advantage of the stop to play tour guide.

"Do you know who used to live around here?"

"Billy the Kid," Shania shouts.

Harlyn scolds her gently. He hadn't asked her the question. She laughs in response. I ask Harlyn if it's possible that Geronimo and Billy met. The answer is yes. They lived in the same region, at around the same time.

"But if Geronimo had seen him, he would have slit his throat," Harlyn adds, imitating the movement across his neck with a hand as precise and swift as a knife.

The girls burst out laughing. I stroke my throat. Wondering whether I would really have wanted to meet Geronimo. The light turns green. Harlyn starts the car again. Now the road surface is grooved. Making a raspy sound, the car starts heaving as if it were hesitating between two furrows. Hup! We're back on smooth tar. The silence returns, troubled only by the AC's heavy breathing. I look at the hills. I imagine Billy the Kid there, under that tree beside the river, his horse tied to a branch, its neck stretched toward the grass. A rabbit is roasting over the wood fire. The grilled flesh is starting to give off a delicious smell. Too busy drooling over his dinner, Billy hasn't foreseen the danger. From the bushes, a few yards behind him, Geronimo is creeping forward, his long knife in his hand. I let out a slight chuckle. Harlyn peers over at me, surprised. I apologize. It's nothing . . .

"So what about your back pain?"

He thinks for a bit, not seeming to remember. Oh, right! he resumes. So he said his prayers to try to relieve the pain a bit, then went to bed. But at two in the morning, he woke with a start. He'd just had a dream.

"I was in the church in Mescalero, and, in front of me, I saw Mother Teresa standing before the altar. So I walked over to her and knelt down, and she asked me, 'How may I help you?' I told her I had a sharp pain in my back and that it had been bothering me constantly for the last several days. I asked her if she could remove it. She answered: 'Harlyn, say four "Our Fathers" and four "Hail Marys, Full of Grace."' That's when I woke up. So I recited the prayers, then woke my wife, Karen, to tell her about my dream. She told me I was right to have recited the prayers."

The following morning Harlyn went to see Father Larry, the priest in Mescalero, to tell him his dream. Father Larry was surprised but wasn't able to explain why Harlyn had had the dream. Father Larry just told him to keep on praying. Which he did.

"The pain disappeared gradually. Three weeks later, I didn't have any pain at all, and I've never had a sore back since."

Harlyn stops. His voice had become a little hoarse when he spoke the last sentence, visibly moved. It has become warmer, like when he speaks softly. I ask him if he has other examples of messages he's received in his dream. He thinks for a bit, seeming to scrutinize the landscape, as if he were suddenly hesitating, out of modesty no doubt, to reveal one more piece of his personal life. But far from worrying about it, I realized how lucky I am. The complicity between us has already allowed us to come so far! And Harlyn's sudden modesty is just proof of how far we've come. Now

I regret not having dared yet to share my vision of Geronimo with him. I'm going to do it. Yes, it's time.

"You see," he finally tells me, his face smiling again, "three times a day, I say a prayer for Yusn, our Creator. And sometimes, during these prayers, I intercept messages, like future events. It's not unusual. I've had those types of experiences for a long time, but now that I am older I take them more seriously. The night of September 10 to September 11, for instance, I had a dream that was pretty terrifying. I saw people screaming. There was the exterior of a building, there was dust, very thick smoke, stones, papers flying everywhere. It was so real I woke up, and I woke Karen who told me, 'It's just a nightmare!' It was two in the morning. The next day, I received a phone call around eight o'clock. A friend told me to turn on the television because the Twin Towers had been destroyed by two airplanes. I turned it on and saw everything that had been in my dream. Then I realized my mind had probably been there and it was frightening."

He grows quiet, apparently lost in thought. Perhaps it's not the right moment to tell him about my vision. He doesn't allow me time for it anyway, but moves on to the topic of another gift. According to him, Apache shamans also have the power to bring to light very dangerous individuals, like sorcerers, who are capable of casting spells that kill people or make them ill."

"But what exactly is the difference between a sorcerer and a shaman?"

"All shamans are potential sorcerers."

"So how do they become sorcerers?"

"By accepting to receive their 'power' from evil sources and by using it to do evil. They do it secretly of course, so no one really knows who they are."

"And shamans can detect them?"

"Yes. When someone who has been a victim of their magic comes asking me for help, I hold a special ceremony, which allows me to see the sorcerer behind all the bad luck."

I frown.

"But how do you see him?"

"In my dreams. I told you, that's how I receive messages from the spirits. So during the ceremony, I ask my powers if the person is a victim of witchcraft. If the person is, the spirits tell me and, in my dreams after that, I can see his face. Sometimes I can even locate him."

"Your power is a veritable GPS!"

He shrugs in response.

"And so, what do you do after identifying the sorcerer's location?"

"Thanks to prayers and secret rituals, I send the bad energies back toward him to destroy him."

"And if you've got the wrong sorcerer?"

A small chuckle from the girls, who have definitely been very quiet for a while. Glance into the back. Shania, thumb in her mouth, head on her cousin's knees is letting her scalp be massaged and, seeing her look of complete ecstasy, it shouldn't be long before she starts to purr.

"The power never gets the wrong sorcerer," Harlyn answers, a little bit drily. "And once the ritual is over, the medicine man cares for the victim of the evil spell by blessing him with pollen. He also says prayers and does purification rituals. It's very powerful."

I feel like punctuating his story with an "Uh huh," the way he does, but I refrain immediately. He'll think I'm making fun of him. That couldn't be further from the truth, though. It's just that it takes me about two hours to internalize the speech patterns of a person and start imitating them despite myself. A bit like picking up a tune from someone. Probably has to do with my musical training. Anyway, as far as inconvenient tics go, I can't hear a clock or a watch without it setting off an internal metronome, and the tick-tock invariably incites a little melody in my head. Harlyn shoots me a look.

"Did you hear me?"

"Uh . . . what did you say?"

Sigh. He continues. "I was saying that the 'power' is as potent as it is dangerous. For instance, it can demand certain sacrifices from the shaman in exchange for its help."

"Sacrifices? But why?"

"To see if the shaman is prepared to do anything for it."

"And what if the shaman refuses?"

"Simple. The 'power' leaves him."

"But that's disgusting!"

Harlyn smiles. That's why shamans are usually feared by those around them, he explains. No one really wants to be their friend because they know the "power" may require such sacrifices at any time.

Thankfully, I don't think it's like that in Mongolia. At least, I hope not. Might Enkhtuya have failed to mention this slight "inconvenience"? Wouldn't be her first omission. She hadn't warned me that the more I practiced trance, my threshold for triggering it would drop and various other stimuli might trigger it too. Like an orgasm, for instance. I sure looked dumb the first time. Luckily, a Parisian neurobiologist cheered me up by telling me that I would learn to control the trance. In fact, my brain would end up remembering the process that set it off, and I would be able to start it or stop it by my own volition. Without a drum, that is. He was right. It took me about a year, but now I'm able to. And it's actually thanks to this new ability that Professor Flor-Henry in Canada will be able to capture electroencephalograms of my brain. With electrodes placed on my head linked to a machine, it would have been impossible to make the recordings if I were playing the drum. So, OK. All I need now is for those Mongol spirits to ask me to sacrifice my loved ones or friends. I swallow. Anyway, this kind of haggling can't possibly exist between us and our environment, can it? I look at Harlyn.

"Do you have a lot of friends?"

"Yes, why?"

"But have you told them that your power might ask you to sacrifice them in exchange for its help?"

With the tip of his right index finger, he pushes up the brim of his hat, which so far he hasn't once taken off, scratches his forehead a bit, just above his glasses, then puts it back, exactly where it was.

"No need, I don't know a single shaman this has happened to."

I exhale. Couldn't he have told me that before?

"But," he continues, "that's still the reason we can't put this power into just anyone's hands. We teach it only to those we know will respect it and not use it for evil ends. Also, the training is very long and rigorous, with many rituals and hundreds of plants to learn."

I ask him again, since he never told me finally, how you become a shaman when it's not hereditary, like in his case. Silence. Silence. Silence. This answer seems hard to craft.

"It's a long story," he says at last. "But again, the person can't simply choose to be a shaman. They have to be chosen. Exactly like you. And like Geronimo."

'Iłk'idą, k ǫǫ yá'édįná'a.

'Ákoo Tł'ízhe hooghéí da'áíná bikǫ' 'ólíná'a.

'Ákoo Tł'ízheí gotál yiis'ą́ná'a.

'Ákoo Mai'áee híłghoná'a.

Gotál jiis'ą́í 'áee, Mai tsíbąąee naaná'azhishná'a.

'Ákoo bitseeí tsínáiłgoná'a.

'Ákoo 'áałjindíná'a:Íquot;Shǫ́ǫ́dé, ntsee dili'.Íquot;

'Ákoo: Íquot;Chéek'e dili'ÁÍquot; goołndíná'a.

'Ákoo bitseeí tsíyóółgee.

Bitseeí bitł'áshį́ k ǫǫ dahiitoo.

'Ákoo 'áí jilą́go nandaajíńt'i ndah gotisá 'áí maií k ǫǫ í kaiłyaanáałghoná'a.

Kaiłnádaadiiłghoná'a k ǫǫ í.

Bikéya 'iładaashdeeskaná'a.

'Ákoo, ndáséshį́, 'Itsá k ǫǫ yaayíńłt'ą́.

'Áshį́, 'áńdeeda. díí dziłí bighe'yá díík'een k ǫǫ í naideesgeená'a.

'Iłch'ágo daagodeek'ąąná'a.

'Ákoo díídíí Tł'ízheí k ǫǫ í daayinłtséés ndah ch'éda'ádaayóół'įįná'a.

Íquot;Ákoo 'áń Ma'yeń ńłch'i'í bijoosndeego deeyolgo,k ǫǫ í,

doobeeshigoda'įįłdago, daadiiłtłáná'a.

Kát'égo, k ǫǫ goosłįná'a. (áó.á)

106

A long time ago, there was no fire.
Then only those we call flies had fire.

One day, the flies held a ceremony.
And Coyote came to the place of the ceremony.
Coyote danced around the fire very close to it.
And he constantly dipped his tail in the fire.

So the flies spoke these words to him: "Friend, your tail will
burn."

"Let it burn!" he told them.
And put his tail in the fire again.
His tail caught fire.

Many flies encircled him,
but Coyote jumped up and fled with the fire.
He ran far away from them with the fire.
And the flies went after him.

Sometime later, he gave fire to the eagle.
Who, in turn, spread fire all across over the mountains.
The fire burned everywhere you looked.

And the flies tried to tame the fire, but it was in vain.

Then, helped by the wind's breath,
the fire became uncontrollable and continued to burn.
And that is how fire came to be.

The Fourth Day

In the raking light, Grandfather, Bald Peak on the Mogollon Rim seemed furred with trees. This was the third sun you had watched melt behind it since your arrival at the summit of this sacred place. Three days during which you hadn't eaten or drunk anything, just prayed, forehead and chest marked with a pollen cross. Just chanted the words conveyed by the eagle spirit to summon the "power." But nothing had happened yet.

Alone in the middle of a small circle of stones surrounded by junipers, you let your gaze soar over the valley, slip into an eagle's wake, climb aboard its feathers, and penetrate the clouds, discovering their color from the other side: where time escapes, where life's inner side conceals its origin and spirits watch over the world, waiting for one of its inhabitants, finally attentive, to hear their words. Why had they not said anything to you yet? You were here. You had been here for three days, ready to receive what the eagle's spirit had promised to reveal two moons ago.

That night you had awoken with an irrepressible need to go walking. There was no moon, but you knew to orient yourself in the dark. Your fingers had wandered the bark of every square inch of this forest, the smells in your mind transforming into images that revealed in a single breath the place your eyes were blind to. This is how you came to the oak in which you had scraped your knees many a time. When you finally settled on the forked branch at the very top on the left, you hadn't been able to hold in a small cry of surprise when you looked at the sky. The air was like the Gila's water during Ghost Face, like liquid ice so crystalline, so limpid you had the sudden impression that all you needed to do was stretch your neck to lick the stars. One of them, slightly reddish, was especially bright, and without knowing why or how you suddenly heard a voice asking, four times, "Are you ready to listen to me?" Surprised, you scanned the darkness. Had a friend decided to play a prank on you? No. The forest's silence was as profound as ever. Yet you did hear a voice. Where could it be coming from? Your mother's words about the "power" returned at once to your mind. Was this voice its manifestation? This vital force of the universe could appear in many different guises, she had told you. Some heard it, it spoke to them; others saw it as a vision in a kind of waking dream. Then it could reveal itself in the form of a person, an animal, a star, the earth, the wind, mountains, the sun, a tree, an insect, a stag, a bolt of lightning, a bird, a horse, or a cloud. But before receiving the power, your mother explained, the individual selected never knew what they would "inherit." On your branch, you had ended up asking the night to reveal the source of that voice. And all of a sudden you had seen it. There was no moon, but very clearly you saw an eagle at the foot of the tree. After staring at him for a while, fascinated by his eyes, you'd heard the voice again. As though it came from him. This time, it was very clear; it told you to go to Bald Peak on the first day of the second moon. After telling you which ritual to perform at the top, it added that you'd have to wait patiently four days without eating or drinking anything. Only then would it disclose all you needed to know. Then the eagle disappeared. You remained on your branch for part of the night to reflect over and over on what you had just experienced. Should you accept this meeting? The only thing your mother had told you on the subject was that, the first time the "power" manifested itself, you could choose either to accept it or reject it. In the latter case, it would never manifest itself again.

What did you risk, finally? You knew well the peak that the eagle had spoken of. It was a sacred place where shamans went to revitalize themselves when they felt their powers waning or had doubts about how to cure someone. A pile of stones in the shape of a cone had been erected there, many harvests back. You had also gone there with your mother. Whenever you had to leave for a distant location, she chose a small stone on the ground, raised it to the four directions, starting with the east, and tossed it onto this pile of stones while praying for your trip to go well. Yes, you would go there. At sunrise you made your decision. You would toss a stone onto the pile in her memory. And you would pray that her eternal sojourn in the other world would continue to be happy.

The first day of the second moon, you set out on the path to the sacred mountain. In the morning, you washed your long black hair with a powder made from the root of the yucca, you used a mescal leaf comb to arrange it, then you rubbed it with grease and pulled it back with the headband you always wore around your forehead. With your nails, you carefully pulled the hair from your chin and upper lip. The Chiricahuas did not like facial hair. When you arrived at the top, you did as the eagle spirit had instructed and cut a juniper branch that you threw onto the pile of stones while reciting an incantation. Then you drew lines of pollen on your body and waited, praying, for the third day to end.

There still, in the center of your stony surroundings, plunged deep in the resinous smell of junipers, you watched as the sun was finally nibbled away by the shadows. For three days, you hadn't eaten or drunk anything, yet your stomach wasn't tortured by hunger. Ever since childhood, you had been trained to eat very little for long periods of time. However, you were very thirsty, and since your ears couldn't help but fasten onto the sound of the stream though it lay far behind you, you packed them with dry grass and wrapped yourself in your blanket to try and sleep, deciding on this fourth night not to stare into the darkness in search of the eagle.

A few hours later, you had a kind of dream. It felt so real that you never really knew if you were asleep or awake. But you saw the eagle again. You stared at it calmly, wondering whether this time you would hear its voice again. And suddenly it broke the silence to announce that, from now on, your body would never fear bullets or arrows. You would never be killed by them. In this way the eagle's spirit gave you the "power" of war. You would see the enemy if you wanted to see him, you would be invisible if you did not want him to see you, you would be able to make him take a different path, you would be able to locate him, to locate his horses, his livestock, you would also be able to protect your tribe from the spirits of the dead and to prolong the night if you were trying to hide from an enemy.

The eagle then taught you a prayer to summon him, adding that, at the appropriate time, he would give you all the prayers you'd need to accomplish your duties as a shaman. He would also teach you how to chant, which rituals to use, at what time, and with which sacred objects, and what restrictions to impose on those seeking your help. For this, all you needed to do was to invoke him by chanting this prayer and smoking some sage. He would recognize your prayer because it was he who had given it to you. He also warned you. It was he, through you, who had the "power." Not you. Everything he would teach you would be useless if he didn't agree. And it wasn't the details of the rituals, the prayers, and the chants that would make them effective but rather that he, eagle, recognized himself in their different aspects and respected his promise to help you accomplish your role as sha-man. You could teach them to no one without his consent. The strength of your medicine would depend entirely on your good relations with him. If you made a mistake and betrayed him, or did not respect his rules, he could make you ill or even kill you.

He ended with one final piece of advice. You should be careful that no one scratched themselves during your ceremonies.

At sunrise, you left the mountain to return to camp. Without truly knowing whether your "power" would manifest itself again. Or if you had simply dreamed the whole thing. But a few moons later, a young boy was bitten by a coyote. The injury was bad, and, since everyone in the camp had gotten wind of your experience on the mountain, his parents came to consult you. Whenever a shaman received his power from an eagle, he was thought to know how to cure an injury or a disease caused by many different animals, including the coyote. The eagle was paramount, but other animals carried specific powers too. A snake shaman knew how to care for snakebite; a person attacked by a bear would consult a shaman whose power derived from a bear; the stag shaman knew the ritual to bring success in the hunt; the horse shaman knew how to heal someone who had fallen from a horse, could find a lost herd, or heal it; the shaman whose power came from the moon or sun could see future events; and finally, some shamans could receive their "power" from multiple sources and draw on them all for their effectiveness. Those were the most powerful.

The day the parents of the young man came to ask for your help, you wondered for an instant whether the eagle would really keep his promise. But, faced with the young man's need, you realized, Grandfather, that you had no choice. So you isolated yourself to recite the prayer that the voice had taught you. You had hardly finished it when the eagle appeared to you and said, I am here, do your work. After having thanked him, you went to tell the parents that you would perform the ritual, that they could make their request in a traditional fashion.

They placed some tobacco rolled in an oak leaf on your right foot. You took it and smoked it to demonstrate your intention to perform the ceremony. It would last four days, from the end of day to the middle of night.

The next day, you built a shelter out of brush. You dug a hole in the center where you prepared a fire and, at nightfall, the young man came, supported by his parents. He couldn't walk without help, and was in great pain from the wound on his right calf. As you had requested, the father had brought offerings to ensure the "power's" cooperation. It was the "power" that would heal the young man through you, so it had to be thanked. The father gave you a knife with a black grip, a small pouch of tobacco, a new loincloth, and a piece of rough turquoise pierced with a hole in which he had placed an eagle feather.

You took the offerings and placed yourself west of the fire, facing east, with the young man. The people in attendance sat around the inside edges of the shelter so as to not block the east. You cautioned them that under no circumstance should they scratch themselves at any point during the ceremony, then you asked the young man to draw a pollen cross on your right foot, to disperse some on your shoulders, to draw another cross on your left foot, and finally to stretch out in front of you.

On a tray, you had placed an eagle's feather, an abalone pierced with a hole, a bag of pollen, symbol of life and renewal, and an eagle's claw. You bound all these elements with a yucca leaf thread. Then you rolled a mixture of sage leaves, juniper, oak, and *Diotis lanata* in an oak leaf that you lit with a brand from the fire. After inhaling the smoke, you blew it to the four directions, praying for the ceremony to go well. You then recited the incantation to summon your "power" and marked the boy with pollen on the base of his neck and on his shoulders. In the brush shelter there was a deep silence. All eyes were fixed on you, watching your every movement. Now came the moment to ask eagle if the young man would be cured. The moment when he must keep his promise and come to your assistance.

But this time, Grandfather, you did not doubt that he would. You took your drum, whose clay bottom had been made by one of your sisters. She had placed a little water and four pieces of charcoal there, and had made four tiny holes in the skin to improve the sound. You yourself had attached the skin to the clay shell after having soaked and stretched it. With a stick of carved wood that was shaped in such a way that one end curved inward, you began to beat the drum, chanting to the four directions a prayer divided into four chants that resembled each other except for the different colors and directions they alluded to. Black for the east, blue for the south, yellow for the west, and white for the north. At the end of each chant, you cried out like an eagle, as he had told you to.

He appeared to you during the fourth chant to announce that the young boy would get well. To achieve this, you had to continue chanting prayers for four nights, but also suck the evil from around the wound with your lips, spit it into the fire while making whistling sounds to the four directions, and finally apply juniper ash to the wound. For the following four days, you also had to make the young man drink a decoction of Mormon tea.

After you chanted a prayer to the eagle, thanking him for his help, he vanished. This was the sign for you to end the ritual. The evening stars were between the horizon and the zenith; the ceremony was over.

You started it again, the following three nights, and, at the end of the fourth night, just as the eagle had told you, you gave the boy an amulet to help him get well and to avoid a relapse. It was a small buckskin pouch containing turquoise beads with pollen and sage. The young man was to wear it until he was fully healed. You had also instructed him on the restrictions he'd have to follow to speed his recovery. Avoid eating liver, entrails, or heart and fruit that had fallen on the ground for four days, and orient your wickiup toward the east.

The night after the end of the ceremony, the boy dreamed that he was falling ill. This was a good omen. In the Chiricahua tradition, this dream was interpreted as a sign that he would heal.

When, hardly a moon later, the boy was able to run along the flanks of the Mogollon Rim without limping, you knew for certain that the "power" had chosen you. You were a shaman, Grandfather, and from that moment on, in slightest rustlings of nature, in the least little clouds placed in the sky just above your head, you would learn to perceive a message from your power. A direction to follow . . .

5

In the blue sky, as far as the eye can see, a few pretty clouds in the shape of cotton balls make little patches of shade on the enormous stretch of desert we're now crossing. Shrubs, stones, cacti. The ones with a white duster at the end. Not even pretty. Harlyn told me that the Apaches had to cross those lands of cracked earth to make their raids in Mexico. Weeks of walking, on foot or on horseback. How did they do it without water? I grab my mug to drink a gulp of coffee. The inside of the car resounds with the crunching of chips. An hour ago, the girls were hungry. We stopped at a gas station in the middle of the desert, at the intersection of four perfectly straight roads. Two signs aged by the sun and the scalding winds pointed toward Carrizozo and San Antonio. Stepping into the store attached to the two gas pumps, I couldn't help but whistle the theme to *Bagdad Café*, the atmosphere of the place reminded me so much of that movie. But after the first few notes the surprised then frankly mocking look of the girls dissuaded me from continuing.

Harlyn bought them four little bags of chips and two large Cokes. I ate an apple I found in my backpack and bought this mug to fill it with coffee. American gas stations are all equipped with places where you can fill travel mugs with coffee, and the cars are equipped with holders designed specifically for them. I unclip the slide-lock lid to access the opening. I put my mouth up against it. Ouch. The coffee is scalding hot.

"Those thermos cups really keep things warm."

115

Harlyn smiles, his eyes fixed on the road. He hasn't taken them off it since the gas station. What is he afraid of? There is no car, no turn, and the cacti aren't going to suddenly get up and cross it.

"Are there any animals here?"

"Snakes, deer . . ."

"Did the Apaches eat them?"

"Only the deer. In our culture, besides biting, snakes bring disease. Merely touching a snake's shed skin or sitting in a place where it was sleeping can make a person's skin peel off, cause sores inside the mouth, on the hands, or on the skin, or make your face swollen."

Behind me the *crunch crunch* of the chips ceases and is replaced by Harlie Bear's soft voice:

"The only good omen is a dead snake lying on its back. That means it's going to rain."

"So you probably don't see that very often around here. It never rains, right?"

Harlyn's head and then his earring go *no*.

"But that doesn't matter. Apaches know how to make the rain come!" says Harlie Bear.

I turn to face her to ask her if she knows how, but with an expression like *I'm not allowed to talk about it*, she points to Harlyn with her chin. I turn to face him.

"Harlyn, do you know rituals to make the rain come?"

His head bobs for a moment, and then his mouth emits a frankly mushy "yes" followed by a "but" followed by silence. I invite him to elaborate.

"Yes, I do. But Apaches don't really need those rituals," he deigns to add. "They know how to find water in the driest deserts."

I look at the sun, the cacti, the loose stones, trying to discover the key to this mystery. Harlyn smiles.

"I'll show you."

He turns his right blinker on, looks into the rearview, and maneuvers the car onto the shoulder. The girls utter a cry of joy, visibly pleased with the decision. Click, unbuckled seatbelts wind back up into their little cases. After having checked that my cowboy boots are indeed on my feet, Harlyn asks me to put on my hat, orders the girls to bring the caps that are in their backpacks, and steps out of the car, inviting us to follow him.

Once we've lined up in single file behind him, we begin to zigzag among the stones and cacti, until we come to a shrub covered with tiny green leaves and little orange balls. Sumac, says Harlyn. "Look at it carefully." I go closer. The girls, wearing identical pink hats on their heads, are already picking the small berries the size of blueberries. Harlie Bear gives me a handful. "Taste, it's really good!" A little cautious, I smell them first. No noticeable smell. I put one in my mouth. Tart taste, between an orange and a plum. Delicious. I swallow the entire handful and start picking too. Harlyn, with a smile, points out other sumacs around us. According to him, it's impossible not to find something to quench your thirst in this desert. He doesn't even understand how the illegal Mexican immigrants can die of thirst crossing the desert to get to the border. For my part, I do understand. So I make a suggestion.

"You should give them survival lessons."

"I've thought about it," he murmurs as he heads toward a low-lying cactus with large oval leaves covered with long spikes and topped by pink flowers.

He kneels. I join him. The girls continue to pluck the sumac berries. "And here's a prickly pear cactus," Harlyn says. You need to pass the flower briefly over a flame before eating it. The fruit that grows after the flower can be also used. Fresh, dried, or juiced when it's nice and ripe.

"It's really good for your health, and full of vitamins. Even the pads."

"With the spines?"

"Of course not! You burn those off first, and then cut the flesh into little squares and fry them in oil.

I reach a hand toward the cactus.

"Don't touch the spines, whatever you do!" cries Harlyn.

My hand pulls back immediately. The needles can cause deadly infections, he tells me. In Geronimo's day, the American soldiers who were always chasing him didn't know that and would die from a simple scratch. Leaning away from the cactus out of caution, I ask if he knows all the plants around us. He gets back up to show me a stunted little tree six feet away from us. I get up. I think I recognize a juniper tree. Harlyn confirms that's what it is.

"So you know this tree?"

"Yes, in Mongolia, shamans burn its leaves. The smoke is supposed to purify a place or a wound, as I said, or their costume before a ceremony."

He smiles.

"A bit like the Apaches then. And are there many over there?"

"Yes. They pound the leaves into a powder, then mix them in water to make 'pure water.' It has to be consumed at the very beginning of the ceremony in order to purify the body of the person consulting the shaman. Is it the same for you?"

His head bobs. More often they make a decoction to induce vomiting in a person to "cleanse" them during a ceremony. But Geronimo ground the leaves into a powder he threw onto embers to purify the air of a home during outbreaks of illness. He said it killed the disease. Today the Apaches mostly use juniper for acne problems, stomachaches, or headaches. They also inhale the smoke for throat and bronchial infections. Its active ingredient strengthens the lungs and provides endurance. That holds true for animals too, and was the reason Apache horses in the past were able to outrun any mount of the American army.

"Just because they inhaled juniper smoke?"

Mischievous smile.

"It's a secret recipe, but I can tell you that we still use it today for race horses."

After ending with his usual "Uh huh," he plucks a few juniper berries and hands them to me. I take one, hard as wood.

He explains, the Apaches would dry those little black beads and eat them when there was nothing else. The women would make bracelets of them too, which they placed around the wrists of their young children before putting them to bed. To pierce the berries so they could string them, they would lay them on an ants' nest. In a few instants, the ants would have dug a hole through the center, the tenderest portion, just large enough to string it with yucca leaf thread. The name of the berries in Apache is "ghost beads." They were thought to protect the child from bad dreams about the dead. He looks at me.

"Dreaming of a dead person was the worst nightmare for an Apache. At night, if you heard voices, if you saw faces around you laughing, if you had the feeling of being touched, or if you were afraid when you were outside, with the feeling of being followed, the elders used to say that you were suffering from 'ghosts.'"

"Was there a cure?"

"Yes, a special ceremony was organized to free you of them. Geronimo received the power for that ceremony too. He'd light a fire by rubbing pieces of wood together, and the first spark was placed in mouth of the person affected. Then Geronimo would pray and sing."

I study the little berry in my palm and once again think about my trance with Geronimo's name. Was it a dream, a vision? When would I finally dare talk about it? I'd decided to earlier, but the conversation went in a different direction. My mind says *don't*. I'd rather start by asking Harlyn if he knows how to interpret dreams. He nods. He knows about the ones that presage bad omens.

"Likedweamingawdwater!" exclaims Shania, who has just joined us and whose mouth is still full of sumac berries.

Harlyn asks her to swallow first. She swallows and starts over: "Like dreaming of water! I get sick every time after."

Harlyn confirms it. Dreaming of fire isn't good either, or dreaming of losing a tooth. But dreaming of green, of fruit, or that you're falling ill is a good sign. Dreaming of your own death is even a sign of a long life. And dreaming of the death of a relative, like a father, a mother, or a brother, doesn't foretell their death but the death of someone outside your family.

"I dreamed that a snake was biting me. What does that mean?" Harlie Bear asks, visibly worried.

"That you'll never be bitten by a snake," Harlyn reassures her.

Still preoccupied by my vision, I finally decide to ask him, as though on a whim, if he has ever dreamed or had a vision of Geronimo. His head says *no*. So how was I able to have one then? All you need to do is ask Harlyn, you fool! But Harlyn continues his explanation. Geronimo had premonitory dreams before battle. The United States Army tried many times to launch surprise attacks against him. But each time, he and his men disappeared, as if he had been warned.

"The soldiers couldn't understand that his dreams were his main informant," Harlyn adds, laughing.

Usually, Geronimo commanded over fifty warriors or more into battle. He was fighting for his homeland and his tribe. It was about freedom for his people.

He turns toward the juniper again, touches its bark. The bark resembles scales. "Its leaves," he tells me, "are often combined with other plants, like osha. Have you heard of it?" I shake my head no. He doesn't offer to show me any, since the plant doesn't grow below ten thousand feet. I ask him how it's used and for what kind of problem. "Its root is crushed into a powder. It's a very black root," he answers. "And then you smoke it, making sure to blow the smoke through your nostrils to purify the sinuses. We also chew the root to help prevent colds." Harlie Bear, who hasn't missed a shred of these explanations, interrupts Harlyn abruptly.

"Can we tell her now?"

Harlyn looks at her, looks at me, seeming to know exactly where his granddaughter is going with this. I wait until he has finished crafting his reply. He finally opens his mouth.

"For asthma, I can tell you now, we use juniper leaves, mixed with osha leaves. You have to cut them in very thin slices and boil them in water for two minutes, then drink the liquid."

He looks at me with a pleased expression. Then he tells me that we have to go back to the car. The next portion of the lesson will take place higher up in the mountains. I jump at the revelation.

"Is that where we're headed?"

The girls start to chuckle. Harlyn shakes his head. He won't tell me. Have a little more patience. On the way to the car, he walks by a cactus with a white duster top. I tell him I've seen them everywhere since El Paso. It's a yucca, he explains. The Apaches boil the leaves for an hour and a half, like cabbage, with some deer or cow ribs.

"Are there yuccas in Mongolia?"

"No, why?"

"Because the Apaches are nothing without yuccas! The fruits, the flowers, the leaves, they use everything, even its fibers as cords to bind the brush covering tipis and wickiups."

"But what's the connection with Mongolia?"

"Well, we'll have to import some if you take me there with you!"

He bursts out laughing. The girls too. I picture the poor yuccas at minus fifteen degrees Fahrenheit, transformed into giant Popsicle shrine maidens. When the laughter has finally died down, our little troop climbs back into the car. An oven. Harlyn starts it up, blasts the AC. Shania opens the window to let the hot air out. I do the same, then take off my cowboy boots and hat, and stare at the landscape. The cacti, the trees, the shrubs. For the first time, I know what to call them. And sitting in my little corner, I realize I'm moved by that. Yes, suddenly this desert seems a little less hostile. The sound of torn packaging in the back. Harlie Bear, who isn't the least bit bothered by the heat, opens her second bag of chips.

"But when they didn't have anything left to drink and the fruits weren't ripe and the cacti were dried up, how did the Apaches survive?"

"They dug at the base of certain plants whose roots trap water."

"And if there wasn't water at the root of those plants either?"

Harlyn smiles.

"You want to know about rainmaking rituals, is that it?"

I nod to the rhythm of the *munch-munch-munching* that's begun again in the back. But since he still won't answer, I ask him if that ritual requires singing out of tune.

He takes his eyes off the road to look over at me. His turquoise earring follows.

"Singing out of tune? Is that a Mongol tradition?"

"More like a French tradition, but it has nothing to do with shamanism!"

I explain to him how, in France, whenever someone sings off-key, we tell them, "Stop, you're going to make it rain!" With a laugh, Harlyn tells me to go ahead and give it a try. If the technique proves effective, he'll be delighted to teach it to the Apaches. So I take up the challenge. Focus. I begin to sing the only song in my repertoire. "Au clair de la luuuuu-nuuh." But Shania immediately starts protesting, "Stop, stop!" She prefers Robbie Williams. Harlyn bursts out laughing. He doesn't like him too much. He's a fan of Beyoncé. A little put out, I reply that *their* songs are impossible to sing in a car. Harlyn concedes the point. For him, the Apache method for making rain is the only effective one. In fact, to prove it, he's going to reveal it to us. Suddenly, there is silence in the car. Pleased with the effect of his words, Harlyn is quiet for a moment, just long enough for his features to assume the seriousness the revelation calls for. He commences: The ritual begins with a prayer to summon White-Painted Woman and Child of the Water. Then you use some sand from Mexico to summon the rain. . . .

"While invoking lightning, you blow it in the four directions and make a sound like this: 'Hoooo, hooo.'"

Shania and Harlie Bear repeat like a chorus, "Hooooo, hooooo." Harlyn tells them to stop it. No joking about rituals! They quiet down instantly. He resumes:

"This ritual can also make the snow fall. But to make the sun reappear . . ."

Harlyn fixes his gaze in the rearview mirror, sending a mischievous smile to his granddaughters.

"You have to draw a circle on your butt with a piece of charcoal and show it to the sky!"

We all burst out laughing. But Harlyn suddenly frowns while looking at the road. I direct my gaze to where his is pointing, trying to discover the object of his attention. I see only the dotted yellow line painted down the middle of the road all the way to the horizon, and . . . Yes, a dark mass, at the very end of it. Some sort of enormous shadow. But no cloud above it. A forest? Impossible in the middle of the desert. I ask Harlyn if there's a problem. No, he answers, reversing his frown. We're just arriving at the Valley of Fire. A huge expanse of black lava that poured out of the ground approximately five thousand years ago.

"Out of the ground? Not a volcano?"

"No, the lava flowed out of a fault line and spread over about a hundred and twenty square miles."

I watch the dark mass grow closer.

"It looks enormous."

"Forty miles long by two to five miles wide."

"And is it deep?"

"Fifty feet on average."

We stare at it in silence. The Apaches know this place well, Harlyn continues. During the wars against the American army, they'd come here to seek refuge and it was impossible to find them. They also used to say that the lava was the coagulated blood of Giant, the monster from our legends. Do you remember him?

"The one Child of the Water killed?"

He nods, looking satisfied that his lessons on Apache traditions have taken hold in my memory.

"Our ancestors," he resumes, "also came to collect clay for their pottery, on the fringes of this lava field. The lava was sometimes carved and used as a sharpening or grinding stone."

Harlyn clears his throat. As he does every time it appears he's about to say something important.

"Geronimo made a prophecy about the lava. He saw in our future a big war taking place when the White Sands area touches the lava region. Each year the sands are moving closer."

"A war? Here?"

"Who knows? Either way, I'll tell you a secret . . ."

My ears perk up.

"The Apaches are starting to prepare for that possibility."

"Because of Geronimo's prophecy?"

He nods.

"I even give Apache survival and combat lessons to all Indians who want to prepare for war."

He shoots me a glance, uttering a hoarse "Uh huh," as if deeply moved. I have never seen him looking so serious.

"Our tracking and camouflage techniques are very effective. They're even being taught at West Point, and I can tell you, they really saved my skin in Vietnam!"

I look at him. In Vietnam? He nods. Uh huh. Then he tells the story: After Haskell Indian Junior College in Kansas, where he did his studies, Harlyn enlisted in the army. Six months of training later, he was sent to a military camp in the northern part of South Vietnam. His unit was tasked with protecting the camp from the Viet Cong and snipers, supporting resupply, monitoring a pipeline the army had installed, and recovering bodies after the fighting. Once, their food was poisoned. Harlyn spent a month in intensive care with a stomach infection. He was also poisoned by Agent Orange. After three years of service, he had to come home. He had a very hard time readjusting to civilian life. He suffered from depression, had nightmares, couldn't sleep, and was afraid all the time that someone might shoot at him. The authorities finally identified these symptoms, which most Vietnam veterans suffered from, and gave it the name Post-Vietnam Syndrome. He was twenty-two at the time and it took him about ten years to get over it.

"Only ten years!" he adds, laughing.

He had Apache medicine, plants, and his willpower to help him. So he fared better than the whites. He clears his throat.

"They still give me free pills to slow the effects of Agent Orange, like diabetes and cataracts, but I don't take them. I prefer my Apache plants. And I'm doing well because of them. I haven't even developed the first symptoms yet, while the whites, despite their medicine, already have for quite a while now."

His face reflects a kind of childish pride now. I can't see his eyes because of his sunglasses, but I suddenly understand the reason for the dash of tenderness and sorrow in his gaze. The horrors of Vietnam must be the cause. With a movement of the chin, Harlyn abruptly directs me to look at the landscape. I turn my head. On both sides of the road, everything is covered in a thick lather of black lava.

"We're entering the Valley of Fire!" shouts Shania.

The lava forms hollows, humps, and little valleys as far as the eye can see. A sea frozen for eternity, in which the gray road with its yellow line suddenly seems like a miraculous opening, formed, for the duration of our passage, by who knows what Apache god. It's beautiful and terrifying. As powerful as life in the act of defying death. I feel tears welling in my eyes. Everyone in the car is quiet. As though, all together, in communion, we were listening to the sound of this magical moment, just before the instant when the sea behind us will close up again. I suddenly feel like withdrawing there. Into a tipi, in the shadow of yuccas that reach high like long totems up to the sky. "Those cacti are sotols," Harlyn tells me, as if responding to my thoughts. They look like yuccas, but they're thinner, with yellow flower clusters.

"Sotol leaves were used as spoons by the Apaches. That's the reason they're called Desert Spoons. But nowadays picking them is forbidden."

I look at the blanket of lava pierced by hundreds of cacti with the need to thrive. The last heroes of the living. Nature seems to have fought so hard here to hang on to life. Humans fight so hard to destroy it. I think about Geronimo's prophecy again. The possibility of a war.

"What's your opinion of the Iraq war?"

After a moment of silence, his voice emerges. It's a little subdued, flat, as if he were speaking to himself. This war is a huge mistake, he begins. Bush and his administration put out the scenario that Iraq was supposedly hiding weapons of mass destruction. But that was false. A governmental inquiry about it proved Bush lied. His only motivation in starting the war was to seize control of Iraq's oil fields. But there again Bush made the wrong decision. He never should have invaded Iraq. A lot of young soldiers have been killed or mutilated, and it's been hell for so many families. We should hunt down Osama bin Laden until he can hide no more. His voice rises a notch:

"But if you look at the history of the Apaches, they too were living in peace a hundred and fifty years ago. Then the whites invaded their territory, killed the members of the tribes who rose against them, and sent survivors to camps. And all that simply in order to take their land, mine for the gold, silver, iron, and copper and exploit the oil, from which the country now derives a little over two billion dollars a year."

He swallows before resuming, his voice quieter again:

"There's a real similarity to what Bush wants to do in Iraq, isn't there? He's only interested in their natural resources, and he wants to take everything from them. That's obvious. But they won't go down without a fight. That too is obvious."

Harlyn abruptly turns on his blinker and parks the car on the shoulder. "I want you to touch the lava," he tells me. We get out. Within six feet, our soles are resting on the black crust. It feels a bit like taking my first step on the moon. In fact, my footsteps make no sound. The lava swallows noise like some carnivorous plant. Very strange. The only noticeable sound is that of insects, a small high-pitched buzzing that occupies at most ten percent of a terribly heavy silence, so deep, dense, and hot to the ears. Harlyn takes a few more steps, crouches down, examines the ground, then picks up a piece of lava, and another, and hands them to me. My hands discover their rough texture, full of sharp irregularities. One piece is heavier than the other.

"The molten lava spread fast at first and then slower and slower. That produced these two types of lava. The one that spread more slowly is the heavier one. We call it *ha-ha* in Apache. The other, as you can feel if you weigh it in your hand, is light, full of solidified air bubbles."

"It's called *pa-hoy-hoy!*" Harlie Bear interjects. "It forms these great big blocks full of holes where the bats like to take shelter. There are a lot around here."

Harlyn nods. The rarest being the big-eared bat, whose distinctive feature is that it likes to hang alone, not in clusters like every other kind does. He also talks about a small lizard called the common collared lizard because it has what looks like a black-and-white collar painted around its neck.

"They're funny," Shania adds. "They talk to each other by making their heads dance up and down, and when they see an intruder . . ."

She stands on tiptoe to mimic them.

"They get on their toes to make themselves look taller!"

We laugh at her imitation. Without missing a beat, she hands me a guide to the local fauna.

"But if you see one, don't get close to it with your finger. It can bite really hard!"

I thank her profusely for the warning, without which I might have lost a piece of my anatomy. That elicits her frowny face.

"What's 'anatomy'?"

Harlyn bursts out laughing. I make an effort not to do the same and attempt an explanation, but Harlie Bear, taking her role of older cousin very seriously, beats me to it. Her definition is perfect. Harlyn congratulates her, then dips his hand into the front pocket of his jeans with an air of mystery.

"We're going to do a little experiment, okay?"

Collective *yes*. He holds his fist out toward us. Opens it. We bring our heads in closer to see. His hand contains some kind of little black seeds. He tells us that Geronimo always carried some in his pocket. Along with a few flowers from the plant that grew from this seed. In Apache, it is called *kaa-yeł-hini*. It's covered with green leaves, is a foot or a foot and a half tall, and its flower is circular in shape with six white petals. The Apaches still use it today to provide relief to cancer patients but also for infections, osteoarthritis, rheumatism, and hernias. It commonly grows in desert along streams or near springs, anywhere it's really hot during the summer months. It needs a lot of sun. The raw flower has no flavor, but when it's boiled it has a sweet taste and isn't at all bitter. Geronimo believed it to have great powers, and in his eyes it was an indispensable remedy. But since it didn't grow everywhere the Apaches lived, he decided to plant it in all the places they might pass, in case they should ever need it. He closes his fist again.

"I know where those places are, but their locations remain a secret. All I can tell you is that my great-grandfather surely carried a few seeds of *kaa-yeł-hini* in his pocket the day he surrendered. Convinced as he was, since he had been promised it, that one day he would be allowed to return to his land and could continue to sow it."

He catches his breath.

"So today, for him, to keep his legacy alive, we're going to plant some."

The girls jump with joy. I remain speechless. Moved. Harlyn must sense it because, before I have the chance to dissolve into tears, he invites us to follow him. In single file, we accompany him to behind a lava dome in the shadow of which we discover a small patch of earth covered with dried grass. He digs a little hole and deposits four tiny seeds in it, covers them with earth, then takes a small buckskin pouch from his pocket and, between his index finger and his thumb, removes a pinch of pollen with which he traces a cross just over the spot where the seeds are. His head bent toward the ground, his hands flat on his stomach, he recites a prayer in a language I've never heard. Choppy, binary. Apache, no doubt. Without grasping the meaning of the words, my ear begins to follow their contours. Far, far away, the words rise into space and for an instant, in his voice, I feel like I'm hearing Geronimo's.

'Ádą, dák'aaná.
nDé hik'a' k'aast'ą
'Áí k'aaí bilátahee tséí hiisk'aashgo k'ádaas'ą.

Daagok'a' dá'áíbee, naagojinłdzoo.
Dá'áíbee, bįį, náa'tsíli, dáhaadí daajiyąí, beenaadaajiłtsee.

Tsébeeshdiłtł'įdéí 'iłdǫ 'ijoondeená'a.
Tséghe'si'ąí 'iłdǫ 'ijoondeená'a.
'Íłą́ą́hdéí dáditsįí dásíntł'izí 'indaa beedaajóóshiizhná'a.

K'adi díídíí dá'ákohégo nDé bik'a'ná'a.
'Indaanałíí goostáńdiłtałí hah'áálgo díík'ehnyá nDédáłeendasijaaí
beenaał'a'áłádą.

In those days, there were only arrows. The arrows of Indians
had feathers on them.
The arrows had flint affixed to their tips.

Indians went into battle with only their arrows
With arrows only, they killed stags, cattle, and everything that
they ate.

Slingshots too were used, so they say.
Stone hatchets too were used, so they say.

The Indians fought off the white man with spears made of a very
hard wood, so they say.

Those were the Indians' only weapons, so they say.
You, white men, in those days could enslave an entire camp of
Indians, anywhere you went, thanks to the six rounds you carried.

The Path of War

ON THE ROUGH black lava your moccasins tore, Grandfather. But you had been taught to bandage your feet in sotol or yucca leaves to protect them from cuts. You had been walking on this broken ground since morning, holding your horses beside you, since it was impossible to ride. Your tribe was headed for Chiricahua, in the north of what is now Mexico. It was your first expedition to that state. In 1846, a war had broken out between Mexico and the United States. Two years later, in February 1848, the treaty of Guadalupe Hidalgo was signed, granting the United States parts of Texas, Colorado, New Mexico, Arizona, and Wyoming and all of California, Nevada, and Utah in exchange for some fifteen million American dollars. The treaty stipulated that from then on the Americans would be responsible for preventing the Indians living in the new territories from making raids into Mexico.

The members of your tribe, Grandfather, hadn't been very pleased with that decision. The Mexicans had always been your enemies, and organizing raids to steal their livestock, horses, and food was an integral part of your way of life. And yet, in spite of everything, your attitude toward them as people had always remained peaceful, for you always went in small numbers and did what you could to avoid confrontations, your aim above all being to rob them, not kill them.

Since the completion of your training as a warrior, you had participated in a large number of such raids against hostile tribes or Mexicans. At first, like all novices, you had been asked to prepare the meals, attend the fire, the horses, and the water supply, service the weapons, and keep watch over the camp. You had also been taught the secret language of warriors, which novices were required to speak among themselves. All words related to war had a sacred meaning. The role of novice was sacred too. You were thought to represent Child of the Water and had to comport yourself with the rigor of that hero, the ancestor of the Apaches. You performed that function with the competence that was required and, after four raids, according to our tradition, you were finally accepted among the warriors.

The Mexicans, of course, saw nothing peaceful about your raids. They would mount punitive expeditions to retrieve their goods. But it had become a kind of established routine, and it was actually during one of those expeditions that you saw your first dead body. You had never been faced with death before that event. Young Chiricahuas were not allowed to take part in funeral processions. So you hadn't even watched your father's. You'd simply been told that his body would be taken to a cave, near the tree where his umbilical cord had been placed, and would then be covered with stones. That very evening you had killed a grasshopper and had covered it with small stones—your way of accompanying your father, or understanding death, perhaps. You had no idea then what it meant. You had even asked your mother what would become of your father, but you had barely uttered his name when she slapped you across the mouth, forbidding you ever to say it again. It might cause his ghost to return. For fear of that, she also destroyed all of his clothing and cut your hair, so your father's ghost wouldn't be able to recognize you and come back to take you with him to the land of the dead. A land identical in every respect to that of the living, with the same terrain, the same sacred mountains, but where there was neither illness, nor pain, nor sadness. Your father would go there, your mother had simply said, by passing through an opening in the ground, a little like a window. Someone would take him to that place, for it was concealed by tall grasses that prevented the living from seeing it and entering too. When the window was open, it looked like a cone of sand, like a tipi with a very large distance between the top and the base. But if a person passed through it, it would be impossible for them to return. They would live for eternity in the land of the dead, where all humans, with no exceptions, must go after their death. The bad were mixed together with the good, and they lived in the same way they had on earth. Your father would eat, drink, sleep, love, and perform the exact same ceremonies. As if each thing in his life had simply been transferred into this other world. He would always remain the same age he was at the moment of his death.

When night came, your mother burned sage and sprinkled the ashes on you and around your bed in your wickiup to discourage your father's ghost from approaching. She also warned you of the tricks that ghosts could use to draw you into the land of the dead. In your dreams, you'd suddenly see that land in all its beauty, with luxuriant vegetation. You'd see your father's spirit. It would offer you fruit of the yucca, and choice bits of roasted game. But you must absolutely refuse to eat them. It was a trap. If you accepted them, you'd die in an instant and immediately join him in the other world.

The following day, the members of the tribe killed your father's horses and burned all his possessions. That way, he'd find them again in the other world and wouldn't be deprived of them. Without this custom, his ghost would return every night to force the tribe to destroy them.

You made your way on the black lava, thinking back to those childhood days, at once so close and so far. You no longer felt the sadness, yet you'd noticed that walking always encouraged such memories to blossom. Shortly after being admitted among the warriors, you had had the pleasure of marrying Alope, a beautiful Nedni Apache. Her father had demanded many horses in exchange for his daughter. But just a few days later you had brought them to him. He must have suspected that you had helped yourself from the Mexicans, but he didn't ask any questions. They were your enemies. You returned to your camp with Alope. That meant you were married. The women of the tribe prepared *tiswin*, the traditional drink made from fermented kernels of corn. You drank, played, ate, and danced for a full day and half the night around a big fire. With a smile, you thought back to what your mother had told you as a teenager to discourage you from having sex with girls. "Watch out! Their sex has teeth." Alope's did not have any! She gave you three beautiful children. Your wickiup, set next to your mother's, echoed with their shrill little voices. You had started teaching them Apache traditions, making them small bows.

On the lava path, you turned to make sure they were following. Alope was quite fragile, but the children already had very good legs. To strengthen them, you'd taught them how to catch butterflies. That very morning, you had asked them to find you a four-leafed clover, as a way to make the march a little less difficult. You knew very well that they wouldn't be able to find any in the place you were crossing, but your ruse seemed to work. Their eyes were glued to the ground, and they appeared to be having fun. It was the first time they'd accompanied you on such a long journey, along with your wife and your mother. Shortly before then, Chiricahua state had expressed the desire to live in peace with the Apaches and had offered to trade goods. Periods of quiet and of war had been alternating for eons. This time the tribe agreed to go and sell buckskins and fur for provisions, blankets, clothes, and glass beads. Alope liked these beads very much, and she'd even decorated your wickiup and blankets with them.

You took the opportunity of crossing that desert land to teach your children skills for fighting thirst. For instance, placing a stone or a piece of dry wood in their mouths in order to salivate. They thought it was very funny. You also taught them to recognize a barrel cactus and cut off its head. They had cried out joyfully when they discovered the water inside. As fresh as the Gila's. They even sighed with delight when they savored its pulp. Then you showed them how to use a stem of carrizo, a kind of bamboo, which you always carried with you, thanks to which you would drink the water captured at the base of mescal leaves. You explained how deer and horses, knowing about that hiding place, would lap it up with their long tongues. They laughed and measured theirs with their fingers—much too short. You even discovered honey for them, hidden by the bees in the heart of a sotol. Their eyes opened so wide on finding such a treasure that they remained speechless for at least three blinks of an eye.

For their benefit, you transformed the journey into a big game. You loved so much to see them discover life, you loved so to pass down the traditions that your mother and father had passed on to you. Deep in your pocket, your fingers felt the small black seeds of *kaa-yeł-hini*. Soon the children would be grown enough to understand their value. You'd share with them your desire to plant it everywhere to allow your people to find it anywhere they might need it. They might even sow the seeds with you. You still had so many treasures you wanted them to discover. That thought alone was enough to fill your heart. There was such joy in it. Pure joy. You couldn't know, Grandfather, that soon you would be living the worst moments of your life.

Two weeks later, you set up camp north of the town of Kas-Ki-yeh, in Chiricahua state. You would go to the town regularly to swap your buckskins, furs, and horses, leaving the camp to the women and children since the territory was at peace. That day, you returned particularly satisfied with a nice sack of beads for Alope and some colorful clothes for your children. They would be delighted. Approaching the camp, you had a bad feeling. A peculiar silence reigned, and the dream you'd had the night before came immediately to your mind. A bison was chasing you. A very bad omen, which you'd preferred not to assign too much importance but which it now seemed urgent to take seriously. You warned other warriors of the imminent danger. Familiar with your predictions, they trusted you, and with you decided to approach in silence.

Hidden among the trees to the north of camp, you crawled to the top of the talus slope that bordered the clearing where it had been set up. At the crest, you couldn't suppress a cry of horror in the face of what you saw. The smell of death and blood wafted from the mutilated bodies of the members of your tribe. Before your eyes, heads without scalps were covered with flies and dried blood. You ran, staggering, toward the tipi where that very morning you had left your family.

When you discovered the bodies of your wife, your mother, and your three children, you couldn't help but vomit. Alope's eyes had remained open and expressed her sheer terror. You closed them with violence. The way you'd slam shut the door of hell. She had surely seen the soldiers kill your children one by one and then take their scalps. They always killed the mothers last. It was one of their techniques for getting the mothers to scream. Otherwise, Apache women died in silence, with dignity, their executioners having to confront their own barbarity. A cry rose in your throat. But no sound came out. How you despised the Mexican soldiers. You, the Chiricahuas, were no lambs, but you never scalped women and children. You didn't rape them either, like the soldiers did and as they accused you of doing. No Apache would ever have committed such an act. In your culture, it brought bad luck.

You don't know how long you remained kneeling next to them, without moving, without even shedding a tear, your hand on your youngest child's. The other warriors finally came to get you. They forced you to let go of your little son's fist. You'd discovered a four-leafed clover in it, his final gift. The first word you uttered was "Who?" Who did this? You were in a territory that was at peace. One of the warriors replied that he'd been able to ask a woman who was still alive. Mexican soldiers from the state of Sonora, who were still at war with the Apaches, had crossed into the part of Chiricahua territory that abutted theirs and attacked the camp. After the massacre, they had left with all the horses, some prisoners, and the scalps of their victims. Their government had passed a law offering one hundred pesos, about a hundred dollars, for the scalp of a warrior, fifty for a woman's, and twenty-five for a child's. They'd receive their rewards and sell their prisoners as slaves to some rich Mexicans once they returned home.

With hatred in your heart, barely stopping even to eat, you'd walked day and night to return to your territory by the Gila. Every one of you had lost some member of their family, but you were the only one to have lost all of them. All of them. When you arrived, you burned your mother's wickiup and your own. Watching the flames, you swore vengeance. In the Chiricahua tradition, death was avenged by death, and nothing could stop you anymore.

The tribal council and chief of the Apaches of the southwest, Mangas Coloradas, decided to launch a punitive expedition against the Mexicans. They asked you to convince friendly tribes to join in. The Chokonen and Nedni Apaches, led by Cochise and Juh, immediately accepted.

You prepared for the attack during all of Ghost Face, and, five days prior to departure, you performed a war dance. A big fire was lit at the edge of camp. Warriors donned the clothes they'd wear in combat, their moccasins, a long loincloth that came down to the knees, and a buckskin headband, along with their weapons: bows, arrows, spears, knives. You didn't have rifles yet. A man standing in the west with the singers began to play the drum. The main singer was usually a war shaman. So you were chosen. Your role was to ask your "power" to help you locate and kill the leader of the enemy. Four warriors walking abreast approached the fire from the east. They repeated this four times. Then two of them went to the south and two to the north to approach the fire from those directions until they stood facing each other. The other warriors joined them and began a dance. Some warriors went toward others, circling the fire to the other side and then returning to where they had started. Four times all together.

The chants began. In yours, you invited each warrior, in turn, to come and dance in the center of the ring and, using his weapons, mimic his deeds and the way he would kill his enemy. The women, in a circle around you, didn't participate in this dance but in unison shouted a lengthy cry in imitation of the one shouted by White-Painted Woman when her son, Child of the Water, returned from killing Giant. With each new chant, the dancers made room for new ones, then went to smoke sage, while standing at the edge of the ring and reciting prayers. A kind of invocation for the spirits to protect them during battle, but also to bring them good luck and food, which they would need throughout their expedition.

When all who wanted to participate in the war finished their dance, they gathered in a circle around the fire, four times, and shot arrows with their bows. The ceremony was over. It was repeated for four nights.

The last day, like all the other warriors, you sharpened your weapons. After sharpening the wooden tip of your arrows, whose shaft had been made out of reeds from the Gila's banks—the best and strongest—you checked the three feathers intended to guide them. You dipped the tip of each arrow, hardened in the fire, in a toxic potion made from the blood of a stag's spleen buried in the ground to rot for about ten days and a vegetal poison made with the juice of nettles crushed with other ingredients whose names must remain secret. You then checked your leather shield. Only the war shaman could have one. Yours was decorated with eagle feathers all around it, and an image of eagle on its face. As a healer, Grandfather, you also had to provide amulets for the warriors, a bag of pollen and *kaa-yeł-hini* flowers. To care for them after battle, you also placed sage, Mormon tea to fight infections, and *i-ah-i* in a buckskin bag. *I-ah-i* was applied on open wounds as a poultice to speed healing. Finally, you sang a prayer to ask your "power" if it would foretell the battle's outcome.

It replied favorably, and you told the warriors that you could leave. The engagement would be successful.

At the break of day, the entire camp gathered to witness your departure. During your absence, every member of the tribe would have to act in such a way as to avoid bringing you bad luck. As soon as the sun was high enough to light the undergrowth, you formed into a line for the march, with two warriors in front, two in back, and scouts on either side. Then you left, carrying as your only item of "comfort" some fabric gathered in a roll around your middle. This would serve as a blanket for the many nights you wouldn't shelter in a tipi. You didn't even have horses for this. Your only advantage in the face of the multitude of Mexican soldiers being your quickness and mobility, those too cumbersome creatures would have slowed you down in the ravines and canyons you had to cross.

You walked fourteen hours a day in order to reach the Mexican border as fast as possible. Each warrior carried a quiver positioned so the feathers were oriented toward the top of the right shoulder, a bow, a spear, a knife, and also provisions and a supply of water in a soft flask made of animal intestines with one end tied off. The provisions were mainly dried meat and mescal leaves. At nightfall, you picked a campsite close to the water if there was any. Each warrior cooked for himself and ate his own food, frequently supplemented by game you hunted along the way.

At the border, the warriors sent by Cochise and Juh met you at the place you had agreed upon. You communicated through smoke signals. You would cut sotol leaves and put them on a fire to produce a large amount of smoke. If the smoke came from a summit, that meant enemies were close by. If it came from a plain, it indicated an illness or an epidemic. To stop the smoke all you had to do was to scatter the fire quickly.

You arrived together in Sonora state, where you sought to locate the Mexican troops that had attacked your camp and killed your families. They were gathered in the town of Arizpe. So you made your camp to the north of town, near a river. The Mexicans quickly spotted you, but you'd made preparations to face them. Before nightfall, you sent out four scouts in the four directions, and they were able to confirm that the soldiers wouldn't attack until the following day. So you placed sentinels around your camp and slept. The battle would be hard.

At sunrise, your men gathered to pray to Yusn. As the "power" had instructed, you prepared a paste with a water base and white pigment. With two fingers, you traced a line on the forehead, the sides of the face, and across the nose of each warrior. An identifying mark intended to prevent any confusion during the battle. Your scouts then came to tell you that the Mexicans were on their way. As you had been the most injured by their attack on the camp, you were invited to lead the battle. The previous day, you had performed a ceremony asking your "power" to tell you which way the Mexicans would take to arrive here. All you had to do was put your arm out, then turn in a circle while reciting some prayers until it told you where to stop. Your arm had shown you the direction they would come from. You went there to scout the terrain and, near the river, noticed a large circular depression behind which you could conceal your men. An ideal spot for them to wait for the enemy's arrival without being spotted.

That morning, the scouts confirmed that the Mexicans would indeed arrive from the direction the "power" had indicated. You led your men there. You placed them in a semicircle wide enough for them to pass behind the cavalry and take them by surprise. When the soldiers were in sight, you said a prayer to the four directions. The men, armed with their bows and spears, shifted the quivers on their backs so the arrows' feathers now faced their left elbow. You made it clear that they should use their spears only when the Mexicans reloaded their long single-shot rifles. That was the only time they'd be vulnerable. You were quick, and you could easily sprint toward them then and leap at them, plunging your spears into their chests.

When the Mexican infantry, advancing two rows, was not quite within rifle range, you sent two men into the open. The soldiers knelt to shoot at them. But you knew your men were out of range, and your goal was to force the Mexicans to fire. You had noticed that, when hot, the too long barrel of their guns warped slightly and became markedly less precise.

While Cochise's warriors slipped behind the cavalry without attracting notice, you called back your two "decoys" and waited for the infantrymen to begin reloading their weapons before ordering the attack. With rage in your loins, you then swept down on them and plunged your spears into the heart of every one of your adversaries. For the first time in your life, you took pleasure in tearing them apart and seeing the expression of terror in their eyes. Nothing could stop you anymore. As your "power" had predicted, you remained invincible to their bullets, and the images of your wife, your children, and your mother, all mutilated, nourished your every move.

When you had not a single arrow left, when your spear finally broke in the chest of an enemy, you jumped on the remaining soldiers and wrestled them to the ground so you could finish them with a knife, until there were none left. Only then did you notice the battlefield covered with bodies and heard the war cry of the Apaches. You had won. An immense shiver of joy coursed through your bloody body. Your own cry joined with those of your brothers.

That day, your Apache name, *Guu ji ya*, spread to the lips of every Mexican, changing a little each time, until it become the name that would make them tremble in fear from that day on: *Geronimo*.

(Library of Congress)

(Library of Congress)

One of the last portraits of Geronimo at Fort Sill, 1905.

An early photograph of Geronimo, taken not long after his surrender in 1886.

Copyright Corbis/AP Images

Geronimo, his wife, and their children at Fort Sill, 1898.

Council between General George R. Crook and Geronimo in March 1886. Crook is second from the right in the first row.

An extraordinary photograph of the last band of "hostile" Chiricahuas, taken in front of the train taking them east, as prisoners of war. Geronimo is in the front row, in the center; Naiche, son of Cochise, is on the far left. This is the only known photograph of the female warrior, Lozen, third from the right in the second row.

At Fort Sill in Oklahoma, Geronimo would dress in costume for the benefit of the tourists who paid for his autograph, as in this studio photograph.

Geronimo at the St. Louis World's Fair in 1904.

Still a prisoner of war in 1909, the year of his death.

Geronimo's daughter, Eva (right), and niece, Emily.

Geronimo (on horseback) in Los Embudos Canyon, March 1886.

Harlyn Geronimo with his wife, Karen, and their daughter, Kate, on the Mescalero Reservation, 1991.

Harlyn Geronimo with the actors Wes Studi and Irene Bedard during the filming of *Into the West*, produced by Steven Spielberg.

Harlyn Geronimo in front of sculptures of *gans*, the mountain spirits portrayed by masked dancers during some Apache ceremonies.

Harlyn Geronimo reciting an Apache prayer before the memorial he had erected on the site of his great-grandfather's birth by the Gila River.

Harlyn Geronimo, his wife Karen, and their granddaughters, Harlie Bear and Shania.

Harlyn Geronimo with his granddaughters, Shania (*right*) and Harlie Bear, holding a photograph of Geronimo's daughter Lana, the girls' great-great grandmother.

Geronimo (on the right) at his surrender in March 1886. He is accompanied by his son Chappo (left) and Fun, a warrior.

Harlyn Geronimo playing his ancestor during the filming of a documentary.

Lana, Geronimo's daughter and Harlyn's grandmother.

In an herbal pharmacy in Ruidoso, next to the Mescalero reservation, Harlyn tells Corine Sombrun about traditional Apache uses for medicinal plants.

Harlyn shows Corine how the Apaches were able to survive in the New Mexican desert, thanks to their knowledge of the flora. Here he's picking sumac berries.

At a gallery of Indian art in Ruidoso.

A tipi and a wikiup, used in the puberty ceremony on the Mescalero reservation.

In Mongolia, the shaman Enkhtuya with two members of her family and Corine Sombrun before a traditional Tsaatan tipi, a form of dwelling still in use.

6

"I'm hungry," Shania shouts to us in the front.

I smile. Since we left, we've stopped approximately every two hours to fill her stomach. This time, Harlyn asks her to be patient, since we're on a highway, but he suggests a stop in Truth or Consequences, a town about fifteen minutes away. "At McDonald's?" Harlie Bear asks. Harlyn agrees. The girls let out a squeal of joy. Not me, but I bow to the general enthusiasm. The land is flat now. Still a desert but only a rocky one. With nothing worthy of note. I take the opportunity to ask Harlyn how the war between the Apaches and the United States began. He looks at the dashboard. 12:25. A quarter of an hour is a little short for the explanation, but he'll try to summarize.

In 1851, the head of the commission charged with drawing the new border between the United States and Mexico announced to the Apaches that the Americans would protect them if they were good and didn't prevent their men from working. The Apaches agreed and in fact no incidents were reported.

"That's when Geronimo saw a white man for the first time," Harlie Bear pitches in.

Harlyn confirms this. His great-grandfather had heard about these men who were measuring the lands south of his territory and paid them a visit. He found them very friendly and even engaged in some trade with them. Skins, game, horses in exchange for clothes and corn. Once they had finished with their measuring, they went westward. In July 1852, the superintendent for Indian

Affairs for New Mexico—Harlyn has forgotten his name—signed a treaty with Mangas Coloradas, who was still the chief of the Indians in that region. In that treaty, the United States committed to respecting the Indians and to punishing American citizens who did them wrong, in exchange for which military and trading posts would be established in Apache territory. The Indians also had to promise to live in peace with American citizens and let them circulate freely on their lands. They also had to commit to ending their raids into Mexico.

"And did they agree this time?"

Harlyn gestures no with his head. Not Geronimo, at least. He found the measures unjust in light of his family's massacre at Kas-ki-yeh, and he led at least a dozen more raids after the treaty was signed. He was all the more determined to exact revenge when the Mexicans, during another surprise attack, had killed his new wife, Nana-tha-thtith, and their only child.

I can't help but utter an indignant, "*Again!*"

And that was just the beginning, Harlyn adds.

I swallow, preparing for the new horrors I'm going to have to listen to. After a deep breath, Harlyn continues:

"But despite those escapades by the Mexicans, which the Americans were pretty much indifferent about, ultimately, the Indians fully honored their promise not to attack the whites.

"So how did the war begin?"

Before answering, Harlyn removes his glasses, massages his eyelids a bit, then the bridge of his nose, places his glasses back in front of his eyes, and inhales, as if he were gathering momentum. He continues: Problems began in 1859, shortly after the discovery of a gold deposit in the mountains northeast of Silver City.

"We'll take the road there later," he adds, pointing his index finger in a vague direction, "but we'll be turning off before that. We're definitely in the same general area, though. Geronimo at that time was living peacefully beside the Gila, just north of Silver City. He was married to Chee-hash-kish, who gave him two children,

Chappo and Dohn-Say. I'll talk about them later. So the Apaches were quiet and no attacks on the whites had been reported."

He interrupts his story, as though to let the suspense build. The town of Pinos Altos, he continues, had sprung up right next to the gold mine. It was like a mushroom, like so many of the towns that popped up everywhere deposits were being discovered. The Apaches didn't understand the whites' interest in the golden metal, which by their lights wasn't even hard enough to make arrowheads or spear points. So they let it happen. The problem was that the newly arrived miners were violent people, fearing neither God nor man, and had no respect for the Indians whose lands they were invading. In addition, little by little, they'd encouraged Mexicans to come and cultivate the land to provide them with food. That was an insult to the Apaches, for whom these people were the enemy. But the miners systematically took the side of their protégés. They unjustly accused the Indians of stealing horses, when the thefts were perpetrated by their compatriots or the Mexicans. He clears his throat.

"So, a latent hostility set in. And was quickly amplified by the miners' aggressions."

"The sign!" Harlie Bear interrupts. "We're there."

Harlyn puts on his blinker to merge onto the lane taking us to Truth or Consequences, then, still focused, resumes his story.

"Mangas Coloradas, the Apache chief in the area, went to Pinos Altos to try to smooth things over. But the miners tied him to a tree and whipped him with cattle whips before letting him go. Furious, Mangas gathered his men and asked his son-in-law, Cochise, to join him. Cochise had always respected his promise not to attack the whites. He even had an arrangement to provide them with wood. But, in the face of this unjust attack, he agreed to join Mangas." Harlyn interrupts his story. His mouth makes an odd pout, his lips pushed forward. I'd never seen him do that before. Then he continues, his voice quiet: "The fighting began in September 1861. The Apaches seized the Mexicans' corn, stole their cattle and their horses, and attacked their homes, as well as a supply train. They also burned the wagons of a convoy of emigrants heading to California."

A glance in the rearview mirror. Blinker. He switches lanes.

"They spared the women and children, but fifteen or so men died. So the miners fought back and the war began."

"And Geronimo?"

"Those events took place far to the south of his territory, but he supported his brothers, and, anyway, another arbitrary act, committed by the military this time, would soon bring war to the Chiricahuas."

"I'm tired of this. When'll we be there?" Shania says suddenly in a whiny voice.

Harlyn reassures her, two minutes at most. He merges at a new fork in the road, then resumes his story, not at all fazed. Along with the cattle, he says, a twelve-year-old boy had disappeared from a ranch. They accused Cochise. The soldiers mounted a punitive expedition, but before they could find him, Cochise presented himself in person with a few warriors and affirmed that he hadn't abducted the young boy. The soldiers didn't believe him. They invited him into a tent, supposedly to talk, but once inside they began to put his warriors in irons. Cochise barely had time to whip out his knife and rip through the wall of the tent to escape. Once outside, he took three hostages with him, intending to use them as ransom in exchange for his men who had been taken prisoner. But the soldiers ultimately refused to barter. So he killed the hostages, and the soldiers hung the warriors.

"Yaaaaay, we're here!" Shania shouts. "I want a Happy Meal with a surprise inside."

Harlyn parks in the McDonald's parking lot, which is virtually empty. Shania immediately unbuckles her seatbelt and opens her door. Harlie Bear doesn't wait to be asked to get out either, but she does pause a second to tell me:

"Geronimo had *lots* of wives!"

Harlyn smiles as he switches off the ignition. Yes, Apaches were allowed to have many, and until the end of his life his great-grandfather often had two or three at the same time. When the tent incident occurred, it seems he had married a woman close to Cochise's family, who went by the name of She-gha, and then a young Biidaa-hikahnde woman by the name of Shtsha-she. The girls, already outside the car, come and open Harlyn's door.

"Come on, hurry up!" Shania tells him, taking his left hand to make him go faster.

He laughs. I get out too. Harlyn locks the doors. Click. The girls skip off hand in hand toward the entrance to the restaurant. Harlyn has his eye on them, checking to make sure no car threatens them. I like his mother-hen aspect, ready to protect his joyous little chicks who are already pushing open the glass door. Harlyn speeds up but when we finally catch up with them they're already at the counter. The room, almost empty, smells like old grease. But that doesn't seem to bother them. Super excited, they order two Happy Meals. Shania is missing one toy to complete her collection. I don't understand very well which one, but Harlie Bear promises that she'll give her hers if she gets it. High five. After propping his sunglasses on his hat again, Harlyn orders a Caesar salad. At fifty-nine, he adds, when he sees my smile, he has to watch his weight.

"Geronimo would have preferred a hamburger," Shania flings at him with a tone of reproach.

"But preferably of horse meat!" answers Harlyn. "That was his favorite. And you know, when the Indians had to get rid of their horses for safety's sake, they ate them!"

Shania utters a cry of horror.

"But I could never eat my horse. I love him so much!"

Harlyn reminds me that he raises horses, and that he gave one to his granddaughter.

"You're missing out, Shania," he insists. "It's delicious on the grill."

New cry of horror, but this time she blocks her ears. So Harlyn assures her he has no intention of cooking her horse. Harlie Bear, probably by way of a diversion, tells her she's lucky. Intrigued, Shania removes her fingers from her ears.

"Imagine, in Geronimo's day you'd have to hunt buffalo to make your burger."

Shania puts on her frowny look.

"And what about ketchup? How would I get that?" she ends up saying, appearing horrified at the thought of a life without that condiment.

We burst out laughing. The waiter places the orders on the counter, asking me if I've decided. Yes. Chicken McNuggets and a big coffee. Six pieces or twelve? Six. Standing on tiptoe, Shania grabs her tray and decides that she wouldn't really have liked living in Geronimo's day.

"I would," says Harlie Bear. "Anyway, it wouldn't be me who hunted. It'd be my husband, and I don't really like ketchup anyway."

Shania shrugs. Harlyn and I pick up our orders with a smile. We're off to a red table surrounded by four tall stools near the window, with a view onto the parking lot. The girls set their trays down on the table before climbing onto their seats. Harlie Bear makes to help her cousin, who refuses of course. And hop! She's settled and trying to open the box that contains the surprise. Disappointment. She already has this toy. Harlie Bear opens hers. Same one. No luck. She digs into the fries. Shania covers hers with ketchup. Harlyn spears his plastic fork into a salad leaf, which falls onto the table before making it into his mouth. The girls make fun of him. For once, he retaliates:

"Geronimo's grandchildren wouldn't have dared say anything to him. A little respect, please!"

Laughing, they bury their noses in their Cokes. I go to grab a pitcher of water. Back at the table, Shania is climbing down from her stool. She needs to pee. Harlyn tells her to sit back down immediately. Apache etiquette says you don't leave your seat before you've finished your meal. She climbs onto her stool, grumbling. I tell her that it's the same way in France.

"But I need to peeeee!"

Harlyn doesn't budge. Shania always has some excuse for getting up from the table. She'll have to finish her meal first. Understanding that negotiations are impossible, she bows her head and grabs her hamburger with both hands. I ask Harlyn to tell me about other instances of traditional etiquette. He thinks for a moment. Harlie Bear takes advantage of this to interject:

"You shouldn't take anything from another child just because you're bigger than them!"

"And a boy shouldn't fight with a girl," Harlyn continues, as if suddenly it were a game of who can come up with the most answers. "During a meal also, you shouldn't serve yourself. You should wait to be served, and you shouldn't eat more than necessary. You also shouldn't ask for food while it's cooking."

"And you shouldn't make fun of an old or weak person, or ride a horse without the consent of its owner," Harlie Bear adds, visibly amused by this little game. "And also, a child shouldn't start to eat or drink before an adult, and, if you don't want a stomachache, you shouldn't use a knife to stir food that's cooking."

I pour myself a glass of water. Without asking anyone else if they want any since everyone seems to prefer soda. Harlyn looks at me.

"You're going to grow old prematurely!"

I look at him too now, surprised. Harlie Bear chuckles.

"In our culture, if someone brings water and drinks it first, you say they're going to age prematurely!"

I smile, grabbing a piece of chicken. Shania is still moping. Her lips just touching her hamburger bun, she stares at her knees. As though he hadn't noticed, Harlyn continues. An Apache should never feed himself in another's camp. If he was hungry, he went home to his own. And in the presence of a visitor, he couldn't cut anything up. Shania spills her Coke. Harlyn seems used to it.

Without interrupting his explanation, he mops it up with a paper napkin. An Apache should also never step over someone.

"Like in Mongolia!" I say. "There, if it happens, you should immediately shake the person's hand to resolve the offense."

No handshakes for the Apaches, Harlyn explains, but when you go to another camp, you can't stand outside the door of a home. You have to go inside and sit down.

"Like in Mongolia!" I say again. Harlyn seems surprised by these similarities. I tell him how hard it was for me, over there, to get used to seeing people march into the tipi without announcing themselves. It always gave me a start.

"Om bon!" Shania announces, cheeks filled with food.

Harlyn asks her to swallow before saying it again. She swallows with a grimace. I want to laugh.

"I'm done! Can I go pee?"

Harlyn motions Harlie Bear to accompany her. With the smile back on Shania's face, they disappear hand in hand. I ask Harlyn if the Apaches smoked. Only the adults, he answers. They rolled tobacco in oak leaves. Wild tobacco. And if a young person wanted a taste, they were told that the smoke would make them lazy and a bad worker.

"And how about the peace pipe, what was in it?"

"The Apaches didn't smoke the peace pipe. Only rolled cigarettes. But we didn't smoke if we had blood on our hands or on our knife. That was bad luck."

"And how about you, do you smoke?"

He shakes his head. The girls come back, with wet faces and hair. They must have doused themselves in water in the bathroom, but Harlyn doesn't get up. He's busy pecking at his salad, apparently not too enthralled by this diet food, and then drinks a swallow of Sprite. After exchanging glances, the girls dip a straw in their Coke and slurp noisily, as if to annoy their grandfather. But still unperturbed, he continues to sip his Sprite, lost in thought. He must have a real ability to focus. Anyway, they tire before he does. I sip a little coffee, which is still scalding hot. Harlyn suddenly asks me if the Mongols suffer from alcoholism as much as the Apaches do.

"They drink a huge amount of vodka. But the shamans use a ritual that is supposed to unhook them."

"A rite against alcoholism?"

"Yes. During the ceremony, the shaman hits them with a sort of whip, then makes them drink a magic potion."

Without letting go of their straws, the girls gawk at me, seeming suddenly very interested. Harlyn asks me what it consists in. I smile, already knowing the response my answer will provoke.

"It's water mixed with juniper and . . ."

A glance at the girls. They're waiting, eyes fixed on my mouth.

"Seagull poop!"

They spit out their straws, letting out a *yuuuuuuuuk*. I burst out laughing. Harlyn too.

"Hard to find anything more dissuasive!" Harlyn says. "That mixture would turn even the worst alcoholic sober. Have you tried it out?"

"Yes. Last summer. The man I was supposed to do the ritual for was already drunk when he arrived. His friends were holding him up and he was looking at me, making these *meeeeee meeeeee* sounds. Since I couldn't understand what he was trying to say, someone ended up telling me. He was promising to give me a goat if the ritual worked."

"They pay you in goats over there?" Harlyn asks.

"Generally, no, they use the *tögrög*, their currency, but in rural areas barter is a common practice."

"So did you get your goat?" Harlie Bear asks, definitely very interested in the subject.

"He didn't drink any vodka for a few weeks, but then he started again. But for him, it was a success, so I have a goat waiting for me in Mongolia!"

Harlyn asks me if the Mongols raise other animals. I list them. Sheep, horses, cashmere goats, yaks. The girls have never heard of yaks. I tell them that it's a kind of cow with long hair, and I suddenly remember the miniature yurt in my backpack. I step down from my stool to open it. All eyes converge on me. I end up placing the model on a corner of the table where it's safe from the ketchup and Coke.

"This is a Mongol home."

The girls open their eyes wide.

"It really looks like a wickiup!" says Harlyn. "Except the covering is made with branches in our case. What's this fabric?"

"Felt, made from the wool of sheep or yaks, actually. The colder it gets, the more layers they put on."

"Around the wickiup too!" says Harlie Bear, touching the felt. "Is it cold in Mongolia?"

"Down to minus thirty in the winter."

A collective cry of surprise. Even in their freezer, Harlyn says, it's not as cold as that. I nod, smiling. He adds that he dreams of coming to Mongolia with me.

"But preferably in summertime!"

The girls chorus their approval. Harlyn takes the yurt into his hands. Turns it, looks at the smoke hole at the top, turns it again, scrutinizes the little wooden door.

"It reminds me of a flying saucer!" says Shania, swinging her legs under her stool.

I ask her if she's ever seen one. Without answering, she shoots a worried glance over at Harlyn, who puts on a mysterious air. The same air he took in the car when I spoke of Roswell. This time, I insist. He ends up telling me that there are a lot of them in this area. But you really shouldn't talk about them. He becomes quiet again. I look at the girls. Quiet too.

"But what's all this mystery?"

After taking a moment to form his reply, Harlyn opens his mouth.

"There are lots of rumors on the subject. The Apaches have known about them for more than two hundred years. But see, if you talk about it too much, the aliens land near your house and abduct you."

I stare at him with my eyebrows like two big circumflexes.

"Have any of your people been taken?"

A shrug of his shoulders, as if I'd asked the dumbest question in the world. Harlie Bear answers for him.

"No, because we don't talk about it!"

Of course. Shania dips her straw into her Coke again. She blows into it this time around. The liquid gurgles, making little bubbles. The topic of aliens closed once and for all, I dig into my bag again to pull out my shaman's jaw harp. They'll want to talk about that at least. Harlyn looks at it carefully. Two big blue-and-yellow silk ribbons are tied to it along with a little brass disc. I explain that we use the jaw harp to summon spirits at the beginning of a ceremony. He looks at the metal circle and asks what its purpose is.

"It's a kind of mirror that's supposed to protect the shaman by reflecting bad energies and sending them back to wherever they came from."

"Like this, then?"

He pulls out the necklace hidden under his T-shirt. The one I couldn't see the end of at the motel. I'm looking at a flat, round seashell about an inch and a half in diameter. An abalone, he tells me. This shell is also supposed to protect him by reflecting bad energies. I add that another mirror of this sort, but bigger, is used by shamans to predict the future.

"How?"

"They point their index finger at the center of the mirror while saying the birth year of the person consulting them, and they can see important events associated with the person's future."

"Are you able to see them?"

"No, I've never been able to."

"For me, it's more with dreams that I can see the future, as I told you."

After reflecting a moment, he asks me if I know how to play the jaw harp. Of course. I show him. *Dzinn, dzinn*, then *bong!* right in my teeth. Probably stage fright from playing in front of an Apache. And in a McDonald's no less. I look around. The room is empty. It's okay. Musicians are allowed to warm up, right? I start over. Harlyn and the girls' gazes are locked on my lips. There. Finally. A pretty melody emerges. Grows more and more bewitching. I suddenly notice discomfort in Harlyn's face, then worry. He keeps glancing behind me, as though he's checking for something. I stop playing to look too.

"Is somebody there?"

"Not yet, but you shouldn't keep playing. If the spirits come, they could be dangerous for you."

"Really? They're not nice?"

He shakes his head.

"Not all of them. I've learned to protect myself. One night, when I was in a hotel in San Francisco for a conference, I felt someone shaking my leg. I turned on the light, but there was no one in the room. So I understood it was a spirit. I smoked a stick of sage, recited a prayer, and went back to sleep. The spirit didn't return. But if you don't know how to protect yourself from them, you could be in trouble."

I feel a shiver down my spine. He's almost giving me the creeps with his stories. But I reassure him about my ability to protect myself from evil spirits. I didn't spend all that time in Mongolia for nothing! Harlie Bear reaches over to grab the jaw harp. Harlyn forbids it, his voice firm. Touching sacred objects is dangerous for those who are unprepared. She pulls back her hand without uttering a word. I tell Harlyn he can touch it if he wants to. He shakes his head. He'd rather not.

"Your protective spirits are inside. We shouldn't disturb them."

Before I can insist, he looks down at his watch and signals that it's time to leave. I put away the jaw harp. Everyone gets up. Harlyn, leading by example, tells the girls to empty their trays in the garbage. The little clan follows his orders. We place the empty trays on a pile. Done.

Climbing back in the car, Harlyn asks me if I've retained the name of Mangas Coloradas, the chief of the southwest Apaches. I have! He then offers a date, saying I should remember that too. I repeat it. January 1863. January 1863 . . .

"The only good Indians I ever saw were dead."
GENERAL PHILIP SHERIDAN

"The more [Indians] we can kill this year, the less will have to be killed the next war, for the more I see of these Indians, the more convinced I am that they all have to be killed or be maintained as a species of paupers."
GENERAL WILLIAM TECUMSEH SHERMAN

"An Apache can stoically suffer death without so much as a grunt, while imprisonment is a terror to him."
NEWSPAPER REPORTER, 1886

"They are the keenest and shrewdest animals in the world, with the added intelligence of human beings."
MAJOR WIRT DAVIS, 1885

A Renegade

JANUARY 1863. THE GREATEST injustice ever committed against the Indians by the whites has just taken place, and you, Grandfather, were on the run with half your tribe.

To prevent the soldiers from following, you walked at night, on rocks, rocky paths, or sod, and erased your inevitable tracks with tufts of grass. You had lost half your people, half your weapons, and your food had run out. And you felt the anger tormenting your heart. All the more because you had suspected the trap. You had even warned Mangas, but he hadn't listened to you. The residents and the soldiers of the little Apache town of Tejo, near Silver City, had invited him to come sign a peace treaty. They promised, if Mangas accepted, to allow him to settle in that territory with his people and to provide him with food, meat, blankets, flour, and finally to live in peace. Which is what Mangas desired most of all. You, Grandfather, you had been opposed to it. You didn't trust them. But, in spite of that, half the members of the tribe had left for Apache Tejo in the hope of at last living in plenty, alongside white men who respected them. If everything went well, Mangas would return to fetch the rest of the tribe. You had agreed on a place where you would wait. A secret place where, in the event of a problem, he and his warriors could reunite with you after splitting into small groups that would have been impossible for the soldiers to follow. This was one of your war tactics. You had also insisted that they not go without taking half your weapons with them. They had finally agreed and, after their departure, you made your way to the rendezvous point.

You had waited for days there. Until you ran out of food. But, just as you suspected, Mangas never returned. You found out later that he had been tortured and murdered. After he was decapitated, his head had even been put on exhibition to satisfy the whites' curiosity. His skull turned up some time later in Washington.

That's why you were on the run. That murder had opened your eyes once and for all to the real intentions of the whites toward your people, and from that moment on you refused to be friendly toward them. Unfortunately, only a few members of the tribe had agreed to follow you into the mountains around Hot Springs, near the Gila. The others, worn out by the soldiers' constant harassment, had finally accepted the whites' conditions. To abstain from all hostilities in exchange for food, the necessities of life, and land on a reservation close to your territory of origin. Far too good to be true. As you had surmised, Grandfather.

Not only did the Apaches never obtain title to any property but in 1875, allegedly for economic reasons, the government decided to put into place what they called a "policy of concentration." As proposed by agents on the ground for the War Department, the new policy sought to collect all the Apaches into a single area. Indeed, every day new towns were popping up out of the ground. Gold prospectors, miners, farmers, and settlers were flocking to the region, and the Indians couldn't be allowed to impede them or threaten the safety of the routes to the better territories of New Mexico, which were now open to settlement.

So the old reservations were closed, and the Apaches were transferred to the one in San Carlos, Arizona. But all those who were against these policies, like you, Grandfather, escaped to the mountains. As a result, all of the tribes that had lived in relative peace on the reservations now found themselves spread out all over the land, outside of the white's control. So the decision to concentrate the tribes had the effect of relaunching the Apache wars. They would last more than ten years.

Now that you were a renegade, it was easy to pin all of the robberies and murders committed in the region on you. Even those you weren't responsible for. Very quickly your reputation became larger than life, and the soldiers tried every way they could to catch you. But since you were impossible to capture by force, they decided to seek your surrender through negotiation. They sent a messenger to relay their wish to parlay. His words seemed to convey a real intention to resolve things in the best way possible for you and your people. So you decided to accept the proposed meeting and begin the process of negotiation. Yet no sooner did you arrive than you were disarmed and taken to headquarters, where you were brought before a court martial. Since the tribunal couldn't prove all the misdeeds you were accused of, you were convicted of refusing to go live on the San Carlos reservation and having fled with your men. They put you in chains and transferred you to San Carlos, where you were kept prisoner for four months. Then you were transferred a little farther north to a place now called Geronimo, where you were made to cultivate corn and lived quietly for two years. Under close watch.

But during the year 1881, rumors were circulating that the officers at San Carlos were planning to try the Apache chiefs again for their past actions. The idea of this bogus trial, organized with the sole aim of getting rid of you to end the danger you represented, coupled with the memory of the injustices committed in the past, led you to decide you were better off fleeing.

Together with two hundred fifty Apaches, you crossed the Mexican border to take refuge in the Sierra Madre, where you managed to hide out for a year. Unfortunately, Mexican soldiers finally located you and began to send troops into the mountains where you had established your camp. It now became urgent to get help, and the only possible solution was to convince your brothers who had remained at the San Carlos reservation to flee and come join you.

In April 1882, with a few of your men, you crossed the Mexican border again. After walking for about fifteen days, you camped near San Carlos. There, you chanted four prayers and questioned your "power." It assured you that the raid would be successful. It would also contribute to the success of the operation by causing the soldiers and the employees on the reservation to remain sleeping. Fortified by this assurance, you and your warriors took the last leg of your journey to the reservation. At daybreak, you managed to make contact with the members of your tribe. But they categorically refused to follow you. They preferred peace to freedom. That was an impossible decision to accept, for, without their help, your own freedom, your own choice, was jeopardized. So you ordered your warriors to take them away by force and to kill any who resisted. Faced with that threat, a hundred men and about three hundred women and children joined you.

But they were slow. Their stay on the reservation and their inactivity had caused them to lose their endurance. The young ones had never even been trained as warriors and didn't hunt anymore, since the area of the reservation had been reduced five separate times to satisfy the rapacity of the miners and cattle breeders. So you found yourself with hundreds of Apaches unsuited to the conditions that would be necessary to escape the soldiers already on your trail. You decided to send your warriors to steal mules and horses, so you could transport your people faster. When everyone was equipped, your order was to travel only at night. But the soldiers had hired Indian scouts, who quickly located your group, for it was difficult to hide them. You decided then to transfer the noncombatants to the top of an inaccessible canyon while you and the warriors lured the enemy's scouts into a trap.

As soon as they'd spotted the path you had taken, you concealed yourselves, then split into two groups. To signal your position to your brothers, you gave low wolf calls. The soldiers, led by the scouts, didn't realize it was an ambush and walked straight into it and kept going. The group lying in wait on the path ahead fired at them with rifles—the time of arrows was long past—forcing them to turn back. Then, your men hidden to the sides of the trail finished them off.

Victorious, you were able to rejoin the rest of the group at the top of the canyon. Yet the danger wasn't over. Other soldiers were after you and, to lose them once and for all, you still had to reach a rocky outcrop. A good hiding place. But to get there, first you had to traverse a long exposed stretch, which according to your calculations would be impossible to cross before daybreak. Which meant the soldiers would inevitably spot you. You had no other choice but to summon your secret weapon. For the day not to break before you'd made your way across the exposed area, you asked your "power" to prolong the night. It had told you before that it could do this. That night, you prayed with all your might, with all your faith. And, at nightfall, putting your fate in its hands, you gave the signal to depart. As you had predicted, you didn't reach the other side before daybreak. But that day, yes, daybreak took its time, and the night lasted two or three hours longer than usual. Just enough time for you to reach the rocky outcrop, where your group was able to vanish and quietly continue its journey to Mexico.

From the Sierra Madre, you launched numerous raids to steal livestock, convoys of supplies, and ammunition. Chappo, your eldest son, who had become an excellent warrior, fought at your side. No one saw you, save your victims. Well-organized, fast, efficient, sleeping only on horseback, and allowing yourselves only brief moments of rest to revitalize yourselves, you managed to wreak havoc on the whole border area between Mexico and Arizona. Newspapers made headlines out of the terror you inspired, and the soldiers were under great pressure because of their inability to stop you. During one of your confrontations, Mexican troops managed to capture and kill your wife Chee-hash-kish, the mother of Chappo and Dohn-say, but rather than prompting you to give up, that act quadrupled your desire for vengeance. Your "power's" help would be all the more precious.

One day, you summoned it. You were on the verge of being trapped by a regiment of cavalry, and it seemed your last option. After the ritual prayers, it told you to make pollen drawings on the path by which the soldiers would arrive. They would be unable to cross the magic marks. When the drawings were finished, you went into the hills to hide. And then the incredible happened. Coming level with the markings, the regiment, for no apparent reason, turned around. You were able to flee and set up camp on a very steep mountain in the north of Mexico, near the border with Arizona. Between raids, you lived there peacefully. You even married Zi yeh, a young Nedni Indian. The women of the camp would accompany her in their chores of drying meat, picking berries, and preparing meals. That ambiance, so similar to the time of your youth, brought you great comfort during the most difficult moments of the fighting. You felt once again that there was a land that was yours. You felt free, invincible, and as long as you were alive, no one would ever force all of you to live on a reservation.

During this time in the United States, however, the government continued to put into place the means to eradicate you. In September 1882, General George R. Crook was assigned command of the military in Arizona Territory. After evaluating the situation, he decided that the only solution for ending your incessant raids was to track you to your Mexican refuge and attack you mercilessly in order to weaken you and finally force your surrender. After obtaining permission to enter Mexican territory, he carefully prepared his expedition.

Completely unaware of that imminent danger, Grandfather, you went to lead a raid in Chihuahua state. Your tribal council had decided to kidnap some Mexicans in order to trade them for Apache prisoners. However, one night, as you were sharing provisions around a fire, you had a vision. Your camp had just been attacked by American soldiers. You told this to your brothers, who were used to this sort of phenomenon from you and immediately decided to return to camp. During the journey, you had another vision. You declared that the next day a man would arrive from the left of your path, and tell you that the camp had been captured. That's exactly what happened: right before you arrived, one of the warriors charged with protecting your people informed you that Crook had hired Apache scouts to find the camp. His soldiers had then encircled it and had compelled your tribe members to surrender.

You gathered your warriors to take stock of the situation. The council quickly concluded that if the Americans and Mexicans had the assistance of Apache scouts, you had no chance of escaping. Your women seemed tired of this life on the run, living in constant fear of attack. You also couldn't count on support from the San Carlos Apaches who had been taken by force the year before. They had never truly integrated into the group and thought only of returning to San Carlos to live in peace. So you had no choice but to surrender. In May 1883, you agreed to meet with Crook.

7

"What's your favorite color?" Harlie Bear asks me.

"Turquoise," Harlyn answers, before I can respond.

"And me, pink," Shania chimes in, pulling on the bottom of her T-shirt.

I'm about to say that mine is orangey-yellow, but Harlyn parks the car. Strange, we just left the McDonald's in Truth or Consequences. I ask him where we're going, but as usual, he responds with a mysterious smile and a "Follow me." I look at the girls. Same smile. OK. We step out of the car and walk a hundred yards or so until we reach a building made of pale yellow concrete.

"The Geronimo Springs Museum!" Harlyn exclaims, with a big smile.

Surprised, I step back to look. A giant Apache is painted on the front. Harlyn invites me in. Inside, a large bookstore of sorts occupies the entryway, with a counter off to the right. Harlyn greets the cashier. She recognizes him, asks him how he's doing. Very well. He introduces me. Corine is going to write a book about Geronimo. Really? she answers, turning to greet me. She hopes I'll enjoy my visit. I know I will. She then hands me a ticket that says, "FREE." I thank her for the kind gesture. You're welcome! she says, looking at Harlyn, who's smiling as if he were at home here and invites me to begin our tour. I have to admit that I feel a certain pride in having Geronimo's great-grandson as my tour guide. The girls are already in the exhibit rooms, I can hear them talking and laughing in the distance.

After passing through the doorway to the first room, Harlyn steps back into the hall, as though he'd forgotten something important. He motions me to follow him into the bookstore. We end up in front of a wall of books. His gaze scans the shelves looking for one I'll need to write mine, he explains. There. From the "Anthropology" shelf, he pulls a book entitled *An Apache Life-Way* by Morris Opler.

"This will give you the details on the life and traditions of the Chiricahuas in Geronimo's time." He smiles. "Since I may have forgotten some things!"

He goes to give the book to the lady behind the counter and then invites me to follow him.

The first room houses a reconstructed Apache home. A wickiup, Harlyn tells me. He steps into the dwelling, and I'm about to follow, but he already steps out, apparently preoccupied. I ask if there's a problem. He shakes his head, then says yes. He asks me to sit down. He has some important things to tell me. I look for a seat. There are none. With his hand, he motions me to sit on the floor, there, in front of the wickiup. OK. He kneels next to me, remaining silent for a moment. I hear the girls' laugh in the distance. I stretch out my legs, then fold them again, trying to find the most comfortable position. Harlyn's voice finally resonates, subdued, monotone, almost in a whisper. His great-grandmother Kate passed down this information, he begins, looking at the palms of his hands lying open on his thighs as if he were about to offer me their contents. But he has never revealed it to anyone. He knows today is the right time to talk about it. He raises his head toward me slightly. These events took place in the 1880s, after the government's decision to concentrate the Apaches on the San Carlos reservation. His gaze searches mine.

"As you know, many Apaches refused to be torn from their land to go live on that reservation, so they fled, Geronimo first among them."

He clears his throat softly.

"The problem," he continues, his voice more distinct now, "is that the United States government had opened the Southwest to colonization. Adventurers and settlers were arriving in droves in this Eldorado, where they were promised land, gold, and the opportunity to make a quick fortune. As a result, the Indians who were beyond the whites' control became too much of a nuisance. For the area's economic development, the government decided purely and simply to eliminate them from their own territory. The methods they used back then defies comprehension sometimes. (His voice rises a notch.) What I'm about to tell you the Americans deny. But it's what my great grandmother Kate told me. And while I can't entirely confirm that it's the strict truth, I still want to share it with you."

Without a word, I open my ears. The soldiers, he tells me, started putting the Indians into contact with people carrying the tuberculosis and the smallpox viruses. They even gave them blankets infected with those viruses. On the reservations, they reduced the food rations to starve them, and they put poison in the food they sold them. But since many Apaches continued to resist, they sent soldiers after them, sometimes taking advantage of when the men were away from their camps to kill the women and children. Harlyn bows his head. He asks me if I'm ready to hear the rest. I agree, with a worried feeling. His voice becomes a muted monotone again, as if no one other than me is supposed to hear it.

"Once, Kate told me, soldiers with bayonets stabbed babies and pregnant women, pulling their fetuses out while they were still alive."

I turn away. I need to get away from Harlyn's eyes, where tears have suddenly started to well. He asks me to listen a little more. Just a little bit. I drop my gaze.

"They . . . they also grabbed newborns by their feet and smashed their skulls against the rocks."

This time, I get up, wanting to vomit, to leave this room. Harlyn seems to understand. "I know, it's unbearable," he says, "but you need to know about it so you can talk about it in your book." He asks me to come back and sit down. I sit next to him again.

"Using these methods," he continues, "the whites brought the Apaches to their knees. All of the survivors finally agreed to live on the reservations, which kept shrinking in size as the colonizers' need for more land grew. That caused famines."

With his index finger, he wipes away a tear from the corner of his right eye, breathes in, and continues:

"From about ten thousand individuals, the Apache population fell to about two or three thousand. But the whites couldn't have cared less. All they wanted was to take our land, exploit the gold and silver mines, and lead comfortable lives. So the Apaches lost the equivalent of three states: Arizona, New Mexico, and Chihuahua in Mexico."

His voice and eyes suddenly harden. And his energy too. I'd never felt energy like this. A bit like a pupil capable of slowly dilating into a cottony cloud or suddenly contracting into a very hard and compact kernel ready to withstand anything.

"Today, the United States earns two and a half billion dollars annually just off the revenue from the natural resources on our lands. But none of those profits are redistributed to the Apaches."

The girls tumble in, faces beaming and red. They must have been running. "Come see!" they tell me in unison. I follow them, grateful for the breather. They stop in front of a wax figure of Geronimo that's about my size. I'm surprised to find myself face to face with him, along with his descendant who has just stepped in and joined us. Do they look alike? Same stocky build. Same square face. Same nose. Their eyes aren't the same, but this wax gaze can't capture reality. Harlyn says that his great-grandfather's stare could make any adversary divert his eyes. In fact, when he arrived at the San Carlos reservation on his favorite horse, many Indians had gathered to witness his arrival. But they diverted their gazes when they were met with his, and their descendants still speak of it today. His implacable strength forced them to face their own cowardice in not having chosen to fight alongside him.

"Can we go and see the videos?" Harlie Bear asks.

Harlyn acquiesces. They're of the local countryside. A way of discovering, from an armchair, the places where Geronimo lived and the historic steps in the region's colonization. I ask Harlyn in what year his great-grandfather arrived in San Carlos. February 1883. But once there, Geronimo noticed that there was no grass, the water was bad, and disease was decimating his people. He asked to return to the land on the Gila River, which was more fertile, with more game, better fields to cultivate, and pure water in abundance. Since no one bothered to give him an answer, he asked General Crook to at least remove the border around the reserva- tion, which had become much too small to feed all the Indians. Why put up a border around a peaceful people?

He also asked that the Apaches who had remained in the hands of the Mexicans be repatriated to the United States. He didn't receive anything more by way of an answer this time and finally understood that he would never have the same rights as the whites. Harlyn looks at me sadly.

"You'll write about all this in your book, won't you?"

I say yes. The smile returns to his face.

"I knew I could count on you."

I look at Geronimo's statue. I look at Harlyn. I think again of the vision that brought me here. I have to tell him. Yes, now is the right moment. His eyes are fixed on me. As if once again he had guessed my questions. So I go for it. I tell him everything. The trance. My vision of Geronimo. He remains silent the whole time while I explain. He doesn't even seem surprised, really. I wonder why I hesitated so much. Then he finally says:

"I already knew you weren't here by accident. And I have other important things to tell you. But later, when we've arrived at the site of our rendezvous."

"Where past and present . . ."

He nods. I ask him if his medicine can provide him with clues about what the future holds for the Apaches. He thinks for a while. It hasn't yet, no. But Geronimo spoke of a vision he'd had in the mountains above the Santa Rita mines, north of Silver City. Deposits of various metals—copper, silver, gold—had been found there. And they were already being mined. Anyway, his ancestor was hiding in the mountains and being hunted by the American cavalry, and one night he had a dream. He saw boulders tumbling, dust rising from the mines, the metals rising up. He also saw animals lying dead along the rivers. The next day he told his warriors that if the land wasn't respected, if it was dug up to extract more of its "sap," the spirit of this earth would rise up in revolt and cause terrible problems that would bring about the death and disappearance of the human race. Harlyn looks at me and nods gently, with his usual "Uh huh."

"That night, Geronimo witnessed the current state of our Earth and in a way predicted the problems that we're grappling with today. The destruction of the ozone layer, global warming, climate change due to air pollution, chemical spills in our rivers. He felt before anyone that the human race's lack of respect for its environment would cause major catastrophes in the future. The state of our earth today unfortunately proves he was right."

That's why, Harlyn adds, motioning me to follow, he has dedicated himself so much to the conservation of nature on the reservation. He even started a campaign to sensitize young Apaches to the problem.

"I teach them that we must never consider ourselves apart from our environment. To destroy it is to destroy ourselves. So don't forget, it's very important: in the book you must speak of this fight to save our earth."

I promise him I will. But I have another idea all of a sudden. I ask him if he'd be prepared to come to Paris for the book launch. That way he could speak of all these things himself. Joy now lights up his face.

"Of course! When?"

"When it's published."

He thinks. Smiles again.

"If it's warm enough, I'll be able to go swimming."

I give him a surprised look.

"Swimming? In Paris?"

He frowns.

"There's no sea in Paris?"

"Um . . . no."

"So where is the French Riviera?"

"Naał'a'ánahałaaí nahí Chidikáágo hongéí doobaayándzįda.
Han k'aa nahá'ágólaaná'ań 'áńá yaayáńzįhálí.
'Ákoo, dííjį. 'indaanałįí 'įłtį 'ił'ango daadiłtałí tsįníntsaazí bééshntł'izí dá'áída
díík'eh ghádaaniidágo nahá'ájílaa.
'Ákoo, nahí Chidikáágo hongéí, k'aa nahá'ájílaaní 'it'ago biyeeshxahyá
doołi'nahá'ánáájídlaada."

We Chiricahuas are not ashamed that you made slaves of us.
Maybe the one who is said to have created arrows for us is ashamed.
Today he has made for you, the white men, all different sorts of
guns that shoot and pierce everything,
Even fat tree trunks and hard metal.
But for us, the Chiricahuas,
Only those arrows were made
in the past.

The San Carlos Reservation

ON THE SAN CARLOS Reservation, they furnished you with pick-axes, shovels, and seeds. And—the height of absurdity for an Apache, Grandfather—you had to train your horse to pull a plow to till the earth. At first, used to open spaces, he'd leave at a gallop for the middle of the field, as incapable as you of adapting to his new life as a beast of burden. You had to grip the handles of the plow with all your might to hold him back, which caused general hilarity. But in just a few months, you managed to become an excellent farmer. One of the best on the reservation, according to certain reports. You were even proud of your harvests of watermelon, barley, and corn.

Some photographers made you pose in front of fake backdrops so they could publish photographs in newspapers showing how happy you were living this experiment. But you certainly were not happy. Lack of respect for your traditions was a daily trial. You had been forbidden from making your *tiswin*, which seemed unjust. The whites were all allowed to drink their alcohol. Why weren't you? They also wanted to force you to eat pork, but you resisted. An Apache couldn't swallow the meat of an animal that some-times fed on snakes. Then you quickly realized that Apache spies working for the American army had been hired to keep watch on your families. A betrayal in your eyes. Since your arrival, two years earlier, you had honored your word to live in peace. Crook was satisfied. So why didn't they trust you?

Because of that deceitful surveillance, the latent tensions wors-ened and small enmities between Apaches turned into full-fledged quarrels. The fact that you were forbidden from following your traditions became harder and harder to bear. As did the sarcasm of the soldiers and the Indian scouts, who, besides insults, fed your fears by whispering threats. According to them, some of you would be hanged or deported. At first you tried to not take the threats too seriously. But when the newspapers, with big headlines, began to clamor for your execution, you finally decided to consult your "power." And it was very clear. You were in danger, Grandfather. So, in spring 1885, you convinced about a hundred and fifty of your people to escape. Among them, your wives, your children, your son Chappo, and some leaders like Naiche, the son of Cochise, who had died in 1874, Mangas, the son of Mangas Coloradas, and Nana, Daklugie, and Chihuahua.

Your disappearance had barely been announced when the newspapers of the Southwest created a general panic with headlines that the Apaches had left their reservation. Settlers and prospectors fled. Others gathered in groups and barricaded themselves in order to prepare for your eventual attacks. But you were already in Mexico. General Crook was exasperated because this was your fourth escape. He placed some soldiers along the borders of Arizona and New Mexico to protect those states from any new attempts to make raids. And troops led by Captain Emmet Crawford departed in pursuit of you in the Sierra Madre.

Once again, thanks to the help of Indian scouts, particularly of Chato, who had been your former comrade in arms and had refused to follow you, the soldiers discovered your camp. In August, an attack by the Apache scouts, the only ones who really represented a significant danger for you, resulted in numerous casualties among your warriors. They took your horses, your food, and some prisoners, among whom your three wives, She-gha, Sha-zi-yeh Zi-yeh, and five of your children, including Fenton, Zi-yeh's baby, your three-year-old daughter, and a son, Little Robe, who died in captivity shortly after his arrival at Fort Bowie in Arizona. You yourself were injured, Grandfather, but you managed to escape with some warriors and your son Chappo, the only member of your family who hadn't been captured.

Once safe in one of your hideouts, you were able to prepare some *i-ah-i* and apply it to your wound and those of your warriors. For four days, you forbade them to eat deer meat. The fourth day, you marked the meat with pollen, placed it before the mouths of each of the injured warriors three times, and the fourth time they were allowed to eat it. Barely recovered, you decided to go rescue and free the members of your family.

In the fall of 1885, with four of your warriors whose wives and children had also been made prisoner, you crossed the border again to make your way to the reservation where they were being held. Taking advantage of the night, you slipped into the dwellings and, before the alarm could be sounded, managed to free some of them, among them She-gha and your three-year-old daughter.

Before crossing the border again, still elusive and impossible to catch, you made a few more raids to steal what you needed, livestock, horses, and food. The army combed the region, but by that time you were already in Mexico, where you remained quietly in your refuge until the month of November. You even took a new wife, Ih-tedda, from a Mescalero tribe. She would later become known as Kate.

Needless to say, by now General Crook verged on apoplexy whenever your name came up. But the threat he posed, Grandfather, far from worrying you, didn't even prevent you from attempting a fresh raid in his territory. You had some scores to settle with the Indians at Fort Bowie in Arizona, the ones who had betrayed you by enlisting in the Army as scouts. Not a single soldier was able stop you before you managed to enter the camp, kill ten or so of them, and take as many prisoner.

This time, General Crook, with the assent of the Army chief of staff, placed all the troops in the Southwest on alert and ordered that your hideout in Mexico be destroyed by any means necessary.

His army, under the command of Lieutenant Crawford, crossed the border in November 1885. It took the scouts almost two months to find your hideout. You were perched on a steep mountain that was difficult to reach. But on a night with no moon, the scouts mounted a surprise attack. Your "power" hadn't warned you this time. You were able to flee, but the soldiers managed to seize all of your horses, ammunition, and stockpile of goods. That day, isolated, hounded by the soldiers, you realized that no refuge would be safe. Your only chance was to agree to parlay. So you let Crawford know that you would agree to meet with Crook, who had remained at the Arizona border, and with him only, to discuss the terms of your surrender.

Two moons later, on March 25, 1886, at the Los Embudos Canyon on the border between Mexico and Arizona, the meeting took place. You explained to Crook what had driven you to escape, the threats, being barred from practicing your traditions, your families kept under surveillance by Apache spies. The general replied that this had never happened. You didn't protest. You understood that the whites would always be right no matter what. And also, tired of your years on the run, you wanted finally to live in peace and be reunited with the members of your family who had remained in captivity. You offered the general to return to the reservation and make a fresh start. Crook refused. Either you and your men remained on the path of war and he would hunt you down to the last one or you must surrender without condition. You asked for time to consider, but two days later, March 27, you told Crook you would agree to surrender.

During the night, Grandfather, you and some of your companions began to doubt Crook's sincerity. Hadn't he stated that the threats against you were pure invention? Once you were in their hands, they would surely try and execute you. That was for certain. So you took advantage of the darkness and the trust the general had placed in you by leaving you your freedom of movement to escape once again. Naiche and Chappo, the only one of your children not to have been killed or made prisoner, accompanied you with about twenty other warriors and their wives and children. As was your practice, you split into small groups after having agreed on a rendezvous point. The soldiers tried to follow you, but they quickly realized they'd never be able to catch up with you. You were too fast, and they couldn't pursue all the sets of tracks left by the different groups. So they retraced their path to the reservation, taking with them the prisoners who had been unable or unwilling to follow you, including Nana and Chihuahua.

Once back to the Sierra Madre, you had to fight the Mexican soldiers. But they weren't much of a threat without Indian scouts. Also, since the arrival of the whites, you had good rifles and a new means of communication. No more smoke signals that the soldiers could spot. Mirrors were much more discreet. You trained their reflection directly at a group to say, "You can come, it's safe." You oriented it toward the right or the left to show which direction they needed to follow.

Once again, you tasted the joys of freedom.

8

I slip my little finger into my right ear. It's ringing. Harlie Bear asks what I'm doing. I explain. That's good, she says, you're about to receive good news! I look at her dubiously. It's true, she insists, that's what Apaches say. I tell her that in France we say it means someone's talking about you.

"And when you sneeze," Harlyn continues, "it means someone's thinking about you."

"And it's going to rain if a dog rolls on the ground," Harlie Bear adds.

"Gas station ahead!" Shania shouts.

Harlyn turns on his blinker, merges onto the access road, and stops with the gas tank perfectly aligned with the pump. Ever precise. We get out to stretch our legs. It's still very hot. I look at my watch. 4:12. The girls ask their grandfather for money. They're hungry. As usual, since they haven't swallowed a thing for two hours. Harlyn gives ten dollars to Harlie Bear, who takes Shania by the hand and drags her into the store, then he steps over to the pump and chooses his fuel. Diesel. He unscrews the cap on the tank, lifts the nozzle, sticks it into the opening, and presses the handle. The air around his hand starts to quiver. It smells of gasoline. I step away for a moment. He asks me if Mongolia has many inhabitants. Three million. He laughs.

"That's all? That's only two times the population of New Mexico!"

I tell him it's the only country with more horses than inhabitants. And he laughs again.

"Geronimo would have loved to live there! How big is it?"

I think for a second.

"About five times the size of New Mexico. But I'll take you there, and you can ride a horse across the vast steppe in memory of your great-grandfather."

He doesn't laugh this time. His hand is still on the handle of the nozzle, his fingers white from pressing down, and he seems dreamy. Or emotional, I can't tell. The piece of turquoise hanging from his ear is motionless. Not for long, though. The girls come skipping back, arms filled with sugary things. Shania offers me some pink-and-blue candy. I decline. I must still have an apple or dried apricot in my backpack. She puts on her pouty look.

"All you do is eat apples and drink coffee!"

I smile. She's right, but I don't really feel like putting on twenty pounds during my stay. My argument doesn't seem to persuade her. She thinks I'm way too skinny. Harlyn is still smiling. Harlie Bear, always conciliatory, tells her cousin I'm right to be careful, that she should do the same because in her class lots of students already have diabetes. Shania looks down, pressing the candy to her stomach. There's a small *click*. The tank is full. Harlyn puts the nozzle in its cradle. After telling the girls to get in the car, he goes to pay. I grab my mug and join him, feeling like coffee. While Harlyn walks up to the cash register, I look for the coffee machine.

"That way," he says pointing to the left. "Can you grab me a bottle of water?"

"OK."

He's already signing his receipt when I join him again. I pay for my purchases. He puts the card back into his wallet, then pulls out a photo and motions me to come closer.

"It's a print of Crook and Geronimo's meeting in Los Embudos Canyon in March of 1886. Right before he escaped again. I have others, but they're in the car."

He hands me the photograph. My heart does a little leap as I discover a group of men in an agave grove and some plucked trees with white trunks. They're sitting in a circle on ground that's covered with leaves. Flecks of sunlight highlight some of the faces. I recognize Geronimo's in the center, with a band across his forehead. His body is partially in shadow, but he looks like he's wearing a buckskin jacket with a kind of light-colored skirt or loincloth and tall moccasins. I'm moved. To see that moment, held in that photograph like a slice of time. Like a still from a movie that you could pile on top of the other stills to re-create the motion picture in which I suddenly feel I'm entering. I hear the sound of the dried leaves rustling under the officers' boots. I smell their sweet dusty scent. I sense the worried breathing of the Indians standing erect around the soldiers. All of their gazes are directed toward the photographer's lens. Not a single smile. In those days, they probably didn't have them say "cheeeeese" to make them look happy. Geronimo is sitting in the leaves, legs folded before him, his arms resting on his knees. He too stares into the camera. But in his gaze I read defiance. Maybe he's already planning his escape? He seems calm, steady, determined. I suddenly understand how he was able to galvanize his warriors. An incredible strength emanates from his entire being. Harlyn's voice slips into this past. As if to form, delicately, the link between Geronimo and our present. He points to one of the soldiers with a white hat and buckskin gloves. General Crook, he explains. His face and uniform are in shadow. Impossible to make them out.

"And the Apache standing next to the horse at the top of the photograph is Nana, one of the leaders. He won't be one of the ones who flees with my great-grandfather."

I study his long hair, held back by a broad white headband. He looks sad. His arms hang down beside his body. He too is wearing a short loincloth. One of his legs, slightly folded, is in bright daylight. The thigh is muscular. Harlyn's voice resumes. Following that escape, Crook was relieved of his duties and transferred to command another military region. General Miles replaced him. He assembled a force of five thousand men—a quarter of the troops serving at the time—to track down Geronimo and his twenty warriors.

But hardly had he left when the general realized that their horses wouldn't be able to climb the steep, rocky flanks of the mountains where Geronimo was hiding. So he ordered all his soldiers to advance on foot. Of course, they didn't have the endurance of the Apaches, who watched their slow progress from their hiding places and laughed, not worried in the least. As quick as they were invisible, their little group could easily evade the soldiers. But since thousands were after them, Geronimo and his men had no choice but to steal, pillage, and kill in order to survive. As he spread terror in his wake, his reputation as a bloodthirsty savage quickly formed. Children would be told, "If you don't behave, I'll call Geronimo!" Harlyn smiles. Since Miles wasn't about to catch him, he decided to redirect his efforts to the Apaches who were within his reach. The ones on the reservations. Harlyn's right hand comes toward me, and I hand him back the photo. He studies it for a moment while he continues with his account. About ten former leaders were arrested and placed in detention at Fort Leavenworth, Kansas. The other five hundred members of the tribe were deported to Florida, the only state that would agree to take these Indians with a reputation for being fierce warriors, which they did because they saw them as a tourist attraction with the potential of bringing in a lot of cash. Harlyn nods. Uh huh. Meanwhile, Miles opted for a new tactic. Harlie Bear suddenly pushes open the glass door of the service center.

"What are you doing? We've been waiting for you!"

Harlyn looks sorry. He didn't notice the time go by. It's always like that when he's looking at old photographs, Harlie Bear reminds him. Geronimo and Crook go politely back in his wallet. He whispers by way of reassurance that he'll show me the other photos later.

We climb back in the car. In the rear seat lie the remains of two bags of candy. The girls didn't waste a second. Shania, still chewing, has already opened a third packet. Caramels. Harlyn takes one. Not me. He starts the car again. I ask him to go on with his explanation, impatient to learn the final tactic used by General Miles to corner his great-grandfather. No response. Harlyn has put on his blinker, checks the traffic before setting off, looks right, looks left. The dangling turquoise follows each head movement. No cars in sight? Nope. We head in the direction of San Lorenzo. He prepares to answer me now, but his jaw's a bit stuck. The girls burst out laughing. The caramel has done its work. I tell Harlyn he's going to lose some teeth. . . .

"And, you know, in Mongolia, when a shaman loses his teeth, they say he's also lost his 'power.'"

He's shaking his head. Then, with a final grimace to get rid of the caramel, he tells me that even with no teeth, Apache shamans retain their power.

"The only way you can lose it is if you don't respect it. Then the power can get angry and even kill the shaman. But you know that already."

He swallows, then resumes his story about General Miles. His tactic was to send two former warriors for whom Geronimo had a lot of respect to his camp. They probably would have a better chance than anyone else of convincing him to turn himself in. So, with an escort of only six men led by an officer, they left for Mexico. When Geronimo saw the two men approaching his camp, he wanted to kill them. But he recognized his brothers in arms. Unable to fire at them, he let them approach. It was August 1886. His former companions proposed that he hand himself in. Geronimo and his men would rejoin the members of their tribe while they waited for the government to decide their fate. If they didn't, they would be hunted down to the last man. The soldiers were everywhere, and they didn't stand a chance.

Geronimo told them that he and his men would surrender on the condition that they wouldn't be hanged and would be able to live on the reservation with their families as they had in the past. The officer told him that he had to give himself up with no conditions. His kin had been sent to Florida anyway. If he didn't surrender, he'd lose all hope of ever seeing them again.

"Do you know how we say, 'It's my house' in Apache?" Harlie Bear asks me.

"No, how?"

"*Shi ku yai.*"

I say it: "*Chekouyi.*"

The girls start laughing. Harlyn spells it out slowly. *Shi-ku-yai*! I repeat, correctly this time. Again the sound of candy wrappers. I don't know how they can eat so many sweets. I ask Harlyn what Geronimo's decision was. With the tip of his index finger, he massages his forehead between his hat and his sunglasses with a circular motion. He then puts his hand back on the steering wheel, ten-and-two as always.

"My great-grandfather," he finally answers, with his subdued voice, "was shaken by the news that his family had been deported to Florida. So he assembled his men in a kind of council, after which he told the officer that they'd continue to fight unless they could negotiate the terms of their surrender directly with General Miles. The officer refused. So the next day, Geronimo had no other choice but to surrender. All the men were tired of being separated from their families. They wanted to rejoin them and finally live in peace. The only one who wanted to keep fighting was my great-grandfather, but he had to bend to the will of his warriors. Still, he continued to try to define the conditions of his surrender with Miles."

He clears his throat a little and speaks louder.

"The officer ended up yielding, and General Miles, alerted about Geronimo's arrival, offered to meet at Skeleton Canyon, a corridor between Mexico and Arizona about thirty miles south of what is now the town of Douglas, Arizona. Miles arrived there on the afternoon of September 3, 1886. He promised Geronimo and his men that they wouldn't be harmed. They would simply be taken to Fort Bowie and would then rejoin their families in Florida. He also promised they would be given a house, livestock, land, and tools to cultivate it and later permitted to return to their territory on the Gila River. The surrender ceremony would take place the following day."

"Do you know words in Mongolian?" Shania asks the moment she's swallowed her caramel.

I do. To say "yes," you say, "*Tim.*" Harlyn says it first, perfectly. The girls too.

"And how do you say 'no'?" Harlie Bear asks.

"*Ogoui.*"

A chorus of *ogoui* and *tim* begins behind me. I don't know if it's because of this sudden Mongolian ambiance, but I think of my drum in the trunk. I ask Harlyn if he uses a drum during ceremonies. Sometimes. A small one, about a foot in diameter. I tell him mine's in the trunk. Much bigger, three feet in diameter and eight inches deep.

"I can do a ceremony if you'd like."

The turquoise stone goes yes, yes, then no, no. Too dangerous, he ends up saying, suddenly stern.

"I'd be glad to watch one in Mongolia but not that you to do one here. Your spirits might disturb the Apache ones."

"Once I moved about like the wind.
Now I surrender to you and that is all."
GERONIMO
(quoted during his surrender to General Cook)

"I will quit the war path and
live at peace here after."
GERONIMO

"The songs and prayers will always
beat at the rhythm of the Apaches'
hearts."
EDGAR PERRY
(White Mountain Apache and
historian)

Your Last Day of Freedom

THE SUN WAS already starting to set, Grandfather, when a soldier came to get you for the surrender ceremony. You and your warriors followed him to a big ochre rock in the shape of a wolf's fang, lit on only one side by sun, which was now low on the horizon. Its warm, orange tint reminded you for a moment of the skies over the Gila. You missed your river, and the idea of seeing it again, as Miles had promised, of hugging your family to your heart again, made you want to get the ceremony over with as quickly as possible. In five days, the general had said. In five days, you'd be with them. You too were tired of this life as a fugitive, and, for the first time, the thought of living in peace like before seemed comforting. True, you had surrendered, but with honor. Miles had granted everything you'd had asked. He would make sure you weren't hanged, he would give you land, livestock, a house to live in with your loved ones, and you would be allowed to return to your birthplace to die in peace, according to Apache tradition. This time, he would be worthy of your trust. When you told him that the whites had never kept their promises before, he concurred. He even acknowledged all the harm done to Indians and asserted that, this time, he was speaking the truth. He would keep his promises. At least, you dared hope so, and you would keep yours.

When you drew close to the rock with the sharp top, you saw the general standing in the yellow grasses, taller than you, with his white hat on his head. He invited you to come sit on a wool blanket spread on the ground. His gaze was honest, full of respect.

Any lingering reluctance vanished. Before sitting down, Grandfather, you went to get a big stone that you set right in the middle of the blanket. You all sat down, and you told Miles that, on this stone, your pact would be sealed. The pact would last until the stone crumbled to dust.

When the time came for you to swear your oath, you looked around at the landscape one last time. Just to say how grateful you were for it having concealed you, fed you, protected you for these eleven years as a fugitive. That's when you noticed a sumac at the foot of the fang-shaped rock. A rush of joy overwhelmed your heart. One day, you would find your sumac again near the Gila. That's all you wanted from now on: to live in peace with your family, on your land.

You swore the oath. Miles too. He then swept the ground in front of the blanket with his right hand. With that gesture, he erased your past deeds and invited you to begin a new life. Then, the soldiers built a stone monument about ten feet wide by seven feet high, in the center of which they'd placed a bottle containing a piece of paper with the names of the officers in attendance.

The following day, September 5, 1886, you followed Miles to Fort Bowie, accompanied by Chappo, Naiche, and three other leaders. You were heading there for the fourth time, which, as you already knew, would be your last.

The five hundred members of your tribe had been deported to Fort Marion, Florida. Crammed into a space that was far from adequate for their number, in a humid climate, with no sanitation and weakened by insufficient food rations—the Department of War had decided to save on costs—your people very quickly began to succumb to malaria and tuberculosis. At the end of August 1886, two of your own family members were already dead, your four-year-old daughter and her mother, Shtsha-she. But you knew nothing of this, since after your arrived at Fort Bowie, you hadn't been sent to Florida to join them, as Miles had promised, but instead to San Antonio, Texas, where you were awaiting trial. You didn't know either that Ih-tedda had given birth to your daughter Lana.

After your sentencing, you were transferred with Chappo and your warriors, about fifteen men, to Fort Pickens in Florida, on an almost-deserted island. The local authorities were delighted by the arrival of the "famous" Geronimo. You arrived there in October 1886. The fort had been abandoned since the end of the Civil War, but they put you to work refurbishing it. It was very hard work that lasted for months, during which, with no news of your family and feeling once again betrayed by the whites, you had no other recourse than to interrogate your "power." Would it help you? What would become of you? Would you ever see your family again? But it didn't answer. It too seemed to have abandoned you.

The only people who offered some sort of distraction were the numerous tourists who congregated at the doors of the fort to at last view the face of the bloodthirsty Geronimo, whose cunning and cruelty had been described in big headlines by the press. They were led into the compound in small groups of twenty. It amused you to see their disappointment when they discovered you quietly cleaning out the fort's ditches or wells. Maybe you were pleased to make a liar of the press.

At the end of September 1887, Grandfather, your family finally arrived at the fort. What was left of it, at least, for your wives She-gha, Zi-yeh, and Ih-tedda were accompanied by only two of your children: Fenton, son of Zi-yeh, and Lana, Ih-tedda's child, whom you were meeting for the first time. They told you that your daughter, Dohn-say, Chappo's sister, had married and had left for Alabama with her husband and the Indians who hadn't been sent to Fort Pickens. They also told you of the deaths of Shtsha-she and your little daughter. You took Lana, my grandmother, in your arms and rocked her for a long time, as you often did later on, to the great astonishment of the onlookers. A savage was capable of rocking his baby?

Emboldened by your family's arrival, you asked, with Naiche's support, to be given what you had been promised: a home and some land. The officer replied that you should consider yourselves lucky that your lives had been spared by a generous government, which you owed your gratitude. You then asked how long you would be kept as prisoners of war, but no one ever answered. Luckily for you, Grandfather, because the answer was twenty-seven years.

Nevertheless, the officer in charge of the camp made a gesture of good will toward your son Chappo. He found him exceptionally intelligent and wanted to give him a chance to rise above his condition by sending him to the Carlisle Indian School in Pennsylvania. You immediately agreed, happy that an Apache would finally be given the chance to acquire the knowledge and skills of the whites. Your joy, however, would once again be marred by tragedy. Shortly after Chappo's departure, your wife She-gha fell ill with pneumonia, from which she never recovered.

In May 1888, you were transferred to the Mount Vernon camp in Alabama, where you were reunited with Dohn-say, your daughter, and the rest of your tribe, together again at last. But because of the deficiencies in diet and the outbreak of tuberculosis, everyone there was very weak. Out of three hundred prisoners who had been transferred there some eight months earlier, twenty had died already. The camp's officers didn't seem concerned about it, though. They found nothing better for your health than to situate your dwellings in a low valley closed in by trees and with no light. It was an extremely unhealthy place, in which, Grandfather, you used to say that the only way to see the sky was to climb to the top of a very tall pine.

Each house consisted of two rooms, with a hard-packed dirt floor and log walls whose chinks you had to fill in with clay to protect yourselves from the cold and humidity. It was poor shelter, though, for despite your best efforts, there was mold everywhere, absolutely everywhere. On food, clothing, moccasins. You occupied one of these houses with Zi-yeh, Fenton, Ih-tedda, and Lana. With no furnishings apart from a woodstove, you had to sleep on boards and eat on the ground. It was cold in winter, hot in summer, and humid all year round, and yet once again your complaints were ignored. However, public opinion on the fate of the Indians began to shift. Organizations started to take shape that would come to your assistance and force the authorities to moderate their treatment of you.

In early 1889, two missionary women were sent by an organization that was friendly to the Indians to set up a school in your camp. You were an enthusiastic supporter, Grandfather. You brought your children to class in the morning and spent a lot of time there, applying the strict discipline that you had used in the past to help form young warriors. You kept order in the classroom, armed with a switch to curtail any attempt to misbehave.

Yet, living conditions in the camp remained catastrophic. Your people simply couldn't adapt to the excessive humidity of the region and, within two years after your arrival, a quarter of you had succumbed to various epidemics of tuberculosis, pneumonia, diarrhea, and malaria. Public opinion and organizations in defense of the Indians were more and more appalled by the conditions in which you seemed to have been abandoned. They started pressuring the government again, which finally agreed to send a few of you to the Mescalero reservation in New Mexico. You immediately decided to separate from Ih-tedda, whose tribe that was, and from your daughter Lana. That seemed your only chance to save their lives. Ih-tedda at first refused. In Apache tradition, separation meant divorce. But you were adamant, and, in February, they finally left for Mescalero accompanied by a group of about ten other members of the tribe. Shortly after arriving there, Ih-tedda remarried.

Under pressure from the organizations, the government finally freed up funds to build a hospital and new homes for the Apache prisoners at Mount Vernon. You were quickly able to settle in a small wooden house, this time furnished with beds, chairs, a table, and wooden floors, with Zi-yeh, your son Fenton, and your last baby, Eva, who was born in autumn 1889.

Tourism didn't really exist in the area, but the passengers who came by train to the nearest city became customers for the crafts that you were now allowed to make. You threw yourself in this commerce, Grandfather, and, with your innate business sense, it has to be said you made good money on the bows, arrows, quivers, canes, and other objects you fashioned with great skill. One day, a tourist asked if you'd sell him your hat, a sort of deerskin skullcap decorated with beads and silver ornaments representing the sun, the moon, the stars. You hesitated, but he offered you a lot of money, so you sold it to him. When he held it in his hands, he asked if you'd write your name inside, as if your signature would give it incalculable worth. Your name was the only word you knew how to write, so you agreed. But as you drew the letters one by one, you thought maybe you could make him pay a little extra for this gesture, in which he seemed to put so much value. The tourist paid without protest. You said nothing, but when he left, obviously extremely proud of his purchase, you realized that your name, which had become legend, was an asset. Never again would you fail to make people pay dearly for it. Your own small act of revenge.

And you would need it because, once again, tragedy would strike. In 1893, your son Chappo, who was still at the Carlisle Indian School, contracted tuberculosis, which continued its rampage, especially among young people. He was allowed to come join you in Alabama, but this son, in whom you'd placed so many hopes, died in your arms shortly after his return. Of all your children, only Dohn-say, Fenton, Eva, and Lana, who was in Mescalero with Ih-tedda, still survived.

9

The girls are asleep in the rear. Maybe because of the sound of the flute. Harlyn had put a disc in the CD player as soon as the road started to wind around Spirit Canyon. It was a narrow, dark place but full of hummingbirds. My favorite bird, Harlyn says, and Geronimo's too. Geronimo often roamed the depths of this canyon, where the sorcerer whose gaze his mother had forbidden him to meet used to live. "Do you remember?" Yes, of course. And I've even begun to guess where we're going. But this time I don't ask, probably to allow Harlyn the pleasure of surprising me. And I could be wrong. We've just reached a high plateau dotted with small junipers and gray rocks. The sound of the Indian flute surrounds us, very sweet. Lulled by its notes, my gaze scans the ravine to our right, skims the cliffs, follows the eagles that are spiraling in the updraft of hot air. In my loins I can feel sensations like when I used to go hang gliding. Harlyn tells me that he plays this flute too. Geronimo also played it during his captivity. It was a way for him to escape to the land of his childhood.

"Do you see the forest in the distance?"

I look at the dark mass in the raking light. The road winds toward it, running alongside an impressive drop-off. He adds that he likes listening to this music when he comes to this area, and then falls silent again, apparently lost in his memories. I watch his white hat move ever so slightly in time to the swells of the music. His lips are moving too, which gives the impression that he himself is blowing into the flute. Maybe he's imagining himself playing a duet with his great-grandfather. As though in response to my thought, he says that sometimes, when he plays, he feels like he can see Geronimo smiling at him. He glances over at me.

"And if you know how to listen, the sound of this flute has the power to open the window between the two worlds."

He again stares at the road, which is now bordered with tall trees. Accompanied by this soundtrack, we quietly enter the forest like a sailing vessel gliding over the asphalt. "Look," he says, pointing to my side of the road. I turn my head and suddenly spy a sign that reads GILA NATIONAL FOREST. So I was right. My eyes about to brim over, I look at Harlyn. "We're in Geronimo's homeland, aren't we?" He nods slowly, almost solemnly.

"I'm taking you on the trip he dreamed of so much. We're going to his birthplace."

On the left side of the road, I notice a small lake, fed by a river. The Gila? Yes.

"That lake is still a sacred place for the Apaches."

All of Harlyn's descriptions from the beginning of our journey come back to my mind. Thanks to him, to his way of having me relive it all, I feel like I'm about to see Geronimo appear, there, around that bend, hidden just behind a bush, tracking a stag.

"Look, beside the river!" Harlyn shouts suddenly.

I turn my head. The girls wake with a jolt. There's a doe over on the right, just where the woods begin above the road, with brown coat, its neck extended toward a young fir. Harlyn cuts the engine. Now only the sound of the flute accompanies our delighted gazes, which are all directed toward the animal. Harlyn activates the electric window. The doe has turned her head in our direction. Its nostrils begin to quiver, its body gathers itself as if to flee, its hooves slightly flexed, and poof, she leaps onto the road. In two bounds, she crosses to the opposite side, into the shadow of some undergrowth, then looks back at us one last time and flees toward the river.

"There's another one by the water!" cries Harlie Bear.

Our eyes search for it. Yes! In a patch of sunlight, in the middle of drinking. We see the first doe coming to join her. As if she'd warned her of the danger, they walk away together, glancing back at us. Harlyn starts the engine again, all smiles. I ask him if he ever hunts deer like these.

"Of course. And stags too. But not here. It's against the law now."

"You mostly hunt rabbits!" Shania corrects him.

"Always with a bow," Harlyn explains, with a hint of pride in his voice.

I turn to face him.

"A rabbit with a bow? Isn't that hard?"

"Not for an Apache," he answers. "I even teach this hunting technique to the young people on the reservation. A few of them are actually becoming quite good. I'm also teaching them how to track. To get close to an animal without being spotted is a much harder exercise."

He takes a long look around, probably searching for another doe. But, finding nothing of note, he stares at the road again. He was twelve when he was taught these hunting techniques, he continues. He learned to compare paw prints and analyze broken branches, flattened grasses, and the direction of the wind so that creatures wouldn't be able to detect his scent. Once, he took half a day just to go a few yards. But he learned patience and observation, qualities that are increasingly rare nowadays. A glance in the rearview mirror. There's a car right behind us. He pulls a little farther to the right to let it pass. The road's narrow here.

"You understand why I insist on passing them on to our young people," he continues. It's because Geronimo knew how to wait for the right moment that he was so often able to escape the soldiers keeping an eye on him. By studying them, he knew their habits, their rhythms, their weaknesses, the moments when they let their attention wander. It was like watching prey for him, and his hunting skills came in very handy."

The car passes. It's some sort of large white 4 x 4. With a hand signal, the driver thanks Harlyn for letting him pass. I ask if Geronimo was a prisoner in Alabama for long. Eight years. Their group became so weakened by illness that the government decided to send them to Fort Sill in Oklahoma.

"They went by train," says Harlie Bear. "And the whole ride, people gathered by the tracks just to see Geronimo and clap for him."

Harlyn avers with a smile. Like they did in Alabama, people wanted to go home with a souvenir, and at every stop they'd ask him to sell them a button from his shirt, a moccasin, or even his hat. Anything would do. So he cut off his buttons and sold them one at a time for twenty-five cents. For five dollars, he'd hand over his hat. People were fighting over them. Between each stop, he'd sew on more buttons and put on a new hat. That really annoyed the authorities and the military, who were incensed at the thought that a "murderer" could be the object of such acclaim. They were also afraid this enthusiasm would reawaken his desire to escape and regretted not having hanged him fifteen years earlier. Harlyn removes his glasses and gently massages above his eyes. Do your eyes hurt? A little, he says, when he drives for too long. He needs a new prescription. After putting his glasses back on, he resumes his story.

The prisoners arrived at Fort Sill in October of 1893. The Comanches and the Kiowas, who lived in that territory, came to welcome them. They were put in little wooden houses in small villages. Geronimo was named the leader of his village and was charged by the officer of the camp to try and sentence misdemeanors committed by any of the prisoners.

"He was super strict," says Harlie Bear.

"It's true," Harlyn confirms. "He even gave a hundred years' detention to an Indian who had stolen a saddle!"

I look at him, surprised.

"And the sentence was actually enforced?"

"No! He was asked to moderate his sentencing. But it wasn't his fault. In the Apache tradition, theft was punished with banishment, which was the equivalent to a death sentence, since in those days a man couldn't survive alone in the wild. But he soon understood that the times had changed and no one ever criticized his judgments after that. People would come to him regularly to solve their slightest problems."

"He also grew watermelons!" Shania interrupts, looking at her grandfather. "Do you have the picture?"

Harlyn asks me to open the glove box.

"Each prisoner owned a little parcel of land," he continues. "And my great-grandfather became an excellent farmer. It's worth noting that the land had never been cultivated, so it was very fertile. Did you find it? It's a little black album, underneath the cell phone."

I find the cell phone and ask what it's doing in the glove box, since he doesn't use it. A shrug of his shoulders by way of an answer, like, *That thing gets on my nerves*. Harlie Bear, sounding exasperated, confirms that it's true. He always forgets it, and when we need to reach him, we can't. Ah, there's the album. I close the glove box. Harlie Bear asks me to hand it to her. She opens it, flips the pages.

"It's this picture, look."

I see Geronimo wearing a work jacket and pants, standing in a field with trees at the edges. He's holding a huge watermelon with his left hand and a hat with his right. His hair is tied in a ponytail. I recognize the same piercing gaze, sun-chiseled face, high cheekbones, closed mouth like a horizontal line, and a slightly protruding lower jaw.

"The woman and little boy next him, who are they?"

She's wearing a long white skirt and a black tapered shirt with white designs, dots or flowers, I can't tell. She too is cradling a watermelon in one arm. The little boy is barefoot and wears a dark shirt and short pants.

"That's Zi-yeh, his wife, and their son Fenton," Harlyn answers. "Geronimo doesn't know it yet in this picture, but they'll soon die of tuberculosis."

I look at him. "Again?" He nods. Death rates remained very high, and his great-grandfather became more and more alarmed to see his people dwindling like that. He said, if Yusn had created the Apaches, it was because they had some purpose. Yet he was convinced that an uprooted Apache couldn't survive for very long, and the only solution was to bring them back to the Gila River area, to their native land. He never stopped imploring the authorities to let them return. But to no avail.

"Do you know what the soldiers of the camp called him?" Harlie Bear asks me.

"No."

"Gerry! But he really didn't like it. The soldiers knew that, and they called him that on purpose."

I flip through the album and stop at a picture of Geronimo posed standing next to the horse of another Indian, who is tall and gaunt. Both are wearing a vest, a shirt, a pair of pants, and a hat.

"Your great-grandfather is dressed like a cowboy in this picture?"

"Yes, he is with Naiche, Cochise's son," Harlyn answers without diverting his eyes from the road. "Do you see the lasso on the horse behind them?"

I look at Harlyn, surprised.

"Do you know each picture by heart?"

"He spends hours looking at them," Shania says mockingly.

Harlyn responds with a smile, and goes on. When they arrived at Fort Sill, the Apaches had no cattle. So Congress disbursed some funds to buy them some livestock. For their part, they had to learn the work of cowboys, how to lasso, brand, care for the animals. His great-grandfather liked that part of his job, but he appreciated much less the fact that for the most part the profits from the sale of the animals were placed in a fund for the Apaches that was controlled by the government. He thought it unjust and complained about it to the officers of the camps. Nothing came of it, of course. Harlyn adjusts his hat.

"But my great-grandfather was able to earn compensation of some kind. One day, an artist was sent to Fort Sill by the president of the Field Museum in Chicago to paint Geronimo's portrait. My great-grandfather's first reaction was to find out how much he'd be paid for the work of sitting. The painter let him decide the amount, and after some reflection, he agreed to pose for three dollars, but on condition that the painter do two portraits. The deal was struck, Geronimo received his six dollars, and on top of that he managed to sell the artist some craft items signed by him. All in all, a really good deal for the times!"

I smile.

"He had an innate sense of marketing, didn't he?"

"That's for sure, and according to Kate, his wife, my great-grandmother, he enjoyed making money. On his death, they discovered that he had eleven thousand dollars in his bank account!"

"Look," cries Shania, "there's another deer over there, by the water!"

'Iłk'idą, dák ǫǫ da yá'édįná'a.

Ditsį naaki łi' niiyá sitágo łi' hikáshį́ 'óó'ágo baa'nádaa'shdiłhisgo book ǫ hanádaaji'áná'a.Ditsį 'áłts' ǫǫ ségo daajiyaak'ashí dá'áí 'Itsįįsbéézhí beehadaajindííłná'a.'Itsįį́ tsíghe'yá jiłt'eesgo 'iłdǫ́ dá'áíbee nábé'ijiyałtsiná'a. Ditsį dáha'á'áłts ǫǫ séí bighe' hadaa'jich'iishí dá'áí gobee'nłndédíná'a. Ditsįntsaazí 'idaas'áí nanshį́go ditsįdijoolí baadahnaas'áį́ bighe' hadaa'jiłndii dá'áí daago'ide'ná'a.'Ikałí 'iłdǫ́ daago'ide'ná'a.Dákí gostł'ish 'isaa 'ádaajilaí beedaa'jiłbéézhná'a. Gahée yá'édįná'a.'Ádą́, 'ik'aneída, gołką́ądeída, bihóóleída, díídíí díík'eh, yá'édįná'a.

K'adi, dá'át'égo nahidáń gólį́í beenndá'ádáį́ baanáágoshndi.

Díídíí:

'Inaada, goshk'an, nshch'į́, 'ighe'éłtsoi, gołchíde, chíłchį, hosh-jishóhé, 'inaadą́ą́', dziłdaiskáné, niigoyáhé, naastáné, hanóósan,'iigaa'e, dzé,'ináshtł'izhee, tséłkanee, deek'oshé dach'iizhé, diłtałé, yóółndáhé, tsinaasdo'é, chííshgagee, gah, góóchi dá'ákodeyáí, téjółgayé, łį́, náa'tsílidiłhiłí, dibéhé, dá'ákodeyáí, ts'isteeł.

'Ádíídíí díík'eh nahidáń.'Áí nahí doobaayándzįda. Jooba'éndéłáį́ yee'isdahóóka.

Long ago, we lacked even fire, so they say.

The Indians had the custom of making fire with two sticks. One was laid on the ground while the other, held vertical, was spun against the first one, so they say. They took the boiled meat

198

from the pot thanks to a thin pointed stick, so they say. With the same stick they turned the meat roasting in the coals, so they say. Their spoons were a kind of slim sticks into which they had carved a hollow, so they say. Their cups were protuberances in the shape of bowls that grew from the trunks of large trees and that they had hollowed out, so they say. Their plates were made of dried skins. They cooked in clay pots that they themselves had made, so they say. We had no coffee, so they say. In those times, there was not even flour, sugar, and beans, so they say.

Now, I'll tell you what food they had to live on.

It was this:

Mescal, yucca fruit, piñon nuts, acorns, prickly pears, sumac berries, cacti, corn, mountain plants, wild potatoes, mesquite beans, yucca blossoms, yucca flowers, wild cherries, honey, blackberries, salt, deer, wild turkey, squirrels, prairie dogs, rabbits, elks, peccaries, mules, horses, bison, bighorn sheep, and turtles.

All this was our food. We're not ashamed of it. Many poor people could live thanks to this.

The Hunt

THE ARROW YOU were testing for sturdiness in front of your house at Fort Sill abruptly broke, Grandfather. These reeds definitely couldn't compare with the ones from the Gila. From the Gila reeds, both supple and hardy, you could make arrows whose accuracy allowed you to reach the most unattainable of targets. All of a sudden you smiled, imagining yourself hunting, all those years ago. There was a doe on the sandy shore, her coat shining in a ring of sunlight, her neck stretched toward the water. The herd often came to drink in this little cove where the Gila grew shallow. Your body hugging the ground, hidden behind the reeds and tall grasses yellowed by the sun, you had spotted this creature all by itself. Inch by inch, since daybreak, you'd been working your way toward her, watching her slightest movements to make sure she hadn't sensed your presence. Ever since you were little, you had been taught to view each animal as an adversary worthy of the deepest respect and, during your first hunts, a warrior had even followed you from afar to make sure you were comporting yourself strictly according to the rules. To kill an animal without causing it to suffer, for example, a hunter was allowed only one arrow. Once, though, you needed three to kill a stag. After that, you had to practice your archery skills for three moons before you were allowed to start hunting again. As he did before each expedition, the shaman then smoked some sage, blessed you with pollen, and prayed to Yusn to give you the mental strength to succeed. The doe had just turned her head in your direction. Had she seen you? No. She walked quietly toward a creosote bush. Her beige coat blended with the earth's hue, making her nearly invisible. Was it to provide her with a chance to evade her predators' eyes that Yusn had given her coat that color? Your enemies never saw you arrive either. You swooped down on them and the shock kept them nailed to the spot as surely as a flash of sunlight in the eyes. When you were close enough to the doe, you adjusted your arrow very slowly and stilled your breathing. The moment you let the arrow fly, the animal brusquely directed her head toward you. Her gaze fell on yours, as if she had understood she would die. As if she had already accepted it. Her body tottered from the impact. She collapsed. With a single leap, you knelt before her to thank her for kindly having offered you her life. Then you said a prayer to Yusn to thank him for help-ing you. Alope would be happy. You would have food for several days. She would cook part of the meat on a piece of wood placed over the fire or would boil it with yucca flowers. The hooves, the liver, the tongue, and the entrails would be placed on the embers, covered in ash, and cooked for a day and a night. The rest of the meat would be cut up in thin strips that she would hang in the sun to dry. You would eat it during raids, along with mescal leaves or mesquite beans, your favorite vegetable.

But what remained of this today, Grandfather, of all your moments of happiness, of those delicious flavors and the reeds of the Gila? Just a few mesquite trees that you've spotted on your arrival at Fort Sill, already five years ago now, and these memories that suddenly emerged from your mind while Zi-yeh was prepar-ing mesquite beans for you. You raised your head, put the broken arrow down next to you, and sighed. Out of your old habits, at least you'd been able to keep calling your horse with a whistle. Seeing him come with his ears back gave you the same pleasure as in old times. But you no longer displayed your archery skills. Except for bets. You would then pin a piece of paper the size of a coin onto a tree and invite strangers to compete against you. Each of you in turn stepped a few yards away to try and hit the center of the paper. You were able to hit the mark every time. This skill at least earned you a fair amount of money. It was your only satisfaction, really, because fate, despite your prayers, was continuing to hound you. What was your "power" doing? Why had it abandoned you? The members of your family continued to die, one after the other. Even Dohn-Say, your daughter by Chee-hash-Kish, had just died of tuberculosis along with all her family. Only her son, your grandson Thomas, had survived. Terrified by the idea that he too might succumb to that accursed illness, you begged the authorities, once again, Grandfather.

"We are vanishing from the Earth," you had told them, "yet I cannot think we are useless or Yusn would not have created us. He created all tribes of men and certainly had a righteous purpose in creating each.

"When Yusn created the Apaches, he also created their homes in the West. He gave them the grain, fruits, and game as they needed to eat. To restore their health when disease attacked them, he made many different herbs to grow. He taught them where to find those herbs and how to prepare them for medicine. He gave them a pleasant climate, and all they needed for clothing and shelter themselves was at hand.

"Thus it was in the beginning: the Apaches and their homes each created for each other by Yusn himself. When they are taken from these homes, they sicken and die. How long will it be until it is said, There are no Apaches?"

Unfortunately, this prayer failed to move the authorities, Grandfather. They still wouldn't grant you permission to return to the land of your ancestors.

10

Now the road runs alongside a campground next to some hot springs. Harlyn tells me that we can stop there on our way back. The girls scream with joy.

"You'll see, you're in the water among rocks that are like bathtubs," Harlie Bear explains.

"And there's steam coming from the water," Shania cries, overexcited.

I ask Harlyn if the Apaches have a ritual connected to water, like a sort of baptism. His head says no. A baby is blessed with pollen, and that's it. The only ritual still practiced is the one I wasn't able to attend at Mescalero, the puberty rite. And as soon as they have their first periods, Harlie Bear and Shania will be initiated as well.

"It lasts four days, and the whole family is invited," Harlie Bear explains.

"At least two shamans supervise the ceremony," Harlyn continues. "A man and a woman. The woman shaman is responsible for teaching the young woman the principal rules of behavior, which she'll have to practice all her future life as a woman."

"What rules?" Harlie Bear asks.

"You'll find out at the appropriate time, but for now you're still a little girl."

Harlie Bear bows her head and sits back into her seat. Out of solidarity, I suppose, Shania does the same. With a worried look, studying her thighs, she starts to trace with her finger the contour of each flower sewn onto her jeans. With five of them on each leg, that's going to take a while. Especially since she's going at it with the same meticulousness as her grandfather.

"The first morning before dawn, the girl is dressed in her ceremonial costume," Harlyn continues.

I ask him if he's allowed to describe it. He says with a smile that in fact he is allowed to describe it to a non-Indian.

"It's made from five pieces of pure buckskin. Two for the tunic, two for the skirt, and one for the moccasins. The sleeves and the bottom of the skirt are adorned with fringes, and the tunic is decorated with beads."

"Do the shamans also have a costume?"

"Just traditional dress. A fringed shirt or tunic, pants, and a headband on their forehead. Do shamans have costumes in Mongolia?"

"Yes, supposedly to protect them from evil spirits. A kind of coat that used to be made of skin but is now made of fabric. On the back there are braided strands of nine different colors representing the ninety-nine elements of the shamanic world. The sky, the sun, the earth, the wind, etc. There are also little metallic pendants that symbolize pieces of the sky, and little bells to allow the spirits to express themselves."

Harlyn shoots me a glance.

"Express themselves?"

"Yes, their tinkling during the ceremony is proof of the spirits' presence and their desire to establish contact with the shaman."

Now he shakes his head affirmatively, gaze fixed on the road, which once again is straight. In the back, Harlie Bear is drowning her sorrows in the last bag of candy, which she's sharing only with her cousin, the sole person here who understands her. I smile discretely—they're really funny together—and then I continue. The shaman also wears a kind of boot made of animal skins and a feathered hat with a fringe that covers the eyes.

"Why a fringe?"

"It's supposed to protect the shaman's eyes from the evil worlds that he or she might cross before arriving in the spirit world."

"Who are your favorite movie stars?" Shania suddenly asks, having swallowed her last piece of candy.

"Tom Cruise and Jennifer Lopez," Harlyn answers.

Shania taps me on the shoulder. "And you?" Me? I ask her if she knows any French movie stars. She frowns. Nope. Harlie Bear and Harlyn don't know any either and simply shrug as a sign of total ignorance on the subject.

"My favorite movie is *Ben Hur*," Harlyn says finally.

My eyes must betray my bewilderment.

"The classic by William Wyler?"

"Yes, yes, I love it! Gladiators, the circus, all that stuff. As a matter of fact, I'd love to be chosen one day to carry the Olympic flame."

The girls start to chuckle. Harlyn sighs, as though lamenting this lack of support for his dream. Then he returns to the topic of the puberty rite. Once the young woman is prepared and dressed, she's led into the big ceremonial tipi with two women from her family. The shamans then chant some prayers that she has to dance to for four days. It's a very physical and exhausting dance that the young woman has to endure without complaint.

"Her first duty as an adult, in a way?"

"Yes, to have a mind of steel."

"Does it really hurt?" Harlie Bear asks, suddenly worried.

"Yes, but the women around her are there to massage her legs. And anyway, becoming an adult is painful, and the goal of the ceremony is simply to make the young girl understand that. After four days, believe me, she has become a young woman who is conscious in her flesh of how difficult it is to act like an adult."

There is the sound of paper crumpling, and Harlie Bear swallows another piece of candy. Probably to console herself for that horrible vision of her near future. We're now driving along prairie meadows where horses graze. I ask Harlyn to explain the stages of the ritual. His turquoise stone follows the movement of his head. No. He's sorry, but he can't tell me more. OK. I ask him if there's a ritual for boys too.

"A small one, yes, just for those close to him. The shaman blesses the boy and gives advice for his future life as a man."

"Harlie Bear has a boyfriend!" shouts Shania.

"That's not true," her cousin corrects, jabbing her with an elbow.

"It is so, it's true. His name is Charly. But he's not in love with her."

Harlie Bear sinks back into her seat and crosses her arms, aiming a murderous look at her cousin. Harlyn is visibly struggling to keep from bursting into laughter. I turn to Harlie Bear, who's staring fixedly at a spot on her window, and attempt to break the ice.

"You know, in Mongolia, there's a ritual to force someone to love you."

She's still staring fixedly at the window. I go on.

"It's a very secret ritual, but I can tell you a little bit about it if you like."

This time, she turns to face me, seeming all of a sudden very interested. That's what I like about children, their ability to change moods. I tell her that you first have to steal three strands of the boy's hair, then have a ceremony during which, among other things, you play the drum while asking the spirits to cast a spell on him so he'll fall in love with you.

Harlie Bear frowns, apparently thinking at a furious pace. Shania opens her mouth.

"But if the spirits get it wrong, the boy can fall in love with another girl, right?"

Harlyn and I burst out laughing. Not Harlie Bear though, who shifts her gaze to me as if urgently awaiting an answer. I assure her that the spirits can't get it wrong, but even so, to do this ritual takes a big sacrifice.

Silence in the car. All ears are attuned to my lips.

"You give up five years of your life."

"Five years!" exclaims Shania, turning to her cousin. "Well, then you better like him. I'd never do that for a boy."

Harlie Bear just shrugs. Harlyn, a smile lifting the corner of his mouth, announces that the Apaches have a similar rite. The girls look at him with wide eyes. But it's not considered a spell, he explains. Anyone can attempt it. You just need to have something that belongs to the person you want to woo. A piece of clothing or a hair, for instance.

"Like in Mongolia, then," says Harlie Bear.

"Yes. But you also have to put a caterpillar in the boy or girl's bed before doing the ceremony."

"A caterpillar! That's disgusting!" cries Shania, sticking her tongue out.

Harlie Bear, not wanting to lose track of this fascinating discussion, asks her to please stop interrupting her grandfather. Harlyn, content with the effect of his words, resumes his explanation. Next you have to say a prayer to the sun because its rays can spread like a spider's web and entangle a person. Lastly, you chant the butterfly prayer, using a little cord.

"A cord? Why? And how do the prayers go?" Harlie Bear asks, eager to glean all the practical information she can.

But Harlyn refuses to provide a single answer. She's perfectly capable of managing without it. Harlie Bear looks disappointed, and Shania says that, anyway, she doesn't care about boys, so she doesn't care about the ritual either. Which earns her a fresh elbow from her cousin. A fight is brewing, but Harlyn quashes it curtly. Silence returns immediately. His eyes fixed on the road again, he tells me that Geronimo asked for the authorization to organize a puberty rite at Fort Pickens in Florida when he was a prisoner there. The officer in charge of the camp gave him permission but treated the ritual as a barbaric custom and invited three hundred tourists to attend. His hat swivels toward me.

"Can you imagine the ambiance?"

I can imagine, yes. He goes on:

"The people were laughing, making fun of their cries and their customs, calling them savages. I'm telling you this so you can understand how the Indians came to have a commercial interest. For the whites, going to see them was something like watching a wild animal in a cage. A guaranteed thrill, but without risk! For example, the rumor that reached Fort Sill before Geronimo's arrival had it that, when he was captured, he had been in possession of a blanket made of—"

"Of the scalps of white men and women sewn together!" Harlie Bear interrupts with a grimace.

No reaction from Shania, who's still refusing to have anything to do with her cousin. Her index finger has begun tracing the edges of the embroidered flowers again.

"Of course, that aroused the curiosity of the whites," Harlyn says, "and Geronimo quickly came to embody a real commercial stake."

We arrive at a kind of village. Just a few wooden houses, a large rectangular building selling Apache crafts, and a fast food restaurant in front of which two chairs, two tables, and two parasols are set up. The place is empty. Harlie Bear would like to stop here. Shania abandons her flowers momentarily, but this time Harlyn refuses. It'll be night soon, and we're nearly there. More crumpling of candy wrappers from the back seat by way of rebellion. I ask Harlyn how his great-grandfather was "commercialized."

"Simple. They put him on a poster promoting different events in order to guarantee their success. He first experienced it in 1898."

That was the year of my grandmother's birth. "When I was born," she always said, "France was rocked by the Dreyfus Affair. Emile Zola had just published J'accuse, it was the tenth anniversary of the invention of the bicycle, the Eiffel tower's twentieth, and in Paris the inauguration of the first auto show." I tell this to Harlyn, who doesn't seem to understand my sudden emotion.

"Isn't it funny though? That Geronimo and my grandmother would have been able to go bicycling together?"

He smiles. To indulge me, I think. He doesn't seem to understand that, for me, it's as though time had suddenly shrunk together. Geronimo was there just before my grandmother. She was even eleven in 1909, the year he died. But she was raising cattle deep in the Landes region of France. It would have been impossible for her to cross the Atlantic. I'm still moved, though. Harlyn appears to be waiting for my inner computations to conclude. I apologize and invite him to continue. I'm anxious to hear the next part of his story. After favoring me with a smile, he resumes.

"The city of Omaha asked the officer in charge of Fort Sill for permission to invite Geronimo to the Trans-Mississippi & International Exposition, the world's fair in 1898, to be the 'main attraction.'"

"Did he agree?"

"Yes."

"And Geronimo too?"

"For the money, yes, he ended up going! During the event, he earned some extra money on the side, and he was even very friendly with all the people who crowded around him. Driven by his own curiosity, he observed everything, learned, asked questions."

We arrive at a fork in the road. Harlyn looks into the rearview mirror, gently engages the blinker, steers the car onto the small road on the left, and resumes his account. His great-grandfather also took advantage of those expositions to plead for a return to his native land. In Omaha, for instance, he was able to meet with General Miles. It was their first encounter since Skeleton Canyon. He had solicited a meeting many times, but the authorities had never let it happen. Now he could finally tell the general what he thought of him. He accused him of having deceived him and having made false promises to convince him to surrender. Miles, with a big smile, admitted that he had lied, but only once. Whereas, he said, Geronimo had never stopped lying to the Mexicans and the Americans.

"And was Miles able to help with his return to the Gila River?"

"Geronimo asked him, but he replied that the inhabitants of that region absolutely did not want to see him return. Now they could sleep soundly at night, without worrying about Geronimo coming to rob or kill them."

"A producer even offered to put him on tour for months to act in a show," says Harlie Bear.

The Wild West Show, Harlyn says. But the War Department would never agree. They only allowed Geronimo to go to expositions. In 1904, he also went to Saint Louis for the world's fair there. He was put in one of the booths in the Indian pavilion where you could watch the members of different tribes engaging in traditional crafts. He made bows, arrows, and quivers. In the booths next to him, Pueblo Indians made pottery and baked bread. His wife, Ih-tedda—Kate—had also been invited. But since she still lived on the Mescalero reservation, she was in the New Mexico pavilion, which was profiting from her former husband's renown to promote tourism. Harlyn clears his voice.

"Kate often spoke of that exhibit. She and Geronimo saw people they'd never seen before. Turks, for instance. Geronimo was very impressed by their way of fighting with scimitars. She also remembered a tribe from the Philippines whose men barely wore any clothes. He was amazed they'd been allowed to display themselves almost naked."

"And he was even in a parade with President Roosevelt," says Harlie Bear.

"In exchange for a check for about a hundred fifty dollars," Harlyn adds, smiling at me.

That meeting took place in 1905, he continues, during Roosevelt's inaugural parade in Washington. Geronimo, who had been chosen to represent the Apaches, had marched along with five other Indians from different tribes. According to Kate, all eyes were on her husband. Only Roosevelt attracted as much attention. But, thanks to the parade, Geronimo finally realized his wish of meeting with the president. He knew it was his one and only opportunity to plead to the country's highest authority for his return to his native land. Harlyn's head bobbles a bit. Unfortunately, Roosevelt answered that the people of the region didn't want him back. But he promised to speak about it with the commissioner of Indian Affairs. A shrug.

"Of course, the military authorities refused. But the following summer, maybe as a way of making amends, Roosevelt authorized Barrett—"

"To write Geronimo's memoirs, which I read?"

"Yes, Barrett spent about a year with my great-grandfather to collect them. Since Geronimo didn't speak English, it was Asa Daklugie who served as interpreter. Geronimo chose him because not only was he the son of his sister Ishton and Juh, the Chiricahua chief who had fought alongside him, Mangas Coloradas, and Cochise, but also Asa had spent eight years at the Indian school in Carlisle and had perfectly mastered the white tongue. Anyway, in the preface, my great-grandfather made a point of thanking Roosevelt for allowing Barrett to make the book and publish it. Of course, its contents were subject to the military authorities, if you see what I mean."

Yes, I do, but I don't have time to say so before Shania's deep voice suddenly rises, finished with moping at last.

"Do you think Geronimo used the ritual?"

Harlyn asks her which ritual she's talking about, but Harlie Bear answers in her stead, having understood exactly what her cousin was referring to.

"The one that makes people fall in love!"

Harlyn smiles, before reflecting a moment.

"Kate never told me, but . . ."

A mischievous smile begins to form at the corner of his lips. Three pairs of ears prick up.

"When Geronimo wanted to seduce a woman, he always tied a bag of mint around his neck."

"Mint?" Harlie Bear echoes, dreamily. "So is that why?"

"Why what?"

"Well, why he had so many wives!" Shania answers, like, *Duh. You're slow.*

Trying to muffle his laughter, Harlyn gets out a "maybe." Shania turns to Harlie Bear, eyes filled with dread.

"Are you going to do it to Charly?"

This time she gets a slap on the mouth. Shania is about to hit back, but, in a very firm tone, Harlyn squelches the outbreak of the hostilities. Harlie Bear sinks back into her seat, but not without another death stare at her little cousin, who sticks her tongue out before focusing once more on the embroidered flowers. The calm restored, Harlyn sighs with satisfaction, content to pick up the thread of his story again. After his interview with President Roosevelt, Geronimo was conveyed back to Fort Sill, where a happy event was to cheer him after his failure. His daughter Eva had just turned sixteen, and he had received permission to organize the puberty rite, this time without spectators.

K'eeshchí sahde 'ájílaa,
Chí sahde 'ájílaa,
Dleeshí sahde 'ájílaa,
Jígonaa'áí bitł'óle sahde 'ájílaa,
Bik'ehgózhóní,
Ts'is'ahnaagháíÁ Bik'ehgózhóní.
Bíká'ájił'įį.

K'eeshchíí yeenidleesh,
Bik'ehgózhóní.
Ts'is'ahnaagháíÁ Bik'ehgózhóní.

Chíí yeenichí,
Bik'ehgózhóní,
Ts'is'ahnaagháíÁ Bik'ehgózhóní.

Dleeshí yeenidleesh,
Bik'ehgózhóní,
Ts'is'ahnaagháíÁ Bik'ehgózhóní.

Jígonaa'áí tádídíń yiłdahdałndi,
Jígonaa'áí bitł'óle yiłdahdałndi;
Shá noóyáshį; ndiibik'izhį nkéńyá,
Goch'įįńyá.

SONG FOR THE PUBERTY RITE

The poles of the tipi have been made with galena*,
The poles of the tipi have been made with red clay,
The poles of the tipi have been made with white clay,
The poles of the dwelling tipi have been made with rays
of the sun,
His power is good,
Long life! His power is good.
And for Her, traditionally, they do it this way.

He will paint you with pollen,
His power is good,
Long life! His power is good.

He will paint you with red clay,
His power is good,
Long life! His power is good.

He will paint you with white clay,
His power is good,
Long life! His power is good.

He holds in the air his hands painted with pollen,
He holds in the air his hands painted with the sun's pollen,
The sun has come down, has come down to earth,
He has come down to Her.

* Lead sulfate.

The Puberty Rite

THE SUN HADN'T yet risen, Grandfather. Sitting on the wooden step of the stoop of your Fort Sill house, you listened to the silence of the night, thinking about the day ahead. Eva was excited and a little anxious too. She knew that the four days of the ceremony, during which she would be the living personification of White-Painted Woman, the mother of the Apache people, would be a real test for her. But she was brave and strong, and you knew she would pass it without showing the slightest sign of weakness. Just as she had overcome the death of her mother, Zi-yeh, and her brother, Fenton. You were so afraid she too would succumb to tuberculosis. Eva was your sunshine, as cheerful, bright, and full of life as the waters of the Gila. Would you see it again with her one day, that land of your childhood? You were seriously beginning to doubt it. Even President Roosevelt hadn't been able to obtain the permission of the Department of War. You would have to get used to the idea of dying at Fort Sill, in this little wooden house, on this land fenced in by barbed wire. But you quickly chased away this thought when you saw the stars beginning to pale. It was time to wake Eva. The first day of the ritual, she had to be wearing her ceremonial dress before the light of the sun touched her skin. This dress was considered a duplicate of the one White-Painted Woman had worn during her earthly passage. The whole time it was being made, you prayed for it to grant Eva a long life, and you blessed it with pollen, whose role in being dispersed in the air is to connect the Earth and Sky.

Your sister Nah–dos–te would prepare Eva for her future life as a woman. No man could be present for this preparation. Before the ceremony, Eva had brought her an eagle feather. She presented it four times to your sister, already an old woman then, who had taken it four times. From that day on, Eva would call her "mother" and Nah–dos–te would call her "my daughter."

Barely awake, having eaten nothing, Eva washed her hair with soap made from a yucca root base. Nah–dos–te next put pollen on her head, traced a line across her nose, and prayed for her life as a woman to be the best possible. It was time to dress her. Eva's outfit, cut from five skins dyed yellow, the color of pollen, had been decorated with beads representing the sun and a crescent moon, the forces that must act in Eva's interest. After having placed her facing east, Nah–dos–te put on her, in order, her right moccasin, the left one, her skirt, and then the fringed tunic. In the skirt's fringes, on the right side, she tied a carrizo stem with which Eva was supposed to drink for eight days. For, touching water with her lips risked causing rain to fall. On the left side, Nah–dos–te tied a stick so Eva could scratch herself if she needed to. Because, during this same period, scratching yourself with your nails could leave scars. She then tied two eagle's feathers into her hair, at the back of her head. From that moment on, no one could address your daughter using her given name. Instead they had to call her White-Painted Woman. She would wear this outfit for eight days.

Nah–dos–te then drew a pollen cross on some yucca fruit, presented them to the four directions, turned four times around Eva, and put the fruit in her mouth. In this way, her whole life, she would have a good appetite. Nah–dos–te also told her daughter how she should comport herself during the ceremony. Whatever happened, she must remain in good spirits, eat very little, speak little, and avoid laughing or making fun of anyone, or she'd end up with lots of wrinkles early on. In order not to remove the traces of pollen, she mustn't wash herself either during the eight days that she wore the costume of White-Painted Woman. If it rained, she mustn't go outside, or it would rain like it had never rained before and the ceremony would be ruined. She mustn't look at the sky either; otherwise the rain clouds would gather and cause a terrible storm. Nah-dos-te also gave her the required advice for her future life as a woman: her duties as a wife, how to satisfy her husband, and how to take good care of her home.

While these preparations were taking place, you and your friends, Grandfather, were expected to put up the big ceremonial tipi, which for this occasion symbolized White-Painted Woman's dwelling. At sunrise, the trunks of four young freshly cut spruces, cleaned of branches except at the top, were placed in the form of a cross in the meadow in front of your house. They would form the frame of the tipi. After having blessed them with pollen, you bound their tips together with a buckskin strap and attached two eagle feathers to it. Then you said a prayer and were helped to lift the poles and place their ends in the holes that had been dug for that purpose. You put the first pole in the hole to the east, the second to the north, the third to the west, and the fourth to the south. Your beloved nephew, Asa Daklugie, was then able to begin the opening song for the ritual. He would accompany each key moment of the ritual in the same way, an important role you had insisted on entrusting to him as affirmation of your family bond. His parents, your sister Ishton and Juh being deceased, you truly considered him your spiritual son.

When the frame had been erected, the women brought dishes of mesquite beans, boiled meat, and mescal and yucca fruit, which they laid out to the east of the tipi. The singer, Asa, drew a pollen cross on each dish and you ate.

After the meal, some oak branches were tied between the poles and sheeting laid over them to cover the structure, leaving an opening to the east. Inside the tipi, in the center, you dug a hearth for the fire, and the women brought spruce needles to the entrance of the tipi. Asa and his helpers spread them over the ground. The home of White-Painted Woman was ready.

Nah-dos-te emerged from the house, followed by Eva. You watched your daughter with admiration. She had become a beautiful young woman. So far from the baby you used to rock beneath the shocked gazes of tourists who came to observe you at Fort Pickens. You so wished that Zi-yeh and Fenton could have been here too to share this moment. Why did fate keep harassing your family so much? Why had Yusn chosen the cruelest way to make you suffer? Eva now walked with her head held high, pride in her gaze and supple body. A true Apache. Without a smile, she traversed the path to the tipi. Her solemn manner in performing the ritual moved you to tears. You saw yourself as a teenager again, on the day when, with this same solemnity, you had been admitted into the circle of warriors.

In the southwest corner of the tipi, your sister spread the skin of a young stag, on which she set a basket full of bags of pollen and all the objects necessary for the ritual. Eva knelt on the skin. After having thrown pollen to the four directions, your sister drew a line with it on Eva's face, from one cheek to the other and over her nose. The line of guests then took their place on the south side of the tipi. Each in turn had to draw a line of pollen across Eva's face, and in exchange she drew one on theirs. During the ceremony, the young girl transformed into White-Painted Woman was thought to possess healing powers, and this gesture was to bring luck, heal, or keep illness at bay. After this, Eva lay down, her face against the ground. Saying prayers for her to have a long life and good health, your sister then rubbed her from her feet to her head and then right to left.

Eva stood up. On the skin of the young buck, Nah-dos-te drew four pollen footprints into which Eva had to step, starting with her right foot. Walking this path would bring her luck and good health. The basket containing the bags of pollen, ochre, spikes of grama grass cactus, or papyracanthus, a piece of turquoise, and a stag's hoof was then placed in the east of the tipi. Your sister invited Eva to run to it and go around it in the same direction as the path of the sun. Then she raised the basket and shook it to the four directions to scatter from each one all of the illnesses that might affect her.

During this time, the women of the family emptied baskets of fruit and seeds behind the skin on which Eva was seated. Mixed together, the fruits now replaced the traces of pollen, and the seasonal cycle was symbolically complete.

It was midday. The beginning of the ritual was over.

Food was passed around to the participants, and your daughter, White-Painted Woman, made herself available to the mothers who wished to present their children to her. By lifting them to the four directions, she was thought to bring them luck and good health.

At the end of the day, a big fire was lit in the meadow. Asa lit the fire in the hearth at the center of the big tipi. It would stay lit until the end of the four days of the ceremony.

When the sun began to set, the *gans*, the masked dancers who symbolized the Spirits of the Mountain—men only—started to prepare themselves. Every night during the four days they would dance to bless the camp and chase away the evil spirits. The whole ceremony (songs, dances, and prayers) was thought to bring luck to all of the guests. With yellow, white, and black pigments, they painted their face and torso with geometrical motifs. Zigzags, four-pointed stars, triangles. They wore deerskin kilts, tall moccasins, and straps of skin decorated with eagle feathers and tied above their elbows. To accompany them in their preparations, you lit a sage cigarette while facing east, blew the smoke to the four directions, then played the drums while singing prayers.

Once they were dressed, the gans spat four times inside their masks, a cowl made of skin that was pierced with three holes for the eyes and mouth, mounted with wooden slats in the form of three-branched candelabras, and decorated with black, yellow, and green triangles. They raised the mask four times above their heads before putting it on, thereby transformed into the Mountain Spirits. From now to the end of the ceremony, none of the guests was allowed to touch them, point at them with their fingers, or amuse themselves by trying to recognize who they were, under penalty of falling ill or dying. Arriving one after the other from the east, the gans took their places around the bonfire. When their chief extended his arms, they began their ritual dance around him, accompanied by drums and the sacred chants of the musicians.

> The chief of the Mountain Spirits
> The home above the sky, the turquoise cross,
> That is where the ceremony began.
> This fulfills me. This fulfills me.
> The tips of his horns are made of the yellow dust of the Mountain Spirits.
> Thanks to them, you can see in every direction.
> To the south, the home made of yellow clouds,
> That is where the Spirit of Big Yellow Mountain lives.
> Yellow clouds come down toward me, and the turquoise cross.
> The ceremony has begun.
> This fulfills me. This fulfills me.
> Human beings were created.
> The Spirit of the Big Black Mountain to the north is made of black clouds.
> His body is made of the black mirage in the sky.
> The ceremony has begun.
> He is fulfilled in my place. I am happy.

During this time, at the back of the big tipi, Nah-dos-te had spread out a skin. Eva entered, circled the hearth, starting from the east, then went to sit on the skin, her torso held straight, her legs folded under her, a little to the side. Asa, the singer, handed her an eagle's feather. She took it in her right hand and in exchange gave him a rattle made from a stag's hoof, which he shook before walking backwards while singing, to go sit to the south of the fire. Your sister sat behind him, your close friends sat to the west, and you, Grandfather, placed yourself at the entrance of the tipi to recite prayers. During this time, Asa set the different ceremonial objects in the ritual places. A piece of oak wood symbolizing long life, grama grass cactus spikes intended to sweep away diabolical influences, and a sort of wick made from juniper and yucca stems, symbolizing the hearth and the fire. With this wick, Asa lit the sacred sage rolled in a tobacco leaf. After having smoked part of it while reciting prayers, he passed it to your sister. Then, to the rhythm of the rattle, he began to sing four chants symbolizing the four stages of life: childhood, adolescence, maturity, and old age. All of this symbolized the journey through which White-Painted Woman was led, during the course of the seasons, into her sacred home and through a long and full life.

During the chanting, Eva got up to dance. Arms horizontal, elbows bent, hands on her shoulders, legs and ankles close together, she pivoted her feet with her toes then with her heels, from right to left and from left to right, following the rapid rhythm of the rattle. The chants were long, and Eva wasn't supposed to stop dancing before they ended. But Asa was watching her and varying the duration of his chants according to Eva's endurance. The aim was not so much to wear her out as to prove her mental strength. You, Grandfather, saw your daughter's features gradually grow taut with exertion, but nothing in her gaze expressed the least weakness. When Asa finally ended his chant, just long enough to smoke a sacred cigarette and sing a prayer, Eva went to sit down. Nah-dos-te massaged her knees, ankles, and feet, swollen from the effort. This first day, Eva danced only part of the night. But each day she had to repeat the exercise for longer each time, and on the fourth night she would dance until sunrise.

As soon as the first rays appeared, she was at last made to kneel on the skin of the young stag, her body turned toward the east, facing the sun. Nothing and no one could place themselves between her and the star. Asa began the twelve chants to close the ritual, then, after sprinkling pollen over his face and head, he put some on Eva. Nah-dos-te had mixed white clay with water, and Asa traced a line of this clay onto Eva's face, then another of red ochre. He turned again to the east to begin the red paint chant and, with a sliver of wood dipped in pollen and a powder of galena, or lead sulfate, he drew a sun and its rays in Eva's left palm. Praying, he placed Eva's hand on her head as if to impress the pollen drawing exactly where the sun's rays made her hair shine, then with white clay he painted her face, arms, and legs as far down as her knees.

During this time, Nah-dos-te returned all of the ceremonial objects to the basket. Then Asa traced four footsteps onto the buckskin and asked Eva to walk in them, starting with her right foot. At the end of the four steps and the four chants, she placed herself at the front of the skin to allow the guests, in turn, to step in the four tracks. Your sister then put the basket a few yards away from the tipi. After a signal from Asa, Eva ran to it and circled it four times, the last time to give her strength and endurance when running. Then the gans, the Mountain Spirits, chanted the prayer of the last day of the ritual.

> I will sing this song that is yours,
> The song of long life.
> Sun, I stand on the earth with your song;
> Moon, I have come here with your song.
> White-Painted Woman, your power shows,
> White-Painted Woman carries this girl.
> She carries her through a long life.
> She carries her to good fortune.
> She carries her to old age.
> She carries her to a peaceful sleep.
> You have set forth on the good earth.
> You have set forth with good moccasins.
> With moccasins of rainbow you have set forth.

With moccasins of sun you have set forth.
Amid plenty you have set forth.

The ceremony over, Eva walked back to your house, Grandfather. She still had to wear her White-Painted Woman costume for four days without washing herself.

On the eighth day, her last task was to offer a horse to the singer. The men then began to dismantle the tipi. The posts were placed toward the east and abandoned. Under no circumstance would the wood be used for fire.

The ninth day, before sunrise, Nah-dos-te mixed yucca root with warm water, then washed Eva's hair, face, and body, which still bore its paint of white and red clay.

White-Painted Woman was now a beaming young woman.

11

The purr of the motor is the only sound in the car. The girls have fallen asleep again, and Harlyn, behind his glasses, appears lost in thought. The turquoise at his ear dumbly reproduces the movement of the shock absorbers, oscillating lazily. If I had a wolf's senses, I might hear it clicking. When I'm a wolf, during a trance, I have the impression of hearing the thoughts of the body before me. And of the surroundings too. As if suddenly I weren't an "I" anymore, enclosed in my ego, but just a particle of water in the ocean again. The waves go through me, I rise, I fall, information circulates, no more than a current to which I'm finally not impervious. Yes, everything speaks. What we call silence here is in fact the sound of a large conversation. Perhaps the one of the spirit world that Harlyn talks about. How that information circulates, on what platform, remains to be determined. Through atoms, electrons, or what-have-you. But it's there, right under my nose, of that much I'm certain, and my brain has the ability to hear it. My head bobs. My brain follows its movement. It's going *boing boing* against my skull. *Booooing booooing*. Harlyn puts his sunglasses back on his hat, squints a bit, scrutinizing the sides of the road, and smiles as though he has finally found what he was looking for. He parks the car on the shoulder covered with tall yellow grasses and signals for me to get out. The girls don't even wake up when the engine stops. Once outside of the car, he points to a mountain range far in the distance above the road, to the west. The Mogollon Rim, he tells me with a voice somewhat veiled with emotion.

"Where Geronimo received his 'power'?"

He nods, smiling. In silence, we let our gazes caress those sacred mountains. In the light of the setting sun, they seem covered in a soft fur of dark green. I imagine Geronimo up there. Waiting for a sign from Eagle. I imagine him at Fort Sill, watching Eva's puberty rite, dreaming of the day when he'd finally be able to bring her here. The light of the setting sun colors the land around us—the very round hills peppered with pines, the junipers, the yuccas—a pink that borders on ochre, warm and dark. It's the same pink found in the stones of Thoronet Abbey in the south of France, a magical place lost in the silence of a sea of green oaks. I spent hours holding my ear, my eyes, my heart to its walls, hoping to feel the sound of the stone cutters, their voices and hammers, imprinted since the eleventh century in those pink walls as porous as blotter paper. I imagine that this ochre land of the Gila, like the stones of the abbey, must hold within itself the memory of Geronimo. It received his steps, his prayers, his anger. His words. The only living memory of his time, could it tell me maybe the emotions he inscribed there? Yes. And suddenly, I want to press my ear against it. To listen to his memories. Hear his regrets. Was Eva able to return to this land of her ancestors, as Geronimo had hoped? The strident cry of a bird of prey traverses my thoughts. As if he'd divined them, Harlyn tells me that Eva never got to know this place. Small shrug. A sign of regret or powerlessness. Uh huh.

He turns on his heels and walks over to a plant with tall stalks and thin, long light-green leaves growing out of them. *I-ah-i*, he tells me, the plant Geronimo used to heal wounds received in battle. It moves me to see it here, as if suddenly it had leapt out of Geronimo's life to appear in mine. A small blink narrowing the time-space continuum that divides us. Harlyn cuts a few stalks. I hold them to my nostrils. Scentless. He takes a few more steps and squats before a tuft of what might be thyme but whose branches and leaves are more supple and fine.

"Here's the Apache tea I told you about at the motel!"

I come closer. The little threadbare leaves, in the shape of a fan, are soft to the touch.

"We infuse them, either fresh or dried, in water. You can pick some."

I cut a stalk, raise it to my nose. The leaves smell a bit like anise, but very slightly. Harlyn picks two large handfuls for his wife, Karen. I scoop up the bottom of my light blue tunic to hold my harvest. Harlyn does the same with his black T-shirt, and we return to the car. Silence on board. The girls are still sleeping. After having deposited the tea in the glove compartment above his cell phone, Harlyn starts the car again. He tells me he has begun the necessary steps with the government to fulfill his great-grandfather's wish of bringing the Chiricahuas back to their territory on the Gila River. All of a sudden, he brakes. He turns toward me, looking sorry.

"My glasses! I forgot them back there."

I glance at the top of his head.

"They're on your hat."

He smiles, then, starting the car again, admits that he's really too distracted. But Geronimo was too! Toward the end of his life, he'd go looking for a knife that was in his hand the whole time. Azul, his last wife, made fun of him all the time and he'd tell his friends: "See how she treats me!" Some paper crumples in the back. Are the girls awake? Nope. Shania has just slumped onto an empty wrapper. Harlyn resumes his tale. Five years ago, when he was a member of the tribal council, his mother told him about the Gila River lands. The Chiricahuas had fought to keep them. They had shed their blood, had known captivity and exile. Harlyn had to make sure they'd be given back to them. He shoots me a glance.

"The problem is that today the entire area has become a national park. As a result, the restitution process for these lands isn't simple at all. But I've thought about doing it for a long time, and then, about two years ago, with a few Apaches from other states,

I finally began to develop a strategy and take the required steps with Congress.

"And would every Chiricahua be interested in returning to their ancestral lands?"

"On my reservation alone, about two hundred of them would."

"But you told me that there were four thousand of you, so isn't two hundred very few?"

"No, because most other Apaches are Mescaleros now. And they're already on their territory. Unlike the Chiricahuas, who arrived in 1913."

"Why not earlier?"

"Because Congress only enacted the law giving them their freedom in August 1912!"

"1912? So Geronimo died in captivity?"

"Yes, in 1909. For him, unfortunately, the law was passed too late. Either way, in 1913, the government gave the two hundred and fifty former Fort Sill Chiricahua prisoners the choice of staying in Oklahoma or leaving for the Mescaleros' reservation. Three-quarters chose to go and join the Mescalero Apaches, who were kind enough to cede land to them. But symbolically, it isn't ours. The Chiricahuas weren't given anything. They were renegades, don't forget. And today they still call us 'The tribe without land.' So you can understand why I'm fighting so hard for restitution of the lands on the Gila."

"And do you have any chance of getting them back?"

"Lawyers are helping us with all of the various steps we need to take. So far without much success, though."

"But if those steps are successful, what will you live off of here? There's nothing. No casino. No ski resort. No supermarket."

"We're determined enough to overcome those kinds of obstacles."

"Where are we?" a sleepy voice suddenly asks.

I turn around. Shania yawns, looking at her cousin, who also just woke up, with a smile. The fight appears to have been forgotten.

"Are we there yet?" Harlie Bear asks.

Yes, says Harlyn. We're driving along the last stretch of the trip, a plateau peppered with ochre stones, cacti, and dry grasses. Shania, who has a finger in her mouth, grimaces in pain.

"One of my teeth hurts!" she ends up whining, looking at Harlyn.

"If you didn't eat so much candy, that wouldn't happen."

Now an air of concern. I tell Shania that, back in the day, in Mongolia, the shamans had a bizarre way of treating cavities. She looks curious.

"What was it?"

"They poured hot yak butter on the cavity to soften it, and then . . ."

Three pairs of ears perk up.

"They put worms on the tooth so they'd eat the decay."

There's an explosion of *yuuuks* in the back. Harlyn bursts out laughing. I tell them this method was used for a long time and I turn to Shania.

"It was really effective, you know! Show me the tooth that hurts."

Screaming, she puts a hand in front of her mouth. Harlyn smiles, looking pleased. My method should put her off candy for a good hour at least.

"Grandfather was in a movie!" Harlie Bear says abruptly.

I don't see the tooth connection, but I turn to Harlyn, who confirms that it's true. He played the role of a Cheyenne chief in a series produced by Steven Spielberg, *Into the West*. It's on TNT and retraces the whole period when the colonists arrived in the West, the negotiations, the wars, the treaties with the tribes, the creation of reservations. But for the first time, told largely from the point of view of the Indians.

"Do they talk about your great-grandfather?"

"Not really. The series focuses more on what happened in the Great Plains, with the Sioux and the Cheyenne."

He stops speaking. Apparently reflecting.

"To get back to Geronimo," he says finally, "after his daughter Eva's puberty rite, during the winter of 1905, he married a fifty-eight-year-old widow. But it didn't work out, and they separated the following year."

"Did he stay single?"

"No! He married Azul, another widow."

He motions me to open the glove box.

"Take the album. There's a photo of her. Geronimo liked her."

I open the glove box. No album. I turn toward the girls. Harlie Bear is rooting with her hand behind Shania, who grumbles.

"But you're sitting on it!" Harlie Bear tells her.

Shania moves over begrudgingly. Yep, the album's under her rump. Harlie Bear takes it, flips through it, and hands it to me.

"It's this photo."

I see Azul and Geronimo posing, very rigid, in front of a wall. They're squinting, probably because of the sun, but they're staring straight into the camera. Azul has long black hair with a center part, which reveals a large forehead. She's wearing a black adjusted corset, with a white collar and fastened with little buttons and a black skirt long enough to cover her feet. She seems tiny. Geronimo is two heads taller than her. He has his hands in his pockets, is wearing a round hat, a jacket, a vest, a white shirt, and a white scarf, tied with a bow around his neck.

"Azul was with Geronimo for the last three years of his life," Harlyn explains.

I look at her again. Her left arm hangs by her body, one hand is placed on her lower abdomen, she has a droopy mouth, and the tip of her nose deviates off to the right. A grimace at the moment of the picture, perhaps? Geronimo's mouth always seems to resemble a large "minus" sign and his aged forehead is marked with three deep wrinkles.

"So he never came back here, to the Gila?"

"No. But he fought for his people to be allowed to return, until his very last breath."

"So it's also to honor his last wishes that you're so keen for the Chiricahuas to return to their lands?"

He agrees.

"Is there anything else you want?"

He raises his sunglasses onto his hat, as though having them in front of his eyes was preventing him from thinking, then holds his breath for a second before beginning to speak. His voice rides on his held breath for a second.

"I'd like for our tribe to function as an independent nation. With real sovereignty, as was the case two hundred years ago. Today, the American government sticks its nose in everything, tells us what to do, and how to do it, and still doesn't consider us equal to the whites or give us the same advantages. I just want all of that to stop and for our tribe to live independently, making its own decisions about the future of the Apache nation."

"Do all Apaches share your opinion?"

"They know their lands were stolen, and, like me, they don't take too kindly to the government sticking its nose in our business."

"But how can you consider independence when the government finances all of the infrastructures on the reservation, and, like you said, unemployment is at thirty percent and the rate of alcoholism is at thirty-five?"

Harlyn's head goes *No, No.* As if my analysis of the situation were grossly mistaken. In his mind, this catastrophic situation would change if the Apaches stopped acting like dependents of the government and if the government stopped keeping them in that position. Drowning in their own fat, constantly fed advertisements for beer or fast foods, day in, day out, they've lost the will to fight for their nation. Or to find solutions to become the strong, proud people they once were. He clears his throat.

"But solutions do exist. I'm fighting for them! We must first become financially independent, which would ensure free rein for the reservation over all management decisions. Of course, we have that ability to be financially independent, with the operation of the casinos and ski resort, but we could also develop businesses like farming and our natural water resources. And like I told you, we must absolutely re-inculcate our customs to the younger generation."

"But how many of you are ready to take that path? You live like every other American, you eat the same food, you watch the same TV shows, and even you dress like a cowboy!"

His hat pivots again from right to left. *No, no.*

"For the majority of us, even if we appear American, our spirit is still the same as our ancestors'. Whenever we can, we ride our horses, we breathe in the clear air of the mountains on the reservation, we reconnect with our customs, our love of nature, deer, bears, and of our great church, the sky. You must write this in your book!"

He looks at me, as though expecting confirmation, then continues, his voice more and more sonorous.

"I can assure you that our appearance is deceptive. It's as if we were playing a role, as if we were actors. So, okay, we live in two separate worlds, but in each of them we try to respect our Mother, the Earth. She is sacred. I'm also fighting so that at least our homes won't be polluted." He clears his throat. "In 1991, for example, the former tribal president allowed the American government, which had promised financial compensation and infrastructural projects in exchange, to conduct a study that would have resulted in nuclear waste being stored on our lands."

"In Mescalero? Nuclear waste? Where?"

Harlyn smiles at my sudden concern, then reassures me. They didn't let it happen, so there's no risk in walking around on the reservation. He explains that the authorities often act like this with toxic waste, targeting the lands of poorest populations and consequently the most vulnerable ones and most likely to take their money. Which still hasn't stopped most of those populations from refusing their offers or at least hesitating over them. He lets out a long sigh and continues:

"But at the time, the tribal president rushed to accept the Department of Energy's offer without consulting any of the inhabitants on the reservation and gave this as an excuse, and I quote: 'The Navajos make carpets, the Pueblos make pottery, and the Mescaleros make money.'"

Harlyn looks at me.

"See what we're dealing with?"

I nod. He continues.

"Thankfully, the members of the tribe massively opposed this project and joined me in the opposition, of which I'm one of the leaders. In 1995, we also obtained a referendum, which rejected the authorities' offer by a majority and at the same time rejected an economic future limited to reprocessing toxic waste and operating casinos."

His voice comes down a notch, as if he were about to reveal a secret to me.

"Do you know what we've been calling the tribal president ever since?"

I shake my head.

"Chernobyl Chief!"

He bursts out laughing. Me too. Then he resumes, serious again.

"But, as you can imagine, the whole business didn't end there. Some members of the tribal council, still 'motivated' by the nuclear authorities, drafted a petition to organize a new referendum. Then they based their campaign on the promise that radioactive waste could bring in some two hundred fifty million dollars for the tribe and that each Apache would receive two thousand dollars if the new vote were in favor of the project. This time, they succeeded in their plan. By nearly six hundred votes against three hundred fifty, the tribe voted for negotiations to be reopened."

"But you told me the waste isn't buried on your lands?"

"It isn't! I fought in the opposition until 1996 to stop the project. And it's a good thing we did because the nuclear authorities,

232

tired of all the complications, ended up finding another reservation in Utah. Which wasn't a reason to end our fight. As you may have noticed, their policy of 'dividing to rule' is very effective and succeeded in causing deep rifts in our community. Today, with the election of our new president, Carleton Naiche-Palmer—"

"A descendent of Naiche, Cochise's son?"

"Yes, he's the great-grandson of the chief and speaks Apache. With his election, maybe all this will calm down. At least, I hope so. But I still have my doubts, and I'm continuing my fight with the members of our tribe. It's absolutely necessary to convince them to remain firmly determined not to be swayed by the astronomical sums and the promises of jobs and aid that the nuclear authorities will offer in exchange for polluting our lands or taking advantage of them."

Harlyn shoots me a glance, as if to underscore the importance of these last statements.

"It's really vital for us Indians. Without that firm determination, the Federal government, invoking who-knows-what national interest, could end up deciding to break the law that still allows tribes full authority over their territory, just as it often did with treaties in the past. And that would be dreadful, because then we'd have no other recourse."

He swallows, shoots me a fresh glance, but this time to see if I have appropriately gauged the importance of his fight. Yes. And I will also highlight it in the book. Apparently satisfied, he starts again.

"To come back to something a bit more general, today with our Western lifestyle we're destroying and wasting more than we need to. Forests are disappearing, the air is polluted, the hole in the ozone layer is growing, the climate is changing, chemicals poured into rivers and then into oceans are killing all of the marine animals, breaking the biological equilibrium and the food chain. The Western world is digging its own grave. It's what Geronimo predicted. But we don't want to dig ours as well."

He lifts up his hat. Sweat is beading on his forehead. He wipes it off with his index finger, puts the hat back into place, and starts again.

"Like most Indians, the Apaches have always taken only what they needed, which is very little, to live in harmony. So my dream for our future is to help perpetuate this respect of traditions and manage the reservation that way. Let's say, a first step toward reestablishing a balanced economy and thereby announcing our independence."

Harlie Bear's right hand appears between my shoulder and Harlyn's.

"Can you give me back the album?"

I hand it to her. She tips back heavily in her seat. Shania, bouncing a little, emits a grunt while looking at the road.

"Yep, we're almost there!"

The car turns onto a paved parking lot surrounded by pines, junipers, and yuccas. I'm surprised. Is this really the goal of our journey? We drive past a white rectangular building. A welcome center, says Harlyn, and a museum about the prehistory of this region. Shania, arms raised, is redoing her ponytail. Harlie Bear pushes the rebel strands of her hair behind her ears and pulls the bottom of her pink T-shirt over her jeans. She doesn't like it when you can see her tummy, Shania teases, lifting her own shirt up to show off hers. But Harlie Bear doesn't react. She simply unbuckles her seatbelt. Harlyn parks the car in front of the building. It's surrounded by lawns dotted with pines, yuccas, and chollas, cacti in the shape of deer antlers. I enjoy recognizing them now, as if they'd handed me a little piece of their history. But I'm having trouble believing that the site of Geronimo's birth has become a parking lot. No, we'll certainly take a little path through the pines, yuccas, and junipers. *The Gila makes a buckle where you were born, Grandfather*, Harlyn said. No buckle and no river here. The girls get out. Harlyn tells me to follow them. He has to change. To change? Why? He simply smiles, motioning me to join them.

I swallow my disappointment and questions and open the door. The girls skip ahead on the asphalt, seeming to know exactly where they're going. I follow them. The dry, end-of-day air smells like a pine woods, because the needles heated by the sweltering sun have released their resin scent, a final mechanism of defense. I inhale deeply. I absorb it. I swell. I shrink. My disappointment. I glance at the girls. They've just stopped in front of a small mound of large gray and pink stones, held together by some sort of cement that's also pink. Probably some type of aggregate the earth produces here. They're looking at something I can't see. I go closer.

"Wait!" shouts Harlyn, getting out of the car.

I stop in my tracks. Still wearing his white Stetson, he runs to join me. He's now sporting a turquoise shirt of a shiny fabric, decorated with ribbons and white geometrical shapes. He has also swapped out his jeans for a pair of black pants, with a black leather belt that has a large oval silver buckle. Once he's beside me, he stops to catch his breath. The turquoise hanging from his ear is making big ellipses. I ask him if his shirt is traditional Apache wear. Yes, it's a ribbon shirt, he explains. Apaches wear it for gatherings or ceremonies. With the mischievous air of a child about to spring a nice surprise, he takes hold of my arm and draws me to the little mound.

I suppress a sob in meeting your gaze when I come to your memorial, Geronimo. Time and distance suddenly vaporize between us. As if you'd been waiting here, hidden in this famous photograph posing as a warrior, to play this prank on me with the help of your descendent. Loincloth, tunic, and tall moccasins, a knee to the ground, your rifle held in both hands, you seem to be watching me. Now, a tear does escape from my eyes. I wipe it off with a swipe of my index finger. And I feel the pressure of the fingers of your great-grandson on my arm. A small gesture to tell me that he understands my emotion. Breathe in. Breathe out. Reassert control. There. The girls seem moved too. Silent, for once, they're standing hand in hand in front of the photo of their ancestor, next to which gold letters declare against a black background:

"I was born by the headwaters of the Gila"
Geronimo
Chiricahua Apache Chief
1829–1909

It's nice seeing them there with such respect in their eyes. Those two certainly won't let the heritage of their traditions fade away. Harlyn takes a little fringed deerskin sack from his pants pocket. The same one he used in the Valley of Fire. He opens it silently, then slips his thumb and index finger inside to remove a small pinch of pollen. Hand raised, facing the photo of his ancestor, locking eyes, legs tight together, body very straight, he begins to recite an Apache prayer. In the quiet of the setting sun, his words acquire a surreal resonance. In their echo, Harlyn seems to take you from his memory, Geronimo, and gently place you here. In fact, now your gaze appears to thank him. Shania's little hand comes and places itself in mine, while Harlie Bear's holds on to Harlyn's. Silence. Silence. Silence. Now I understand the meaning of Harlyn's words regarding our destination. I really feel, I do, like I'm at the place where the past meets the present. The four of us, eyes locked with yours, Geronimo, make promises to you. Mine is to continue this journey to the roots of Apache tradition by taking Harlyn to Mongolia with me one day. That's what you wanted when you appeared in my visions, wasn't it? For Harlyn, it was obvious. You had picked me to reconnect the Apaches with their Mongolian roots.

"You'll take me with you to Mongolia, won't you?" Harlyn asks me, as if once again he had a tap on my thoughts.

I promise. But all of a sudden, he seems concerned. He frowns.

"Is the trip dangerous?"

"No!"

"Are you sure?"

"Of course, why?"

"Race?" Shania shouts at her cousin, pointing at a large pine. They scamper off.

"Are there terrorists in Mongolia?" Harlyn continues.

"No."

"And what about bird flu? Is there any bird flu?"

"Of course not! There aren't even chickens. Enkhtuya has never even eaten an egg."

He nods slowly. Not surprised, but still concerned.

"We won't go in winter, right?"

This time I burst out laughing. Not him. So once again, I promise. The anxiety finally fades from his face, and, his voice full of emotion, he asks me to tell him about Mongolia.

"Like the landscapes?"

His turquoise says *yes, yes.*

"Well . . . There are enormous plains, covered with rivers, lakes, and hundreds of horses. We'll live in Enkhtuya's tipi. In the morning, you'll light the fire in the stove, then you'll take your horse to round up the herds of yak and reindeer. Sometimes, before the sun rises, you'll go off with the men to hunt wolves.

"Wolves?"

"Yes, there are still lots of them, and they're always attacking the young in the herds."

"And what will you do?"

"Enkhtuya and I will gather wood, fetch water from the lake or river, prepare Mongol pasta."

"Pasta? They know how to make noodles?"

"The best I've ever had! Marco Polo is even said to have brought the recipe back to Italy with him after his journey through Asia."

"And are there T-bone steaks too?"

"It's his favorite meal!" says Harlie Bear, who has just joined us, still red from running.

She beat Shania, whom we see dragging in the distance, arms and legs absolutely uncoordinated.

I explain that there's no steak over there. The meat and its fat are cut into strips and dried on small cords above the stove.

"So they still live like our ancestors did," Harlyn remarks. Harlyn appears more and more excited at the idea of soon attempting this adventure.

"Yes, and you'll sit in on shamanic ceremonies. Enkhtuya will explain all the traditions to you. She'll take you to gather medicinal plants and will teach you how to use them."

A broad smile spreads across his face. Shania comes to an abrupt halt in front of us. Looking put out, she slaps her cousin's arm, yelling a furious, "You cheated!" Harlie Bear just shrugs.

"You know," Harlyn continues, signaling Shania to keep it down, "I consider this trip to Mongolia, to the source of our Apache roots, as a further step in my struggle to heal my people. And I'll make it my responsibility to return with those teachings."

He stops, thinks. Shania walks off, moping, to go fiddle with the bark of a pine tree. Harlie Bear goes back to the car. She's hungry. But Harlyn doesn't seem to notice. Still focused, he continues:

"Geronimo has given us a beautiful gift in allowing us to meet, hasn't he?"

I agree, moved.

"But if he picked you, it's surely for another reason too."

I raise my eyebrows and invite him to go on.

"My great-grandfather was buried at the military cemetery of Fort Sill in Oklahoma. His wish, like mine, has always been for his remains to be brought back here one day, to the place of his birth. But a little more than a year ago, I was made aware of a letter in which it is said that Prescott Bush, the grandfather of our current president, George W. Bush, committed a very serious act."

"Serious? What act?"

"I'll tell you, but if this fact turns out to be true, I first want you to promise to talk about it in our book."

"Of course."

He smiles. As though relieved.

"So what they dared do to my great-grandfather will be known publicly. And after that I'll be at peace and we can to go to Mongolia."

"It is my land, my home, my father's land, to which I now ask to be allowed to return. I want to spend my last days there, and be buried among the mountains. If this could be I might die in peace, feeling that my people, placed in their native homes, would increase in numbers, rather than diminish as at present, and that our name would not become extinct. […]

"But we can do nothing in this matter ourselves—we must wait until those in authority choose to act. If this cannot be done during my lifetime—if I must die in bondage—I hope, that the remnant of the Apache tribe may, when I am gone, be granted the one privilege which they request—to return to Arizona."

GERONIMO

Your Last Journey

In the middle of Ghost Face, Grandfather, the water in the torrent you'd just fallen into was truly frigid. Luckily, it wasn't deep where you lay. Luckily, all the whiskey you'd drunk in that poker game still gave you that sweet sensation of being far away, unreachable, out of that body, out of those bones, out of that memory, so tired from eighty years of fighting. Prisoners weren't allowed to drink it, but bottles of contraband circulated on the reservation and sometimes you liked to abuse it a little, refusing to submit to those stupid restrictions to the very end. In the dark night, you pushed against your arms and legs. One last effort to get your body up from the water and walk the short distance to the sandy shore. There. Head finally resting on the bank, you tried to catch your breath. But already you could feel the cold of death beginning its work in your chest. You couldn't help laughing, Grandfather. For the fierce warrior to die after falling off his horse was Yusn's ultimate joke, then? The echo of your laughter drowned in the current's eddy. From the Gila to now, water had marked your life.

When your teeth began chattering from the cold, you asked Yusn to grant you a little more time in this world. You wanted to be able to say goodbye to your loved ones, those who had survived at least. This left only Azul, your wife, Kate, and Eva and Lana, your daughters. Even your grandson, Thomas, at barely eighteen had been claimed by tuberculosis. Though you had placed all your hopes in this brilliant boy, who had been admitted to the best boarding school in the region. Eleven moons had passed since this new tragedy. Unable to get over it, you had begun to suspect that an evil spell had been cast on your family. All the more since Eva, your adored daughter, also seemed to be developing the first symptoms of the disease. You asked a medicine man to perform a ceremony to discover who had cast this evil spell. But after four or five chants, he declared that it was you. You, Geronimo, were responsible. He accused you of having asked your "power" to give you a long life in exchange for your loved ones' sacrifice. You never spoke to him again. It was completely unjust. You would have given anything to go in their stead.

And so there, that night, you were suddenly glad that Yusn was finally granting you permission to die—unless it was the Christian god. After Thomas's death, you had turned to him somewhat. At Fort Sill, Pastor Wright of the Reformed Church was making more and more converts among the member of the tribe. All of your friends, or almost all, had been converted. Including Naiche, the only survivor among your faithful comrades, for Nana and Chihuahua were dead too. Your wife Zi-yeh and Eva, while still a baby, had been baptized. But you, Grandfather, had always hesitated. Yusn had often protected you. He had also punished you cruelly. Did that mean you should abandon him? The pastor had spoken with you about it at length. You told him that your loved ones' deaths gave you the impression more and more of walking alone in the dark. He had finally convinced you to come and attend a worship. You had listened attentively to the sermon, hands flat on your thighs, and were finally convinced that this path toward Jesus and the principles taught by his religion would be the only way to assuage your conscience. The pastor later baptized you.

You tried moving your fingers, but the cold had completely numbed them. You couldn't even feel your legs, your buttocks, or the muscles in your back. Eyes turned toward the starry sky, you tried to hear your horse's presence above the noise of the water. You finally heard its hoof raking the stony ground. He always did that when he was worried. He was indeed there, waiting for you, your old companion. You tried to purse your lips and whistle for him to come. He would come instantly. All of your horses were trained to do that, a practice that had often saved your life in battle. Not on this night. Your completely numbed lips only made these *fffff, fffff* sounds, barely louder than a small draft of wind. Was the cold the most effective prison? Locked inside its grip, only your eyes could still move. If at least your horse had returned to the village . . . But you knew that fool wouldn't leave you. You had trained him to wait, so that's what he would do. Anyway, Azul would grow worried and sound the alarm. You had never come home after nightfall, even when you were playing poker. Unfortunately, she wouldn't be able to come to your aid at night. The road was too dangerous. You'd have to wait until daybreak. Someone would spot your horse, and they'd come to your rescue.

To give you the strength not to succumb completely to the numbness, you recalled again the leaps into ice-covered rivers that you'd had to make during your training as a warrior. That endurance forged by harder and harder challenges, that power of will to dominate your body's suffering, instilled from your earliest childhood, would allow you once more to pass this test. Under no circumstances would you die here. No. Not before you made your final wishes known. Or had prayed to Yusn. And Jesus too. After all, both would bring you, each in his own way, a certain comfort. Religion and mingling with Christians had even improved your character, you used to say. But your "power," it was clear, was much more talkative than their Jesus, who had never answered a single of your questions. Nor did he whisper the prayers or actions you needed to heal the people who continued to come and consult you. The missionaries didn't actually look kindly on those pagan practices, as they called them. So you didn't speak of them. An alert warrior knew how to adapt to a given environment to take the best from it. No one would prevent you from taking the best from each of those practices. Jesus or Yusn, their teachings were a gift simply intended to enrich your beliefs.

★ ★ ★

You were still very much alive when they found you the next day after spotting your horse. As in each of your battles, your will mastered your body's endurance. Once again, you would be the one to decide when to leave the fight. Three days. You needed to hold on for three more days, which was the time it took for your children to make the trip to Fort Sill. On the condition, of course, that they were notified by telegram. Unfortunately, the soldier in charge of the camp sent them a letter. And when Azul told you what he had done, you realized they wouldn't be able to arrive in time. Your strength was diminishing. It would be impossible to fight any longer. One last time, though, you found the strength to become angry at the inability of this army to at least bring you your children. You would so much have liked to tell them how proud you were of them. How they deserved a beautiful and long life. Eva was soon to be married. A happy life would allow her to withstand this illness whose symptoms were already sniffing about her. You felt Asa's hand take yours and the little pressure of his thumb inside your palm. So cold. You could count on him. Yes. He had promised that he would take care of Eva, still so young, as if she were his own daughter. He had also promised to tell her your last wishes. They hadn't granted you the privilege of dying a free man, but you wished that one day the survivors of the tribe would be granted the privilege of returning to their land on the Gila River. Then Lana and Eva would be able to discover the place where, once, their people lived happily and in harmony with nature. And when they got there, Asa would ask them to go and sit in one of those puddles of red earth that looked like the sun's bloodstains. In the very spot where, when you were very young, stretched out on your back, your gaze perched in the sky, the smell of dry grass and rabbit droppings in your nostrils, you felt the exact moment where past and present, suddenly freed from the constraints of time, could meet and all worlds connect. You were almost certain

243

that's where the window between the world of the dead and the world of the living would open. From sunset to sunrise, according to Apache belief, those two worlds were superimposed. It was the only moment where the deceased could communicate with the living and where your girls would come find you.

Although you didn't exactly know into which world you were going to pass, Grandfather. Was it the Apache one or the Christian one? At death's door, everything was muddled in your mind. For the pastor, you were a murderer, and, if you didn't repent, his God had the worst of welcomes in store for you. But what did you need to repent? You had killed only your enemies, and for the Chiricahuas that wasn't a sin. Actually, at night, when the two worlds were superimposed, no enemy ever came to take revenge on you—that was the only time when the dead could come and harm those who had killed them—which meant that they didn't blame you. Killing them had therefore not been a sin. Just the law of war. You had explained this to the pastor, but for him, you remained a murderer. Your chest lifted a bit. Filling it with air hurt you more and more. You still found the strength to smile. A pale smile, at the idea of soon having an answer to your questions. The spirit. The spirit of the man the pastor spoke of, for instance, had remained a completely incomprehensible notion. You had seen many men die, many decomposing bodies too, but you had never seen what they called the spirit. So which part of a man did it refer to? Your chest lifted again. A little less this time. As surely as the sun scorched the flanks of the Mogollon Rim, pneumonia was consuming your lungs. Suddenly, you saw yourself climbing those mountains of the Gila with your mouth full of water, to strengthen your lungs and improve their endurance. How many times had you filled them with air since then? Breathing was an indispensable act, yet you never thought about it. Except when air was becoming scarce. Life was like the lungs. You didn't feel it. You didn't see it. Until the moment it escaped from you. Your chest tried to lift. But the air was unable to enter, this time, Grandfather. The cave slowly closed.

In a final reflex, you squeezed Asa's hand. It was in the land of the Gila, at the foot of the sumac where your umbilical cord was laid, that this journey had begun. Close by is where it should end. But condemned to die at Fort Sill, how were you to close the great cycle of your life? Your lips moved a little. Perhaps a final prayer to fulfill your wish? Like a bow about to let an arrow fly, you felt your whole body tense. Rocking backward, your eyes saw the reed arrow depart for the Gila. Your strength clinging to it, together you went to meet the shores where both of you had been born and where, beyond a doubt, the best and sturdiest reeds grew.

12

Harlyn finishes tracing a pollen cross on his great-grandfather's face, takes a step back, utters a short prayer in Apache, then turns to face me. And my tears start to fall.

"At six A.M., on February 17th, 1909, he left for his last raid."

Inhale. Exhale. With the back of my hand, I wipe my eyes.

"And his girls, what became of them?"

"Eva married the following year. She had a daughter, who died a few months later."

"Did Eva have other children?"

"No, she died in 1911, just a year after her daughter's death."

"Of tuberculosis?"

"Yes. She was buried at Fort Sill, near Geronimo's grave."

I look at Harlyn and then at the photo of the old chief.

"So, of all his children, Lana, your grandmother, was the only survivor?"

"Yes. Lana was the only offspring of Geronimo born in captivity who had any descendants."

Harlyn watches the sun as it disappears behind the mountains. The parking lot is already in shadow. He asks me to follow him. We walk past the car where the girls are disposing of the last pieces of candy. Harlyn asks them if they want to come with us. No. He doesn't insist. He walks along the parking lot, then turns left to take a narrow dirt path. I ask him what finally became of Asa Daklugie. Harlyn turns to face me to answer, interrupting our walk. After he was freed from Fort Sill, he begins, pushing the front of his hat off his forehead, since it's still hot, Asa became a very good stock breeder. He also set down his memoirs in *The Odyssey Ends*, a book he wrote with Eve Ball, a historian born in the 1890s who specialized in the Apaches. His entire life, Asa remained a fervent admirer of Geronimo, whom he said was the very incarnation of the Apache spirit. His death in 1955 marked the end of an era. After having fought with some of the greatest chiefs, Asa was the last Apache— Naiche having died in 1919 in Mescalero—to have known a time when his people still lived free and happy. After an "Uh huh," Harlyn moves his hat back into place and resumes walking.

A few steps farther, I notice a tuft of Apache tea to the right of his foot. I squat down to pick a little, then catch up to him, proudly brandishing my loot. He looks at it sadly.

"You might get serious diarrhea with an infusion of *that* plant."

"It's not tea?"

He shakes his head. He starts walking again without a smile. I bow my head. This apprentice Apache is definitely not ready to graduate yet. Not the Mongolian apprentice either, as a matter of fact. Once, Enkhtuya instructed me to bring back the leaves of a kind of wild onion. The Mongols chop them onto their food, like a condiment. When I returned with my harvest, she burst into laughter. The whole family would be sick on my leaves! In my defense, I told her that they did look a lot like the actual thing. She conceded that they did, but after that incident, my botanical efforts have always been double-checked. We arrive at the top of a small knoll. Harlyn seems to be looking for something. He touches a tree, walks around it, looks at the ground, motions me to follow him. He's walking into the sun, the quarter circle that's left of it, anyway. His body trails a long shadow as if it were following him. I walk at the tip of the shadow, trying to not fall behind, when suddenly I hear a small cracking sound behind me. A broken twig? My head pivots ninety degrees.

Concealed behind a shrub, I notice the girls tracking us. Harlie Bear puts a finger to her lips as a sign to keep quiet. I say yes with my head, then pivot again toward Harlyn, whose shadow is already two yards away. He's walking fast. A short trot, and here I am again at the tip. But the shadow suddenly stops sliding along the stones and becomes still in the middle of a stain of ochre earth surrounded by little junipers and strewn with . . .

"What kind of droppings are those?"

Harlyn looks at me, seeming surprised by my lack of knowledge. But it's not my fault. I was raised in Africa! Still hoping to impress him with my resolve, I squat down to observe closer up these small droppings in the shape of black olives. Harlyn awaits my verdict with a smile. I give up.

"I'm sorry, but the only droppings I know are elephants' and these seem a little too small for them."

He bursts into his staccato laugh. Ta-ta-ta-ta-ta. As choppy as the Apache tongue. Could a language possibly shape the rhythm with which we express our emotions? OK, Harlyn asks, how on earth can I be an expert on elephant droppings? I tell him about my childhood in Ouagadougou, Burkina Faso, where my parents initiated me into this sort of thing, very useful in life. Still squatting, I look again at the little olives.

"So what type of droppings are they?"

"Rabbit!" shouts Shania, jumping into the middle of the circle like a devil on a spring.

I topple to the ground. Harlyn places a hand over his chest as if a heart attack were imminent. And Shania laughs to tears, delighted with the results. The little scamp! And I'd seen her hiding, too. OK. Breathing again, getting up, now let's evaluate the damage. Shania looks at the seat of my pants. Are they OK? No squished poop? No. Let's brush off this dirt. Harlyn, finally recovered from his surprise, glances over the tops of the junipers. He shows me the bottom of the valley. The Gila. Moved, I observe in silence the flowing water that meanders amid a jumble of shrubs and reeds. I picture Geronimo as a young novice running along the flanks of this canyon, mouth full of water, forced to better control his breathing.

"So is that where he was born?"

Harlyn nods.

"Probably on one of those large terraces overlooking the river, at the confluence of the west fork, somewhere over there."

"And where is his sumac?"

"There are dozens of bushes in this area. Unfortunately, the one where his umbilical cord was laid is impossible to find. Too much time had gone by before the Chiricahuas were allowed to come back, and any memory of the tree's location was lost."

"Is that a problem?"

"No. The most important thing for the cycle of life to be complete is to be buried in the area where your birth tree is located."

His right index finger draws a circle around the river and right up to us.

"By not being buried here, near his sumac, my great-grandfather still hasn't been able to complete his life's great cycle."

"But if his remains were brought back here, he could?"

Harlyn nods. He's even initiated the process with the authorities in order to obtain the authorization to transfer them back here.

"But Geronimo's bones were stolen!" Shania proclaims, now sitting on the ground next to her cousin.

My eyebrows go up.

"Stolen?"

She looks at Harlyn, as if she isn't allowed to say more. Harlyn nods his head slowly. That's the matter he was referring to and what he wanted us to talk about in the book. It's a matter linked to the Skull and Bones secret society, located at Yale University. A very powerful secret society too, both in politics and in business and industry. Founded in 1832 by William Huntington Russell and Alphonso Taft, it has counted among its members some presidents of the United States, including William Howard Taft, the son of one of its founders, George Bush and George W. Bush, but also John Kerry, financiers like William H. Donaldson, numerous CIA agents, members of Congress, two Supreme Court Chief Justices, and the founder of *Time* magazine, Henry Luce. Harlyn stops talking. He massages his forehead with his index finger, just between his eyebrows, then resumes. For a while now, there's been a rumor that Prescott Bush, the grandfather of the second President Bush, and some of his Yale friends, all members of the secret society, might have desecrated Geronimo's tomb at Fort Sill and stolen his skull and femur bones. Harlyn glances at his right boot whose tip has just bumped into a small stone, then starts again, his gaze aimed straight into mine.

"The members of the secret society have always denied it, saying that it was just a legend."

"But it isn't?"

"Without proof, no one has ever dared to push for an investigation. The case first came to light in 1986, when Ned Anderson, at the time the tribal president on the San Carlos reservation in Arizona, requested that Geronimo's remains be repatriated to his native land, right here. But shortly after his official request, he received a letter from a member of the Skull and Bones society, claiming that the organization had Geronimo's skull and that the members were ready to hand it over. There was a photo enclosed, with a skull in a glass case, Geronimo's according to the letter. Some time later, Anderson went to New York as had been proposed, so it could be returned to him. Once he was there, Prescott Bush's son, Jonathan Bush, and other members of the society did indeed present him with a case in which there was a skull, but it was much too small to be an adult's, according to Ned Anderson. So he refused to take it, saying it was the skull of a child and not the one in the photo that had accompanied the letter. Jonathan Bush is said to have answered that this was the only skull their society possessed and even pressed him to sign a document stating that Skull and Bones was not in possession of Geronimo's skull. Anderson obviously refused to sign. But then Endicott Peabody Davidson, the society's lawyer entrusted with the matter, told him they would take legal action if he didn't return the photo that had been enclosed with the letter. All the while continuing to insist that the organization did not possess the said skull."

Harlyn looks at me, apparently checking to see if I've understood everything.

"But a little more than a year ago," he adds, mischievous this time, "Marc Wortman, a writer specializing in the First World War who also used to be a professor of literature at Princeton University and editor of Yale's alumni magazine, discovered, during his research in the archives at Yale's library, the Sterling Memorial Library, a letter that confirmed the desecration of Geronimo's tomb. This letter, authenticated by Judith Schiff, head archivist of the library, was written in 1918 by Winter Mead, a member of the society, to Trubee Davidson, another of its members. It clearly says that Prescott Bush, helped by other members of the Skull and Bones society, desecrated Geronimo's tomb during their military service at Fort Sill that same year. The letter also says that his bones are in a secure place referred to as *The Tomb*, a tomb built by the society in New Haven, where Yale University is located."

"So that's proof that the legend isn't one."

Harlyn's head bobbles.

"Even so, a doubt was raised, because the author of the letter could have just made up the facts."

"Is that likely?"

"Judith Schiff, who, by the way, published a *History of Yale*, tends to doubt it, and her justification is that the members of the Skull and Bones swore to be completely honest with each other in all matters relating to the society. Out of respect for that oath of honesty, Winter Mead, the letter's author, couldn't have made up those facts."

"But there's still some doubt?"

"A tiny one, yes. In the meantime, though, some researchers confirmed there were clues strongly suggesting that the members of Skull and Bones who had volunteered at Fort Sill had desecrated the tomb of an Indian, whom they believed was Geronimo."

I frown.

"But for what purpose?"

"According to Alexandra Robbins, author of *Secrets of the Tomb*, this society is apparently very focused on death and uses symbolic objects, such as macabre illustrations and skulls and bones, preferably of famous people, in their initiation rites."

He lowers his voice a bit.

"Even satanic rites, according to some sources."

I look at Harlyn.

"Are you sure?"

He sighs.

"It's what I've been told. Unfortunately, it's impossible to prove. The members of this society are bound by secrecy and none of them will talk."

"But what do they have to say about the letter that was authenticated?"

"No comment on that either."

Suddenly concerned, Harlyn looks around for the girls. It's true, they're being way too quiet not to be up to some major mischief. As if synchronized, we both turn around. But everything's fine. They're being good, sitting on the ground a few feet away from us and completely absorbed in building a small rock pyramid. OK. Harlyn, reassured, resumes his explanation.

"So a few months ago, I wrote President Bush to ask him to help me recover those remains. If his grandfather had indeed stolen them, it would only be normal for him to do what was needed to have them restituted to me. I know the contents of that letter by heart, as you can imagine. It went . . ."

Harlyn closes his eyes, as though to remember better, then recites: "I am appealing to you so you may assist me in obtaining restitution, if they were indeed stolen, of my great-grandfather's skull and femur bones. According to our traditions, the bones of the deceased, especially when the tomb was desecrated, must be buried again according to the proper rituals. This is to restore their dignity and let the spirit of the deceased rest in peace. It is an important custom." He opens his eyes, satisfied. I ask him what the president's answer was, but he shrugs his shoulders.

"So far, not a word. Nothing."

"But in the meantime, can't you get access to those bones, just to check that they are indeed Geronimo's?"

"No, since they're on display in this tomb that belongs to the secret society. I don't have the right to go there without permission."

"What are you going to do then?"

"I alerted the media. Back in June, I was invited on Fox News, ABC News, BBC News, and by the *Washington Post*. I also formed a coalition of people who were moved by the matter, and enlisted historians, anthropologists, archeologists, and geneticists."

"Geneticists?"

"Yes. To sample my DNA and compare it to that from the bones displayed in the secret society's tomb. If I obtain permission to access it, of course. But since I highly doubt it, I've also contacted lawyers, including the former attorney general of the United States. According to them, the best strategy would be to ask permission to go to Fort Sill and have Geronimo's tomb opened. If it's revealed that the skull and femur bones are missing, then we could initiate proceedings in federal court against the Bush family, the government, and the US Army."

"And if the bones are still there?"

Harlyn thinks for a minute. Opens his mouth, closes it again as though hesitating.

"You know," he ends up saying, "I had a dream I haven't wanted to tell you about yet. But in this dream, somewhere between Demming and Silver City, my great-grandfather came to tell me that his skull and femur bones were no longer in his tomb at Fort Sill. So I'm convinced that in fact they aren't. But if, despite everything, they were there, then we'd ask for the Native American Graves

Protection and Repatriation Act to be applied. That law was voted by Congress and went into effect in 1990. Its aim is to compel museums and federal institutions in possession of bones or Indian ritual objects, whether they're being exhibited or lying in the basement of a federal building, to be returned to their tribe of origin. Using that law, we'd seek the authorization to transfer Geronimo's remains in the area of the Gila, where they could finally be buried according to Chiricahua tradition."

Harlyn looks at me, as though pondering something.

"You know, there are still fourteen thousand Indian skulls stored in the basement of the National Museum of Natural History, all awaiting restitution to their tribe of origin."

My eyes widen.

"But why does that museum possess so many skulls?"

His lips show his pique.

"Well, would you believe that, in 1868, the Smithsonian Institute, an institution founded in Washington 'for the increase and diffusion of knowledge,' funded a study whose goal was to try and prove by measuring skull sizes that Indians were physically inferior to whites? So money was offered to anyone who could provide Indian bones for the study. Ironically, the money ended up proving that there was no difference in size, but the fourteen thousand skulls that were purchased are still there."

My jaw must be agape with bewilderment because Harlyn bursts out laughing.

"I told you this journey would be full of surprises!"

My poor head nods, *yes, yes*. But it's as though suddenly this journey were a microscope shoved under my eyes to force me to observe, down to the most infinitesimal cell, a reality that my little ego, always quite content in its little world, would obviously have preferred never to notice. OK. Inhale. Exhale.

"And Geronimo's bones, is there any hope you'll recover them someday?"

"I'm pretty confident I will, because many people are supporting me. Including the African American community."

He starts smiling and points at the sky turning red.

"And the old warrior too is helping us. He even came to see you in France!"

"Do you think that's the reason for my vision?"

"Who knows? Either way, it will be thanks to your book and my account that this whole matter will be made known in Europe!"

"Will we be able to come with you to France?" Harlie Bear asks abruptly, still quietly seated on the ground next to her cousin.

"For the time being, you guys just go to school and that's that!" Harlyn answers, a little harshly.

A frowny face from Shania, who's fiddling with a rabbit dropping.

"It's not funny."

"But it is funny. It's only by working hard in school that you'll realize your dreams!"

"No."

"What do you mean, no? And drop that poop, will you?"

Harlie Bear chuckles. Shania shrugs, lines up the little black ball with six others that form a circle around the stone pyramid that's finally finished, then contemplates her work of art, not at all in a hurry to answer her grandfather. He doesn't seem to mind. He even seems touched by his little granddaughter's sculpture! I smile. Maybe he feels that his talents have been passed on? He admitted to me that he was a sculptor. He'll even show me his work as soon as we get back to Ruidoso. His work sells very well, but he refuses to exhibit in galleries, he told me. Those "racketeers"—that was the word he used—had wanted to take a fifty percent commission on each of his sales! I think that reaction is certainly the best proof of his lineage. Geronimo would probably have said the same. Her head still inclined over her pyramid, Shania finally answers Harlyn.

"You worked a lot, and you didn't get your dream."

He frowns, tilting his head slightly, as if to move his left eye first in the line of sight. A sign of wariness with him.

"Which dream are you talking about?"

Shania raises her head. A big smile lights up her round face.

"You know, your dreeaaaaaam. To sing an Apache song in the middle of the stadium at half-time at the Super Bowl!"

We all burst out laughing. Harlyn's laugh is loudest and sends its salvo ringing deep into the valley. Ka-ka-ka-ka-kaaaa. And we laugh even harder when suddenly its echo, like a duck call, returns in the sky.

"It's true!" Harlyn finally manages to say. Singing the national anthem at the Superbowl is a dream I really hope to realize one day. But first we must finish our journey."

He's suddenly quiet, as though waiting for our entire group's full attention. There. Our three pairs of ears are back in listening mode. He turns to face the west. The sun's red disc is about to disappear behind the Mogollon Rim. Its last rays, like magic wands, come and strike the earth where we're standing. Its hue, like an old bloodstain, turns a still darker red. "It's time," Harlyn says. "Lie down on your backs." The girls start to laugh. We have to get rid of the rabbit droppings first! Harlyn sighs, but I think they're right. "OK," he concedes, "but hurry." Frantic sweeping. Even Shania's sculpture vanishes, which doesn't seem to bother her, conscious as she must already be of the ephemeral nature of works. There. Everyone can lie down now. Like sardines, nice and tight, we lie on our backs all right next to each other. Only the songs of insects now fill the sound space around us. And then, with eyes finally lifted toward the blazing sky, in the suddenly deep and heavy silence, so characteristic of the moment when the sun disappears, we hear Harlyn's voice rise.

"At sunset, the land of the Gila turns in places the color of an old bloodstain. Even as a young child, I would come sit in those reddish puddles. The earth smelled of heat, dry grass, and rabbit droppings, with a bit of the taste of the poplar buds we used to chew for hours. In those endless sensations, stretched out on my back, gaze perched in the sky, I sometimes felt like I was in the exact moment when the past and present, suddenly freed from the constraints of time, could meet and all worlds connect. . . ."

"We must never consider ourselves apart
from the environment and disturb it."

"Be brave, as your ancestors were brave,
standing in front of the enemy."

HARLYN GERONIMO, BIIDAA-HIKAHNDE
(one of the Chiricahua Apache tribe)

Epilogue

Ruidoso, August 2012

The sign is still there, standing like a warning on the forest road. I'm about to drive on land that no one has the right to enter without permission. I slow down, more out of respect than fear. Because this land, up in the mountains of New Mexico—the reservation where I'm meeting Harlyn today—is all that's left of Chiricahua territory. The last time we saw each other was four months ago at the Metz Book Fair in eastern France, where we'd been invited to sign copies of the French edition of this book. Four years have passed since the launch in May 2008, and Harlyn still hasn't gotten over all the attention the book received. "You know," he admitted, "I didn't know how popular Geronimo was in Europe. And if I was losing hope before, I'm convinced our struggle is worthwhile and I have to keep going." I turn onto the stony drive that leads to Harlyn's home. In a clearing backed up against the forest, the house finally appears. Did he repaint it? Looks like it.

I park next to Harlyn's cherry-red pickup. The sun is setting, and the house is already in the shadows. Two dogs wagging their tails come to greet me. I open my door. The door to the house opens, and there's Harlyn's smile.

After petting the dogs, I walk up the stairs of the stoop to meet him.

"Come in quick," he says after hugging me, "there are Bigfoots in this forest."

I look at him like, *Are you kidding me?*

"Bigfoot? I thought that was a myth."

He shakes his head.

"One of them knocked on this window the other night. Hurry."

Not giving my Cartesian mind the time to reassure me, I go inside. Karen's smile welcomes me into the living room, which is furnished with two large black leather couches and a large flat-screen TV.

"Sixty-two inches," Harlyn says, having followed my gaze.

"Did you have a good trip?" Karen asks.

"A bit long. I came through Pittsburgh. Are there really Big-foots around here?"

Karen points at a table in the living room's extension.

"Sit down. I'll be right back."

I pull out a chair. Harlyn sits at the head of the table, to my right.

"Did you notice? The house is finally renovated. We weren't able to stay here for months!"

Karen returns carrying a photo.

"Look, we took this right behind the house."

I swallow as I make out a huge footprint in muddy ground.

"Your land is always full of surprises!"

Harlyn's laugh is like a volley at the wall. Ka-ka-ka-ka-ka. It's good to see him again. I hand the photo back to Karen.

"Would you like something to drink?" she offers.

"Water, please."

"Wouldn't you prefer wine?" Harlyn asks. "I brought a lot back from Europe, you know!"

I smile, thinking of all the cities where he and Karen were invited for book signings.

"Ten trips in all!" Harlyn says, as if he'd read my mind. "It was fantastic, and I really loved French cuisine."

He looks at me.

"The French spend a lot of time at the dinner table!"

I concur with a smile. Harlyn gets up.

"Well, I'm going to open a bottle. We have to celebrate the good news, don't we?"

Agreed. Francis Geffard, our French editor, just told us that the rights to *In Geronimo's Footsteps* were acquired by Skyhorse Publishing, a New York publisher. Harlyn disappears behind the door. I ask Karen where things stand with the legal proceedings they've started to win restitution of Geronimo's bones. Harlyn's voice comes from the other room.

"We began them in federal court in DC in February 2009, because my great-grandfather was born in February 1829. The date seemed important."

He reappears with a bottle of wine in his hand. "Bordeaux!" he proclaims, placing it under my nose. I look at the label. Médoc 2005.

"A good year," Harlyn notes. "But it doesn't come close to the price of the bottle we had at Paul Bocuse's restaurant in Lyon."

He sits down.

"Did you know that he was voted 'Chef of the Century'?"

I nod. He continues.

"You couldn't join us, unfortunately, but when we arrived in the limousine outside his restaurant, L'Auberge du Pont de Collonges, Bocuse greeted us in person. The twenty chefs who work under him made a guard of honor for us. Uh huh. We were told there's a two-year waiting list to eat at that restaurant but that Mr. Bocuse had made special arrangements for us. And a special menu too, with eight courses! A lot of food, I know. But it was so delicious. Especially the racks of lamb. And the wine I was telling you about that Paul Bocuse opened for us was a Peter Falke cuvée that goes for more than five hundred dollars a bottle. I'd never tasted a wine like that, but my taste buds really enjoyed it, I can tell you that. To thank him, I signed a copy of our book for him. He was very touched, and gave me a bottle of a grand Bordeaux."

He sets the Médoc gently on the table.

"It's not this," he says, "I'm waiting for a special occasion to drink that one. Like a victory in court, for instance."

His voice drops.

"Twenty of us family members received permission from the others to represent them in this trial. We're claiming the remains under the Native American Graves Protection and Repatriation Act, which requires that ritual objects and human remains be restituted to the tribes when they're exhumed."

He walks over to the sideboard to his right.

"You know, we began our complaint against Skull and Bones, the Department of Defense, and the government of the United States in November 2008, when George W. Bush was president. We filed the suit after Barack Obama had become president, but it wasn't directed against him. He understood that. Unfortunately, from that suit we learned that we would do better to file in a different jurisdiction. Since the known remains were in the Fort Sill cemetery, we had to start new proceedings in Oklahoma City."

He opens a drawer.

"So six months ago we took stock with our lawyer, Ramsey Clark. He was US deputy attorney general between 1965 and 1967 and then the attorney general from 1967 to 1969, when Lyndon Johnson was president. He told us we were going to need more funds because this trial would be costly. Not because of his fees—he supports our cause and is working for no fee—but because the state of Oklahoma has never been in favor of repatriating my great-grandfather's remains to the Gila River area."

He opens a second drawer.

"Actually, his grave at Fort Sill has become a tourist attraction and generates a lot of revenue and they aren't ready to give that up. To raise funds, Ramsey Clark advised us to open an account at the First National Bank in Ruidoso, which also supports us, where people who want to take part in this fight can make a donation. I also have to collect more signatures from the members of our family. We need at least twenty-five more to begin the new proceedings, and I only have twenty so far."

He turns toward Karen.

"Where's the corkscrew?"

Karen gives me a knowing look.

"Right in front of you."

She sets three wineglasses on the table. Harlyn comes back with the corkscrew in his right hand.

"In Lyon, we were put up at the Grand Hotel, which was a palace, and we were given the presidential suite. The bedroom alone was bigger than our house, and there were huge windows that opened onto a balcony where we could see the Rhône, the cathedral, and the whole city. Magnificent. We had two days there. Did you know that Lyon existed back in Roman times, more than two thousand years ago? But the most amazing thing is that there are still monuments from those times, like the two Roman arenas. They're ruins, granted, but we were able to walk in the amphitheaters and the stands. We also visited the old town, which hasn't changed in four hundred years. And the cathedral is the twin to Notre Dame in Paris. I lit a candle there for my grandfather."

He opens the bottle and expertly fills our glasses.

"A limousine took us to the site of the Foire Internationale," Karen continues, "We were the guests of honor."

"Uh huh. And the book signing afterward was unforgettable. There were so many people, some waited for up to two hours for me to sign their book. Some were in tears when they saw me. They had driven hundreds of miles with their children just to meet me. Some people of Native American heritage came with lots of gifts. We signed the book and gave autographs for two days in a row. Unfortunately, a lot of people in line never reached us because there were too many. And in the end, the crowd was so big that the guards had to escort us out.

"At the restaurant they had to put up barriers when we had lunch, but people were still climbing over them to take pictures. The guards would push them away, and they'd come back. It was incredible!

"Anyway, it felt really good to see how much people respect the name of Geronimo over there. Uh huh. Then we were invited by a national TV channel, France 2, to be on the one o'clock news, a peak time for viewers.

"Dignitaries from a number of other countries were there. The ones from Tanzania and Algeria even invited us to visit them, but we declined the offer because of the social unrest there. It seemed too dangerous, and we didn't want the Navy Seals to rescue us. Anyway, we'd prefer to go to Mongolia, as you suggested, Corine."

I look at Harlyn.

"Even at minus fifteen?"

"Didn't you say we'd go in summer?" he corrects me, with a smile. "So when are we going?"

"I'm still getting the budget together, but I haven't lost hope."

Harlyn proposes a toast to the American edition and our trip to Mongolia. We raise our glasses. Karen adds how much they enjoyed meeting Enkthuya, my teacher, on their trip to the book conference in October 2009 that was sponsored by the city of Le Mans, in the east of France.

"We were so glad to finally be able to meet our distant relatives from Asia!" Harlyn continues after setting down his glass. "But it was even better than we expected when we met Enkthuya for the first time at the restaurant and saw that her hair was as black as ours and her eyes weren't the usual Asian shape but more Apache-looking. Rounder, with eyelids that go straight across.

"And when she spoke, it was like the world of the Apaches was speaking through her. Can you believe it, Corine? Their words of thanks and welcome use the same consonants as ours. Like *Yat he hé*. Other words sound like old Apache words, and there are lots of similarities between our consonants and our verbs.

"We were amazed to hear that a twitch in the eye has the same meaning in Mongolia. In the right eye, it means good news, and in the left eye, it means bad news. Enkthuya also mentioned the blue birthmark their babies have. And juniper too, which is used in both our shamanic practices to purify a place or a person."

"And the umbilical cord," adds Karen. "They put it close to where the baby is born, like us. They also know a lot about stars, the cosmos, its meaning, and the importance of respecting it, and, just like we do, they honor the sun so harmony reigns in our lives."

"Not to mention the tipi they still live in even today. But I'll stop there, since we talked about our respective traditions and compared them all night long! I gave Enkthuya a shaman's necklace made of sacred red and white seeds, turquoise beads, and a ring of abalone. She gave us ceremonial scarves made with blue silk. It was really wonderful. Enkthuya said she was looking forward to our visit to Mongolia. We'll stay in her tipi, and for the first time I'll be living like Geronimo!"

Harlyn drinks a swallow of wine, looking happy.

"Even though I knew about our common ancestry with these people, I couldn't help but be surprised by so many similarities. Right down to the cigarette Enkthuya gave us, rolled in paper and made of specific wild herbs like those Apaches use during ceremonies."

He looks at me.

"Would you like to smoke one?"

I put down my glass. Sure, why not. He gets up. Karen invites me to follow her over to the terrace. We sit on a bench with its back to the wall of the house, shielded by an awning. I ask Karen whether Bigfoot might come and pay us a visit. She smiles without answering. Harlyn arrives with the rolled cigarette in his hand.

"We smoke this medicine to purify ourselves before a ceremony, but also in the evening sometimes, to relax after a long day."

He lights the tip, which crackles in the silence. The smell of sage and mint fills the air.

"It smells good."

"And it is good!"

He takes a few puffs before handing it to me. It really is delicious. And smooth.

Karen tells me that the conference where she, Harlyn, and Enkthuya met again the morning after their first meeting was unforgettable.

"The Mongols and the Apaches together for the first time in front of an audience!" Harlyn continues. "I got teary-eyed there too. And we received lots of gifts. Products from the region like potted pork meat, sweets, but also portraits of my great-grandfather."

"And wool socks that a woman knit for us!"

I smile, handing Karen the cigarette. I have a wonderful memory of that historic event myself.

"You signed more than a hundred books, didn't you?"

"Yes," Harlyn confirms, "and the next day, the mayor of Le Mans, Jean-Claude Boulard, gave us eight bottles of one of the best wines of the region. Uh huh. We brought them back in our suitcases to share with our friends here. None of them had ever drunk a French wine before, but I think I've hooked them now."

"And what about the surprise?" Karen asks him. "Do you remember the surprise?"

Of course, he remembers. The mayor took them to city hall, and, when they entered his office, there was a portrait of Geronimo. It had been hanging there for years.

"I signed it in front of all the elected officials and the celebrities. The local press took pictures. It was a beautiful moment."

Harlyn takes a final drag on the cigarette. We listen to it crackle in the gathering night. A cricket responds in song. Then another. Then another. The concert will go on until daybreak. Harlyn puts the butt on the cement floor.

"And there was the trip to Normandy."

He turns toward his wife.

"Two thousand nine or two thousand ten?"

"Two thousand nine for the Foire Internationale of the city of Caen."

"That's right. The morning of the opening, spectators were waiting in the bleachers. As guests of honor, we entered on horseback, on spectacular creatures. We received a standing ovation! There was a minister, the mayor of Caen, and some members of the US consulate. All the people who came to greet us afterward told me how Geronimo was a legend for them. They also spoke of my father, Juanito, Lana's son. My father was one of the million soldiers who came to liberate France in 1944."

His gaze rests in the starry sky.

"They surprised us with a trip to Omaha Beach, where my late father disembarked on June 6 with his comrades of the Third Army Field Artillery and the 501st Infantry Regiment. He was in eight major battles by the time his company had reached Belgium at the end of the war. I was quiet for a long time. Just crouching with my hands in the cold sand. Uh huh. . . . My father was twenty-nine, and it was his first time in combat. Like his comrades, he was sick on the boat. The sea was rough that night. In the morning, they got to the beach. The Germans were shooting from the top of the cliff that they had to climb. Juanito told me that to avoid the artillery fire they had to run without stopping and use their comrades' bodies as shields. It was hell, and he told me he would have died if his Apache medicine hadn't been there to protect him. Lots of whites think that's impossible, but I know he's right, because the same 'power' protected Geronimo."

He looks at me, smiling.

"You believe me, of course."

"Where are you," Karen asks me, "with your scientific research on the shamanic trance practiced in Mongolia?"

I clear my throat.

"They took electroencephalograms of my brain at Alberta Hospital in Canada under the direction of Professor Flor-Henry. It's the first time ever that a study has been done on this type of trance, which I can now induce intentionally. They managed to prove that it altered quite a lot the behavior of the brain circuits. And that's probably why perceptions are different during a trance. It's as if we could suddenly access abilities that are seldom or never used in the normal state. The results contributed to a significant advance in our knowledge of the brain."

Harlyn emits an "uh huh," pondering it all.

"You know," he says finally, "at first I couldn't see the point of proving these ancestral techniques scientifically. Indians have experienced them successfully for thousands of years. But thanks to the experiment you initiated, now it's difficult to put them in doubt. I wasn't able to read your book about the experiment because it's in French, but when we talked about it, I understood what it's about. You're talking about the 'power' I have and that Geronimo had, I mean, the abilities developed by shamans. Like the ones that predicted the army's imminent arrival to my great-grandfather and enabled him to escape. The ones that allowed you, Corine, to have a vision of Geronimo and to meet me. The ones also that protected my father on Omaha Beach. It was really moving to be there to honor him with the military men and dignitaries who accompanied me. The press, TV, radio—around ten different media organizations were present! Afterward, we went to collect ourselves at the American cemetery of Colleville-sur-Mer. Then we visited the Airborne Museum at Sainte-Mère-Eglise and the memorial honoring the American soldiers who died to liberate France."

The turquoise hanging from Harlyn's ear slowly starts to oscillate to the rhythm of his emotions.

"We stayed that night in Servigny," Karen continues, "the city where the German general von Schlieben signed the surrender. That was the first time we slept in a real castle. The room was huge, with two king-sized beds."

"And there was knights' armor in the halls. They're impressive, real metal shells, but they would have been much too heavy for an Apache warrior."

He turns to me, smiling again.

"Strong legs are your best asset against the enemy, aren't they?"

I look at mine, all skinny. Harlyn and Karen smile.

"We had dinner with the mayor and some dignitaries," Harlyn continues. "They gave us lots of cakes, souvenirs, fruits, flowers . . . and another case of wine!"

We laugh.

"The next day we went to Mont Saint-Michel. Amazing—on top of a huge rock surrounded by water at high tide and flat sand at low tide. At the top, we visited the beautiful abbey that dates back to the eighth century and then the walled city that grew around it. There are thousands of stairs, and no car can drive in there."

"We were the guests of chef Michel Bruneau at the La Mère Poulard restaurant. He's known around the world for his famous omelet."

"Yes, and I signed Barack Obama's photograph," Harlyn says. "Someone told me he'd eaten there. They asked what I thought about the fact that the message, 'Geronimo, Enemy Killed in Action,' was used by the Navy Seal team to notify the White House that bin Laden had been killed. It's true, I was really shocked when I heard about it, and I immediately petitioned President Obama and Defense Secretary Gates to explain how it was possible for my great-grandfather's name to be used in such a disparaging manner. Uh huh. I heard two different versions. One was that the mission's official code name was 'Operation Neptune Spear,' referring to the Seals' trident insignia, and that bin Laden's code name was actually Jackpot. 'Geronimo' was the code to report his capture or death. However, in the book *No Easy Day*, a former Seal who took part in the mission claims that 'Geronimo' was in fact bin Laden's code name. That remains to be cleared up, but meanwhile I've asked for an official apology for what amounts to a grave insult to all Indians, and also that Geronimo's name be expunged from all official documents relating to the operation. Anyway, I don't hold a grudge toward the army or Barack Obama. Our president doesn't foster ill will toward us, I know that. In fact, he seems to support the Indians' cause and is a good president. I want to say that. But I still want to know the truth, and I'm going to keep searching for it. Because if bin Laden was just a terrorist, Geronimo was always fighting for his people's freedom. Uh huh. And actually, the US Army honored him when they named the 501st Parachute Infantry Regiment 'Geronimo.' It makes me glad, because the name I bear belongs to those who have always fought for freedom and against terrorism."

"The chef of La Mère Poulard in Mont Saint-Michel even reminded us of that by making a special menu in our honor!"

"Uh huh. And when people found out I was Geronimo's direct descendent, they came out to greet me. The crowd kept growing. There were about two thousand people, I was told. Many just wanted to shake my hand, but when they began trying to touch my clothes, the bodyguards told us to get out of there. We were evacuated through a secret passage and escorted back to our limousine."

"That was really scary," Karen says.

"But when we took the limo back to site of the Foire Internationale in Caen, do you know who welcomed us, Corine?"

I shake my head.

"Miss France! And I can tell you, she's really pretty."

Karen looks at him, shrugging her shoulders.

"A few days later," she continues, "we discovered Vincennes, the town and the castle near Paris, when we participated in the America Festival. It brings together around sixty North American writers every two years and thousands of people interested in those cultures. We took part in discussions about Indian issues, met with schoolchildren, and got to meet many writers."

Harlyn gets up, suddenly looking worried.

"Let's go back inside."

I follow right after him.

"Is there a problem?"

"Sssssh," he answers, motioning me to hurry. "When the humidity falls, Bigfoot comes out."

Still not sure whether this is some sort of a joke, I beat a hasty retreat. And when the door closes behind us, Karen and Harlyn burst out laughing.

★ ★ ★

When we're seated around the table again, Karen asks me if I'm hungry.

"I could eat as much as a Bigfoot!"

She disappears with a smile, while Harlyn serves us all another glass of Bordeaux.

"I'm sure Geronimo would have loved wine."

He drinks a sip.

"Fleshy and soft on the palate. . . . With hints of wood . . . leather. When I'm signing books during autograph sessions, I always ask for a glass of wine."

Karen sets three plates and a bowl on the table. Inside the bowl are small berries about the size of chickpeas.

"Apache cherries," she says. "Do you want a taste?"

I look at the red–brown fruit.

"They're cooked. Have some."

I put one in my mouth. Acidic. Seeing my grimace, Karen says she never adds sugar, just like their ancestors.

"That's why they stayed slim, and I wish our children would follow their example."

"How are Harlie Bear and Shania? I haven't seen them since the book came out in France. They must have changed a lot!"

Karen replies that they've become beautiful young women and still excel in school. But it's their dream to go to Europe with them.

"First, they'll have to finish their studies!" Harlyn grumbles.

Karen smiles.

"Yes, Grandpa Hen!"

"We'll take them to the Disneyland near Paris," Harlyn says with a smile. "We had a wonderful time there, didn't we?"

Karen nods, placing a few cherries on her plate.

"They picked us up in a limousine, and we stayed in a palace that looked like the White House!"

Harlyn swallows a cherry.

"We had lots of interviews but were still able to try some of the attractions, like a boat ride, a walk through It's a Small World, then Space Mountain and Rock'n'Roller, a huge rollercoaster where we went at the speed of sound."

"It was scary!" Karen pronounces, spitting a pit into her hand. Harlyn smiles tenderly.

"On Friday night we went to see *Buffalo Bill's Wild West Show*. And because we were in the celebrity seats, we were able to go backstage and meet the actors. Many of them were actual Indians from the American West, from Montana and New Mexico. Some were from Canada. For the show, they were riding bareback and were dressed like in Geronimo's times. We had the opportunity to take pictures with them. And then we were invited to the traditional dinner of barbecued ribs and corn. It was very good. Very 'western.'"

Karen puts another bowl on the table.

"Here's some Apache food instead."

I look at the yellow-brown mixture, surprised.

"It's cooked yucca. Taste."

I put a piece in my mouth. Harlyn and Karen are waiting for my reaction. It has a soft, stringy texture. The taste is bland, slightly sweet. I have trouble swallowing it because of the fibers, but I end up smiling.

"It's good!"

"Geronimo was crazy about it," Harlyn says, looking relieved. "But I prefer T-bone steak!"

Karen raises her eyes to the ceiling, taking a piece of yucca.

"And Swiss wine!"

"Another great trip," Harlyn says with a smile. "When was that again?"

"October 2011."

"That's right. This time, we were the guests of honor at the Foire Internationale de Mar ... gny ..."

"Martigny in the Valais."

"Yes. And one of the most memorable moments was when we arrived at the site of event, a sort of arena surrounded by bleachers. There were thousands of people and the moment we entered, wearing our traditional Apache costumes, the crowd rose to give us a standing ovation."

"It was really lovely," Karen says, moved. "That was followed by some photo and autographing sessions. And then one of the organizers, who owns a plane, took us on a ride to see the Swiss landscape and the Alps up to the border with Italy."

Harlyn drinks a swallow of wine.

"That's where we visited one of the most famous vineyards in Switzerland, the Farinet vineyard in Saillon. They received us like distinguished guests, with drum rolls, flowers, a guard of honor, and a gun salute. Uh huh. Only celebrities like Sean Connery or Claudia Cardinale had been given that honor before us!"

"And in the evening the national Swiss TV received us. Harlyn mentioned the issues our tribe is facing and our fight to repatriate his great-grandfather's remains."

"The next day we were invited to the German-American Institute of Nuremberg in Germany, where there was a speech during the reception in our honor. We spent the night in Stuttgart in a beautiful castle."

Karen gets up. I ask Harlyn if Paris was as he had imagined it.

"It's so big, with so many different neighborhoods! For starters, our hotel was in Montparnasse, the artists' mecca, and I learned that back in the day we might have crossed paths with Hemingway, Scott Fitzgerald, or Peggy Guggenheim."

Karen places a box on the table.

"We also visited Montmartre. A cameraman from Canal +, a national TV channel, filmed us exploring the little cobblestone streets, the art galleries, and the Place du Tertre, where Gauguin, Picasso, and Van Gogh used to hang out."

"And the Sacré Coeur basilica, at the top of the Butte Montmartre."

Harlyn bows his head.

"I don't know if I should tell you this, but I lit another candle for my great-grandfather. Uh huh."

"If we don't win the trial after all that!" Karen says with a laugh.

Harlyn nods, smiling.

"In the evening we were invited to the set of *Grand Journal* on Canal +, and again the audience gave us a standing ovation!"

"And then they showed the segment filmed earlier that afternoon in Montmartre," says Karen.

"Yes, and I spoke some more about Geronimo, about our fight to bring his remains back to his birthplace. The journalist Michel Denisot asked me which candidate I was going to vote for in the presidential election. That was in May 2008. I said, Barack Obama. George W. Bush had never answered my letter asking for an explanation of Prescott Bush's role in the Skull and Bones matter."

I look at him, sorry for that.

"Skull and Bones still hasn't given permission to have the skull examined by an expert on their premises?"

He shakes his head.

"But I haven't lost hope. During the trip to Paris, we were invited to the United States embassy, where I was also able to talk about our fight. And then we went by train to the Astonishing Travelers festival in Saint-Malo, in Brittany."

A smile returns to Harlyn's face.

"The beaches along the coast were shimmering like gold. We discovered that the town of Saint-Malo was surrounded by ramparts, the oldest dating back to the twelfth century!"

"And do you remember the red cars?"

"Lamborghinis, yes! They were on display in front of city hall, which was a castle, where the mayor received us. He suggested that

Karen go sit in one with him, and they were photographed by the local press."

"You would have liked it to be you, wouldn't you?" Karen teases.

Harlyn concedes with a smile.

"Then there were autograph sessions. People had come from all over France to meet us."

"We were also able to meet Sherman Alexie, the writer of Native American origin. He gave us his contact information, and we've seen each other since. It was good to meet him."

Karen opens the box in front of her.

"Look," she tells me. "It's an herbarium of plants that we use in our traditional medicine. Harlyn already showed you a few in the desert."

She takes out a first sheet.

"Here's *i-ah-i*, to repair a broken bone."

She takes out another sheet.

"This plant relieves stomachaches . . . and this one, osteoarthritis . . . And this one brings down a fever."

Karen lowers her voice.

"Don't say their names because it's a secret, but I'm teaching them to our young people, and, despite what we might have thought, they're very interested."

"My Apache wrestling and bow hunting classes are also very popular."

"And the Apache language!" Karen continues. "My classes keep getting bigger and bigger."

"You know, Corine, we finally have real hope of saving our traditions. And if we're able to reconnect with the traditions from Mongolia, I'll be able to teach them too. Isn't that good?"

I cross my fingers. Karen nods.

"Do you know the date of the launch of *In Geronimo's Footsteps* in the United States?"

"Autumn 2014."

"Do you realize," Harlyn says, "our book is going to be published here, in my own country?" He pauses, visibly moved.

"I'm sure it'll rally lots of people to our cause and help with repatriating my great-grandfather's remains."

His voice chokes suddenly.

"All I want is for his final wishes to be respected."

He looks at Karen, his eyes brimming with tears. But for the first time in a long while, I see in them a glimmer of hope.

Afterword

by Ramsey Clark

Harlyn Geronimo's passionate commitment to return the remains of Geronimo, his legendary great-grandfather, from Fort Sill, Oklahoma, where he died a prisoner, to his birthplace and native home at the headwaters of the Gila River in New Mexico is a profound revelation of the endurance of the Native American spirit. It was Geronimo's desire to end his days and leave his remains in the land where he had been born and had lived a life unaffected by alien intruders until he reached manhood.

There was a widely known claim that Geronimo's skull had been stolen from its grave site at Fort Sill toward the end of World War I by a group of Yale students in military training there, including Prescott Bush, father and grandfather of future US presidents. When Harlyn asked me to represent him in recovering his great-grandfather's remains, the first step was to determine whether Skull and Bones was in possession of the skull. We filed a lawsuit on February 17, 2009, in US District Court in Washington, DC, against President Obama, the Secretary of Defense, the Secretary of the Army, Yale University, and Skull and Bones, in part to determine the truth of that claim without a trial. After the suit was filed, I met with two representatives from Yale. They made a persuasive presentation, on the basis of the long history of contention over the issue, that the Skull and Bones story was mere legend, and the society never had Geronimo's skull.

This claim meant the only practical way to proceed was by an action to recover Geronimo's remains at Fort Sill by administrative proceeding in the Department of the Interior, or a case filed in Federal Court in Oklahoma's Western District. If the skull was not there but Geronimo's other bones were, then we could go back to Yale. This was preferable to delaying our proceeding by several years in court to determine whether the skull was at Yale.

In order to recover the bones, artifacts, and other properties of an early Native American, the statute enacted by the US Congress requires a majority of the living adult lineal descendants to file the claim. This has caused a lengthy delay, because lineal descendants who chose to remain in Oklahoma and have an interest in gambling casinos at Fort Sill oppose the move. And the present burial site at Fort Sill is a major tourist attraction. Harlyn has twenty descendants who have joined the claim but needs more.

Geronimo's fervent wish to return to the still pristine headwaters of the Gila, within the first national forest preserved by US law and far away from the military and gambling chatter at Fort Sill, Oklahoma—where his remains presently attract tourists to a scene of captivity, force, and frivolity—can still be fulfilled.

What is required is a claim by a majority of his direct descendants to the government of the United States, demanding that the last journey of Geronimo be to his birthplace, still in the primeval state of nature he loved and in which he was born and had lived all his years in freedom.